16 00

D0205746

A CASTE OF DESPAIR

Migrant Farm Workers

A CASTE

Ronald L. Goldfarb

The Iowa State University Press / AMES

OF DESPAIR

© 1981 Ronald L. Goldfarb. All rights reserved
Composed and printed by The Iowa State University Press, Ames, Iowa 50010

First edition, 1981

Library of Congress Cataloging in Publication Data

Goldfarb, Ronald L.
  Migrant farm workers.

  Includes bibliographical references and index.
  1. Migrant agricultural laborers—United States.
2. Migrant agricultural laborers—Law and legislation—
United States. I. title.
HD1525.G64   305.5′6   81-6024
ISBN 0-8138-1790-0   AACR2

Unless otherwise indicated, all photographs are courtesy of the Archives of Labor and Urban Affairs, Wayne State University.

C O N T E N T S

Foreword   vi
Preface   viii
Acknowledgments   2

1. The Migrant Streams   3

2. Bosses of the Stream   19

3. Health, Housing, and
   Education   33

4. The Neglected Minority   52

5. Judging the Employment
   Service   60

6. Foreign Competition   114

7. Exclusion from Social
   Benefits   147

8. A Miracle in the Making   176

9. The End of the Stream   209

Notes   221
Index   233

F O R E W O R D

THE AUTHOR of this thoughtful, clear-headed analysis of the political, economic, and, inevitably, legal situation of an exceptional American working "population," our migrant farm workers, does well to make mention of the other books, all too many of them, that have preceded his own. I am one who wrote such a book, and in it I did likewise—referred with a sense of mixed gratitude, admiration, and despair to colleagues who had tried to tell others of a particularly grim and shameful story, as I hoped to do. I fear that I knew then, what I also now know, that my book would not be the last one written, even as this one done by Ronald Goldfarb will not be because, unfortunately, there seems to be little prospect that this nation is yet prepared to do what is so urgently required: once and for all bring justice to an extremely hard-working segment of our so-called "labor force."

Migrants confront us dramatically with the dreary, banal side of our pietistic avowals with respect to work and its value. Migrants are, after all, men and women (and, alas, children) who are quite anxious to work, who are willing, as a matter of fact, to travel hundreds and even thousands of miles in pursuit of a job. Nor are their efforts anything but strenuous, dedicated, productive. Here are Americans who toil in the fields from sunup to sundown so that the rest of us may eat vegetables and fruit. Here are Americans who shun welfare rolls in favor of an insistent, earnest working initiative. Here are Americans whose hands are deeply calloused, whose backs are constantly bent because they choose to do sweaty, demanding work rather than trying one or another means of making a living or, for that matter, trying to obtain money without working for it. Yet, for so doing, for exposing themselves to the strain of difficult, often dangerous work (pesticides can be lethal), for enduring a life of continual movement, these Americans get, often enough, virtually nothing.

Put differently, migrant workers are significantly denied the various protections and benefits millions of other Americans have learned to take for granted. Migrants live in squalid shacks, often without even a minimum of sanitary facilities. Migrants are herded across our land like cattle, denied the right to organize on their own behalf, and even treated as virtual peons. (There have been, in recent years, repeated cases of "peonage" argued in our federal courts.) These are families living brutish lives—in their sum, a scandal to this nation of ours. Yet we seem unable to rectify this injustice even though it is not hard, as the author of this book demonstrates, to imagine what steps might make all the difference in the world. The issue is a matter of laws, as was the case in the 1930s when other American laborers had to fight hard for the kinds of protection they now enjoy.

One can only hope that this book makes its way across the land, gets read by students, by young lawyers and doctors, by journalists, by legislators in our state and national governments, and not least, by ordinary citizens who deserve to know what terrible tragedies are connected to the daily food we all enjoy having available. Maybe this is not a very favorable time, as far as needed legislation on behalf of migrants goes. Still, sometimes at least, voices in the wilderness have a way, historically, of being heard and heeded—or so one wants to believe.

Here is a strongly worded, trenchant, discerning, fair-minded analysis of a major American social problem. Here, too, is a kind of exemplary witness—what it means to be a compassionate, high-minded lawyer and what it means, as a matter of fact, to remember in one's mind and heart, in one's working life as an attorney, as a citizen, those words engraved on the Supreme Court Building in Washington, D.C.: "Equal Justice under Law." One concludes the reading of this book wishing (hope against hope!) that it will be the very last one written and wishing, too, that those who practice the law could claim more colleagues such as Ronald Goldfarb—a moral example to a profession, to all of us.

ROBERT COLES

P R E F A C E

IN 1975 a federal court in Washington, D.C., appointed me to monitor how well the Department of Labor provided government services to migrant and seasonal farm workers. One afternoon when I was traveling in the home base of what is known as the East Coast "migrant stream," I stopped unannounced at a union hiring hall in Avon Park, Fla. With a small group of state and federal labor officials, I was traveling throughout farming areas of Florida to learn about the lot of farm workers there. This world was strange to an urban man with only the vaguest notions about how crops were planted and harvested and found their way to my table.

Avon Park is a poor, scruffy, agricultural town; paradoxically, it is not far from the luxury of Miami and Palm Beach. The union building was spare but well used. The young woman in charge of the office there seemed wary of us; she was plainly skeptical about our interest in her union's affairs. We persuaded her to accompany us to a modest luncheonette on a nearby back street and to sit and talk with us awhile.

On first impression she seemed to be a contentious if not a surly person—one not to be taken seriously. She wore a tight Mickey Mouse T-shirt and dungarees. Her body was thickset, and her language was coarse. But as she spoke, it was clear that, however rough-hewn, she was a bright and engaging person, full of insights, convictions, opinions, and commitment. She was a forceful, challenging, and compelling advocate with a one-track mind that governed a one-track life. She was a child of farm worker parents who had committed herself completely to the union movement. Her whole life was devoted to getting farm workers the justice they deserved. Without stint, single-mindedly, she pounded at strangers about the needs and problems with which her impoverished but dedicated union was engaged.

First impressions of a brazen dame faded fast; they were replaced by the reality of a savvy, sensitive, probing, and extraordinarily dedicated working woman. We spent several hours debating life and labor over a simple lunch of collards, crackers, and tea; then we returned to the union hall where we watched the operation work. When my party had to leave, the tough, cynical woman we had met upon arrival embraced us, imploring us not to forget the farm workers' needs. The memory of the magnetism and energy of this committed woman remained long after we left Avon Park and Florida.

Because she had asked to have one of my books, I sent her a copy of my most recent one (about jails) along with a note thanking her for her hospitality. A short time later, I received a friendly letter from her. She thanked me for sending the book and said she looked forward to reading all my books, "including the one I hope you'll write someday about farm workers." Then she wrote:

This note was really prompted by my thinking about the possibility of such a book and my wondering how people write books about very different subjects, and know enough about all of them to write a book. Then, I thought, maybe you—being pretty expert on prisons—are already an expert on farm workers. There are all kinds of cages, maybe. Some have stones or bricks for walls and some have iron bars. Some have only systems and prejudices and traditions (like slavery) to hem folks in. But, like all cages, you can't get out except for an occasional and unique escape. It would really be neat to read about those cages and how we might tear down the walls. . . .

We would meet again and become friends in later years. I kept her letter and thought often about what she had said.

Her words reminded me of an excerpt from the story one of my children showed me, *The Confrontation* by Raymond Barrio:[1]

No matter which way he turned, he was trapped in an endless maze of apricot trees, as though forever, neat rows of them, neatly planted, row after row, just like the blackest bars on a jail. There had to be an end. There had to be. There—trapped. There had to be a way out. Locked. There had to be a respite. Animal. The buckets and the crates kept piling up higher. Brute. He felt alone. Though surrounded by other pickers. Beast. . . .

At first, I hesitated to write about migrant farm workers. The sad story of their tribulations bursts upon the American conscience periodically; genuinely, we resolve that something must be done, and then interests wane and we forget. "What

could I do that others had not already done?" I asked myself.

The novel, *Grapes of Wrath,* by John Steinbeck was a landmark in American social history; it is a classic in our literature. The titles of other comparable books are a recurring indictment of a society that countenances the continuation of the pathetic problems of farm workers:

America's Own Refugees, No Harvest for the Reaper, The Forgotten Minority, Uprooted Children, Sweatshops in the Sun.

The advent of television highlighted even more profoundly the horrors endured by migrant farm workers in America. In 1948 Edward R. Murrow broadcast into millions of American homes the grim picture of our country's *Harvest of Shame.* In a white paper on migrants 22 years later, Chet Huntley rediscovered the same situation; he recalled *Harvest of Shame* and wondered if a decade later the same problems would still exist. They do. In the 1970s, the Public Broadcasting System depicted these same scenes in perhaps the most damning of all these television programs: *A Day Without Sunshine,* the story of the human and economic problems of farm workers in the orange groves of Florida and the powerful political process that deadeningly defeats periodic attempts to improve their lives.

One wonders what it is about this group that leaves them so ignored, so immune from reform measures. Why is it that their problems remain today when they have been so thoroughly illuminated in the past? Why does a country whose ideals and social conscience are normally touched by problems like these fail to take meaningful steps to find real solutions? Why does a country that is characteristically so overloaded with social welfare programs fail to deal with the needs of one worthy client group? Why is this government of so many laws so lawless in its administration of programs designed to benefit this group of needy people? Why have other disadvantaged groups been able to assuage as well as dramatize their problems, while this one isolated caste of workers has suffered so long? Why has the labor movement traditionally been able to overcome strong

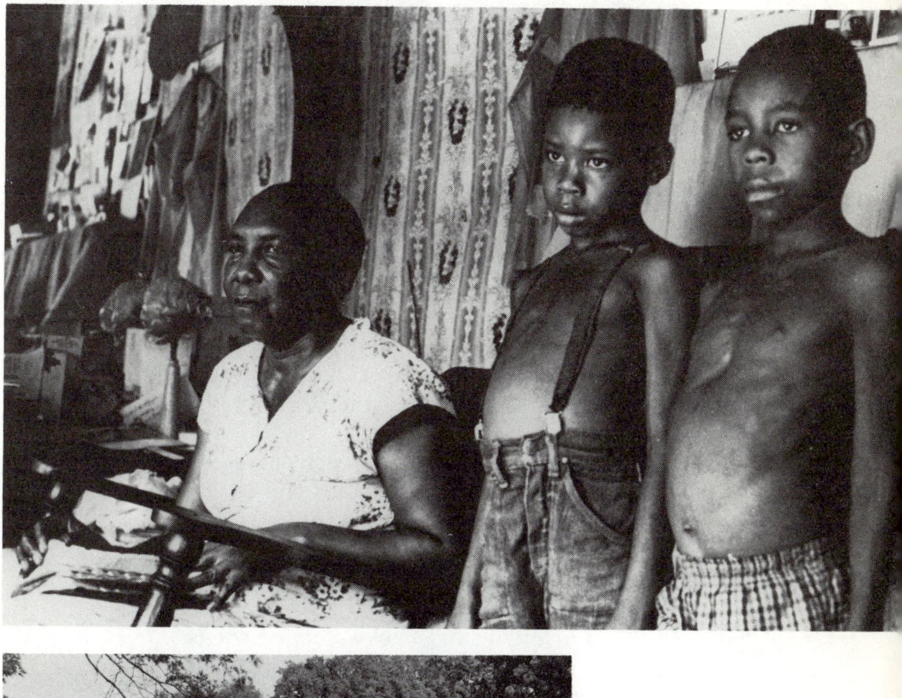

Library of Congress

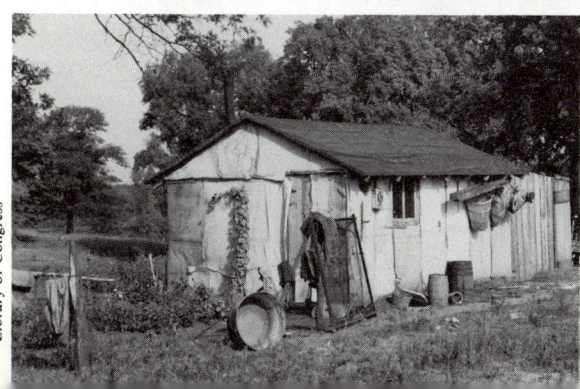

economic opponents and hostile public opinion against its actions for others but has only just begun in the 1970s to attend to the problems of farm workers?

Other disadvantaged groups received recognition during the social revolutions of the 1960s; farm workers have remained invisible, while public perception of other groups has heightened and their just claims have been publicized. Without place and without power, farm workers have remained in the dismal backwaters of society. Occasional attempts to call attention to their plight have been short-lived and ineffectual. Ironically, other groups, whose cases were harder to make, have received more public attention simply because cases were made for them. But farm workers—who toil so hard and cause relatively few problems for society at large, who do the grueling and important work that brings the food to our tables, and who ask only to be treated decently—have been treated contemptuously, when they were not being ignored. Their dilemma should be a challenge to all our consciences; apparently it is not.

One wonders just what it takes to bring about reform. If it is the need to highlight information and gather documentation of grievances, farm workers long ago should have been able to claim redress. If it takes the passing of laws designed to solve problems, again farm workers can point to some that should have helped and were meant to benefit them although they have been administered in ways that have defeated their noble purpose. If litigation is needed, there has been ample precedent to provide remedies to redress farm workers' grievances. If a widely published understanding of the justness of a group's cause is necessary, their lot should have been improved long ago. If the inherent fairness of their claims was the key factor, farm workers' grievances could be pushed to the head of the line.

All these ingredients of reform exist in this compelling situation. Yet, farm workers' problems have continued, have been exacerbated, and for the most part remain untended. Americans who take pride in their social system and reap the greatest bounties in the history of any civilization cannot account for the inequities they permit. America has allowed a caste of despair to continue in a land of plenty. It has created a migrant caste because it has permitted injustice in its fields.

Eventually, one who was drawn into this serious social drama had to try again; not trying, giving up, would be a more serious, personal failure than losing any battle. So I wrote this book in the hope that it would help the cause of human justice to which people like this moving young woman and others like her give their lives. I dedicate the book to that cause, and more personally to my children—Jody, Nick, and Max—in the hope that their sense of what is just will flourish in a better and a fairer world.

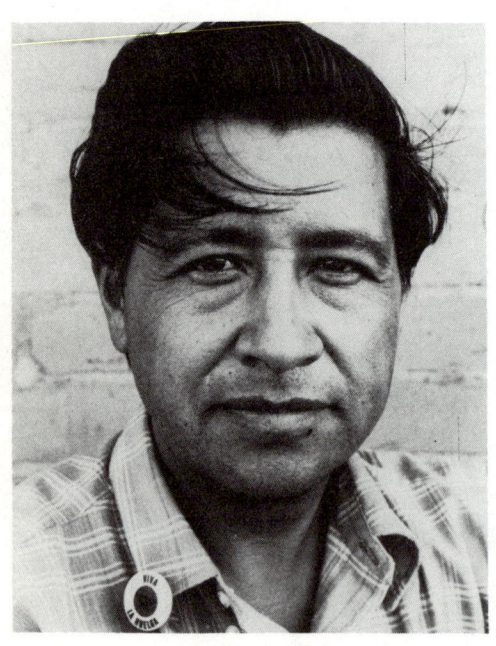

Migrant Farm Workers

A CASTE OF DESPAIR

ACKNOWLEDGMENTS

Numerous people in my office—lawyers, law students, and secretaries—helped me write this book. Janet Zaccari, Lise Larson, Alverda Boyce, and Frances Michael kept my records and typed and organized my manuscript. Frances did the index as well. David Schiller, Michaela Mudre, Liz Siegel, James Altman, Ronald Schechter, and Kevin Carey did research for specific parts of the book. Dick Fortman checked all footnote citations. Nick Kotz and Linda Singer read and critiqued the manuscript. Jocelyn Gutchess, Fred Romero, Larry Sherman, Marc Grossman, Caryl Pines, and Jim Lorenz provided helpful critiques of various chapters. Countless people educated me about the world of farm workers, and I am indebted to them all. I offer special thanks for the invaluable attentions of Frances Michael and Nick Kotz. A Ford Foundation grant made it possible for me to take the time I needed to write.

1

THE MIGRANT STREAMS

THE PHENOMENON is unique: three streams of people—eventually hundreds of thousands—flow and fan northward, traveling from their homes around Florida, Texas, and California to distant places, where they will pick and pack crops throughout the agricultural centers of the United States. For months they travel thousands of miles, stopping for brief periods to work in fields and sheds with the fruits and vegetables that grow seasonally in states that supply the nation with food but need labor to bring it all in. With their families, alone, or in random groups they pick the fruit in Florida's citrus groves, the cukes in the Carolinas, the tobacco in Connecticut, the tomatoes in Delaware's Delmarva Peninsula, and the apples in Virginia. They trim sugar beets in Colorado, collect cherries in Washington's Yakima Valley, gather avocados in California, and prune and tie grape vines in the vast vineyards there. As part of the nation's life-giving force, they harvest and gather the lettuce, melons, asparagus, potatoes, blueberries, strawberries—all the rich and varied products of the land.

The crops are varied and seasonal; therefore, so is the work. Like the season the work is rhythmical and sure, but it is subject to the cruel vicissitudes of weather and pests as well as the human ones of greed and competition. Some of the work is skilled, some not; in every respect it is gruelingly hard. Worse still, it is often accompanied by inhuman and exploitive conditions.

The work day is long—when work is available—from sunup till past sunset and with little rest. Whole families pitch in, including infants and children. Crops cannot wait when they are ready. The pay is usually meager, often below the minimum standards required for all other work in this country. The bitter irony is that these people who labor to bring food to this nation's bounteous tables often go hungry—they are often denied food stamps.

The conditions these workers endure are harsh; they are subjected to special dangers and hardships: unsafe equipment, unhealthy sprays and pesticides, crude and unsanitary living conditions, exploitation in infinite ways by their crew bosses and employers, lack of care of any kind by anyone. If this charge seems dramatic and general, the real shock lies in the specifics that support this indictment. These will be described in later chapters.

Yet the migrant farm workers' labors are critical—preparing, harvesting, and readying for distribution the bounteous, billion-dollar collection of crops that feeds the richest country in the world. They work where local labor is unavailable or unwilling to do the job; yet the conditions and standards of their employment have always been a national scandal. As a group they are politically naive, without public voice or power to make their way or improve their lot.

Their work forms a symbiosis with nature, the earth, and the elements—not in the phony romantic sense of happy laborers romping in the sun, as some would depict them, but in an arduous almost pantheistic sense of man giving his life to encountering, perpetuating, and participating in the balances of nature. Farm work is employment that is real, necessary, and fundamental. But ironically, farm workers have been abused, humiliated, and profaned by their fellowmen, by the human forces of commerce and economics, and by greed.

Some observers say that the migrant streams are drying up and this human flow will soon end. Analysts attribute this change to evolving mercantile conditions such as mechanization, to challenging social forces such as unionization and agribusiness, even to the perversities of welfare legislation that was intended to be protective and ameliorative. To the extent that this is so—that we are witnessing the end of the migrant streams—it is instructive to understand from whence they came and why they have waned. Because there is always likely to be a significant population of migrant workers who will perform vital work for the consuming public, it is necessary to understand their needs, problems, and expectations and most importantly to seek ways that assist them in realizing their just aspirations.

THE MIGRANT PHENOMENON

Migrant farm work is a historic phenomenon in the United

States.[1] During the first half of the nineteenth century, there were vast population shifts westward. New waves of immigrants from Europe, along with other poor and landless industrial workers, left eastern cities and migrated west in search of work, wages, and land. There was a difference between these migrants and those who are the subject of this book. These workers did not move constantly; generally, they would take their families to a new place and settle there. Some hired hands would go from farm to farm and work alongside the farmer—clearing land, ditching meadows, and helping with the harvest. But generally they stayed in one locale for longer than a short season. The chief similarity to today's migrants was that they also were poor, dependent, and without promising opportunities.

During the period after the Civil War, changing economic and social factors led to the evolution of migrant streams with the characteristics that continue today. Cornell historian Cletus Daniel described "the development and expansion of large scale, labor intensive commercial agriculture in various regions of the country beginning in the late 19th century and idly accelerating during the early decades of the 20th."

In scale and structure, this industrialized agriculture was fundamentally unlike the family farming operation. . . .[U]nlike the family farm, which typically depended on family members and an occasional hired man or two at harvest time to meet its labor needs, the industrialized farm was perennially dependent upon a large, cheap labor force which was abundantly available during seasons of peak labor need, and either sufficiently mobile to move on when that need no longer existed or to remain in the vicinity and sustain itself through other means, including public assistance, until such time as there was again work to be done on the farm.[2]

An industrial commission on agriculture at the turn of the century described a "floating class" of workers—"beggars and vagrants who moved as the harvest progressed from the more southern to extreme northern grain fields." As sharecropping declined in the south and cotton picking became mechanized, large numbers of southern workers became unemployed and regional wages and prices became depressed. These displaced workers went east to the large fruit and vegetable farms, where refrigeration advancements had given rise to expanded production, and west to California, where the groves and fields were vast and the growing season was longest.

One social phenomenon that evolved during the first half of

this century (and no doubt contributed to the evolution of the farm workers' union movement) was concerned with the nature of farm life. In our country's early history, most farms were small and tended by families aided by small numbers of hired hands who, working and living with the family, felt a personal stake in the success of the farm; as a result, they neither were exploited nor felt so. Farm workers were not very different from working farmers. They lived similarly; were from the same class; and enjoyed close, personal, stable relationships with each other.

As agriculture became an industry and its enterprises became large in scale, the principles of farm operation changed radically.

Picking peas, 1941.
(Library of Congress)

Mechanization.

Land ownership grew in scope and was concentrated in fewer hands. The owners often were distant corporations, and relationships with employees became distant and impersonal also.

Farm work was becoming a big profit-making business more than a way of life. Owners often were interested in the farms only as part of a bigger, diversified list of holdings. Wages became matters to be calculated on ledgers, not personal contracts to be discussed and negotiated. Workers were laid off or imported for impersonal reasons governed only by economic considerations. Their welfare was neglected. Their social status became alienated from the agricultural community. As growers and farmers organized, workers were forced to act collectively to improve their individual bargaining positions.

Improved transportation facilities, including the advent of the automobile, provided growers with distant labor forces and migrant workers with equally distant job opportunities. The penultimate example of this phenomenon is the modern agribusiness that imports large numbers of workers from all over the country and the world, placing them in positions in which they will have no bargaining power. The high levels of mechanization and specialization that followed from this form of concentration changed and exacerbated the farm workers' situation.

The two basic elements of migrant farm work are the need of some people to move from place to place in search of work, because it is not available in one location, and the seasonal character of American agriculture, which requires a short-term influx of workers during the varied harvest seasons.

THE THREE STREAMS

During the first half of the twentieth century, three discernible streams of migrant farm workers evolved: an East Coast stream, a midcontinental stream, and a West Coast stream. These three human streams are based upon similar phenomena of labor and economics, although their ethnic and sociological makeups are different.

Originally, the East Coast stream was composed of Irish, Italian, and Scandinavian laborers who lived along the mid-Atlantic coast. More recently, the East Coast stream has become populated by native blacks, along with imported Puerto Ricans and West Indians from what has been called "a new migrant stream, this one airborne." Native workers live inland in Florida (Belle Glade is their winter capital) during the winter months; but they travel, often with their families, up the East Coast in spring and summer to pick the local crops as they are ready. They travel alone as "freewheelers" and in groups known as "crews"; they migrate in broken-down cars filled with people of all ages and their earthly possessions or in crews in old buses and trucks run by crew bosses. They make these seasonal pilgrimages because they must; they cannot earn enough money in the season at home to support themselves, even by their modest standards. So they travel from place to place, from farm to orchard, from field to grove to packing sheds, readying the crops of the East Coast for delivery to the dining tables of America. They travel through the Carolinas and Virginias, to New York and New Jersey, all the way to Maine. With the onset of winter they return home to Florida to work there at odd jobs or to rest and wait for the seasonal stream to begin again.

This toilsome, nomadic life was described by Salvador Herrera, National Association of Farmworker Organizations official, in a poignant speech to his organization.

Each year when the harvest begins, thousands of buses and cars haul thousands of crews to fields across America as millions of migrant farm workers hit the road. They ride in flatbed trucks, on old condemned school buses patched together for just one more season. They go by car: old cars, with engines knocking, laying a smoke screen of oil; old

Travel patterns of seasonal migratory agricultural workers.
(Office of Migrant Health, U.S. Public Health Service)

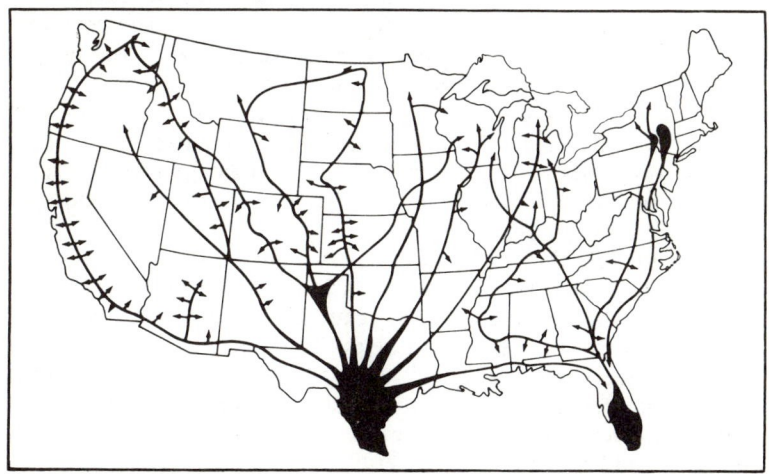

cars packed with bags, bundles, pots and pans, children crying. They go in pickups made into mobile tents—a home for the season. . . . The circus and the college house parties leave Florida after Easter. The first week of April, the major league clubs wind up their spring training to go home to play ball. The snowbirds start back to the cities of the north with their tans. And the migrants and farm workers form crews and follow the sun. Sometimes a single bus will carry a crew; sometimes they pass in ragged convoys as the migrant battalions rumble out of Florida and up the Eastern Seaboard. . . . The worker finds little to do in November. It is after a lean Thanksgiving and a bleak Christmas that hands are needed again in the fields and groves of the winter gardens.[3]

The midcontinental stream is based in the Rio Grande Valley in southern Texas and is composed predominantly of Mexican-Americans. One recent article reported that there are 200,000 migrant farm workers in Texas, about 140,000 of them in the Rio Grande Valley. This stream of labor was initiated in the late nineteenth century by cattle and sheep ranchers who were able to satisfy their needs for temporary herdsmen and shepherds by importing Texans and Mexicans. In the early twentieth century, Mexican and Chicano workers were recruited to pick cotton in Oklahoma, cut sugarcane in Louisiana, top sugar beets in Colorado, and harvest wheat in Kansas and Missouri. They now live in their own small homes and on farms for half the year in and around Texas. They travel in large family units in trucks, seeking seasonal farm work and the opportunity to earn money to sustain them through the rest of the year.

This stream follows two basic geographic patterns. One group travels solely within Texas, working only on the cotton crop from July to December. The second travels to the Great Lakes area (Michigan vegetable farmers are said to be the biggest midwestern importers of migrant labor), after working in Texas in the pepper, cabbage, cauliflower, and onion fields. Some also travel into the Rocky Mountain and northern Pacific areas to harvest tomatoes and pick cherries. On their journey back to Texas, some stop in the Panhandle to harvest peanuts and soybeans.

About half the migrants in this stream go only to one location in or outside Texas; often this is the same place year after year. The others move around, changing locales and employers as opportunities present themselves. Both groups are led either by crew leaders who handle all their arrangements or by a family patron who represents the small nuclear group. Deals are struck with employers privately, or work arrangements may be made through the U.S. Employment Service.

The West Coast stream has a unique ethnic base and history also. The abolition of slavery in the midnineteenth century left a labor vacuum in the vast farm and ranch lands of California. This was filled with imported Chinese laborers in the 1880s; with Japanese laborers in the early 1900s, and later with southern Europeans, many of whom settled and became landowners in this appealing land of plenty. In the 1920s and 1930s, Filipino laborers were brought to California farms in large numbers; in the early 1930s, they made up 14 percent of California's migrant labor force. Others followed from faraway Mediterranean countries and the East Indies.

Seeking employment during the Depression, hordes of men came to California from the Oklahoma and Arkansas dust bowl and from elsewhere in the Midwest where mechanization had displaced many corn belt farm workers. Presently, about one-fourth the migrant population in California is Mexican; during different periods, the number of Mexicans has risen and fallen, reflecting the changing economic circumstances in Mexico and the United States.

Migrants in the western stream move throughout California, which employs by far the largest number of farm workers of any state. Some move northward to Oregon and Washington to work on the large cherry, strawberry, and apple harvests there.

It is clear that there is no single profile to describe migrant farm workers. A *New York Times* report quite accurately noted:

The stereotype of the farm worker is of a Mexican-American stooped over a lettuce field in California, or weeding a row of cantaloupes in Texas or Arizona. Actually, a migrant farm worker is almost as likely to be a southern black who follows the harvest from Florida to upstate New York, or into Maine. The work is also varied: Some farm workers are skilled equipment operators who drive combines through the wheat fields of Kansas; others tend sheep herds in Idaho or round up cattle in Texas or harvest corn in Iowa.

The migrant streams are generated by the seasons of the crops and the economics of the farm labor market. The workers are drawn like human tributaries into areas of expanding work, and they vanish from places where work opportunities have dried up because of mechanization or other local phenomena. The streams are composed of poor and hard-working people, usually of similar sociological and ethnic backgrounds.

Their work and work conditions are similar whether they are gathering blueberries in New Jersey, picking avocados in California, cutting cotton in Texas, or packing tomatoes in Michigan. All face certain inherent problems: grueling, back-breaking work, poor pay, dilapidated housing, a displaced life in changing and often hostile surroundings, subjection to dangerous pesticides, and exploitation by growers and crew leaders who have almost total control over their lives. They endure all the inevitable problems of being uprooted: inadequate representation, few meaningful legal protections, no security, little opportunity to get out of the stream or to direct their children to a better life.

MECHANIZATION AND CONCENTRATION

The inherent difficulties encountered by migrants in their arduous lives have been compounded by the intervention of one specific, perplexing phenomenon that has narrowed their job market. This problem—mechanization—is the product of broad, impersonal forces over which farm workers have no control, and it cannot be legislated or administered away.

During the middle decades of the twentieth century, three fundamental factors have affected farm labor practices: the number of farms has decreased significantly, the size of farms has increased, the number of hired farm workers has decreased. All have resulted from the trend toward mechanization. Ingenious machines have been developed to speed the picking of crops that new fertilizers and pesticides have enlarged. Migrants have suffered the brunt of these technological advances; and they have received few of the benefits.

The available information is incomplete and inadequate; it is impossible to assess precisely the extent to which farm workers have been displaced by machines. Labor data, for example, deal with the number of man-hours required to produce a particular crop. These statistics cannot be translated precisely into numbers of workers. However, according to a U.S. Department of Agriculture (USDA) study, the number of family farm workers (nonhired, nonmigrant) has decreased from 7,597,000 in 1950 to 4,128,000 in 1965 to 3,330,000 in 1975. The number of hired (nonfamily) workers also shrank from 4,342,000 in 1950 to 3,128,000 in 1965 to 2,638,000 in 1975. The number of migrants in the hired farm worker group decreased from 466,000 in 1965 to 209,000 in 1974, largely because of mechanization. In the half-century since 1920, the man-hours employed in agriculture have decreased by two-thirds, about one-third of the cutback occurring since 1955. At the same time, the costs of paying farm workers has increased 40 percent—from $2.8 million in 1950 to

$5 million in 1973. Capital spent on mechanization rose from $2.8 million in 1950 to $4 million in 1965 to $5 million in 1973.[4]

The reasons for this increase in reliance on machines causing a consequent decrease in the use of farm workers should be obvious. Consider several examples. In Florida it is reported that a crew of 19 fruit pickers can hand-harvest 2.32 acres a day. A 16-member crew can mechanically harvest 8 acres a day. By virtue of maximum mechanization of oranges 16,200 fewer citrus pickers (36 percent) would be used during a season.[5]

Farm workers can pick 8.5 bushels of apples in an hour. Mechanical harvesters can pick 120 bushels in that time. Mechanization of fruit and vegetable farms is on the increase in Michigan. In 1964, for example, 5 percent of the state's blueberries were harvested by machine; by 1969 the amount that was machine harvested had risen to 90 percent. In 1965, 10 percent of the tomatoes in California were harvested by machine; by 1967, 95 percent were harvested mechanically.[6] A USDA study has concluded that mechanization of tobacco crops will drastically cut the need for seasonal workers for harvesting. By 1978, the report speculated, about 200,000 fewer people would be needed to harvest a 1972-size crop.[7]

The impact of mechanization on farm workers is a problem the United Farm Workers union has attacked head-on in California. Mechanization has become a priority issue for the union; it has replaced the grape boycott in expressions on bumper stickers, campaign buttons, and public platforms as a union issue. Cesar Chavez, president of the United Farm Workers, has referred to farm machines as "los monstruos—the monster . . . mechanical behemoths that threaten to decimate the farm worker force and turn California into another Appalachia."[8] The union cannot be against progress, Chavez says, but the perversities of this progress can and should be brought under control.

Cotton was once the major crop in California. Several decades ago, 100,000 farm workers labored in cotton fields. In the late 1950s thousands of families in the cotton-growing San Joaquin Valley were laid off because of the advent of cotton-harvesting machines. Sugar beets, almonds, and other field crops have been mechanized almost completely in recent decades. Again, thousands of workers and their families have endured misery and poverty as a result.

In 1977 an electric-eyed tomato sorter was introduced into the tomato fields of California. In the first year of its use, 7,500 workers were displaced. Chavez has pointed out that 50,000 people worked in the tomato harvest in 1964; by 1972 the work force had shrunk to 18,000. Each mechanical sorter in use reduces the number of workers from 66 to 90 percent. Chavez has predicted that in the harvest of 13 crops alone more than 120,000 California farm jobs will be lost to machines, raising the unemployment rate 1.2 percent and the consequent rate of social problems with it.

The impact of machines not only is felt by farm workers but consumers also have been harmed because food prices have risen disproportionately. Since 1964 the consumer cost of canned tomatoes has risen 111 percent compared to an overall food cost rise of 90 percent (and a rise of 76 percent for other produce). Furthermore, some vegetables are too fragile to be machine harvested. By genetically reprogramming plants to the needs of machines, such crops as the "square-round" tomato have been developed; and Chavez has noted that other new varieties of tasteless, pulpy, nutritionless fruits and vegetables are the result.

Chavez has pointed out another irony of the mechanization phenomenon. Research has been conducted by state-supported schools such as the University of California, which has developed machines without thought to their implications for the lives of farm workers. At an increasingly swift pace, the university has developed farming equipment that will lead to the mechanization of the bulk of such labor-intensive crops as wine grapes, lettuce, fresh tomatoes, peaches, apricots, cherries, melons, and celery, to name only a few. About 75 percent of the cost of the research that develops these new machines comes from public funds, with the growers seemingly the greatest beneficiaries.

When Chavez challenged the University of California Board of Regents about its role in conducting research and development for farm machinery, the Vice President for Agriculture, J. B. Kendrick, Jr., responded, "The University is an agent of change. It does not decide public policy or compensate losers among conflicting societal interests."

Former Secretary of Agriculture Bob Bergland had a less laissez-faire attitude about this subject. Late in 1979, Bergland announced he would cut off federal research funds for agricultural mechanization if the project would result in loss of jobs, dispossession of small family farms, or monopolies of food production.

The United Farm Workers union is pushing state legislation in California to deal with the impact of mechanization. One proposed bill calls for social impact studies before public money is spent for mechanization research. Another would create a state fund to compensate farm workers who are displaced by machines. As yet, neither of these bills has become law.

The union is not against progress or even against mechanization. It is concerned about reckless technology and the need to design complementary social programs to help workers who may lose their jobs as a result. In a lawsuit filed in January 1979, lawyers for farm workers called the phenomenon of mechanization publicly funded "welfare machines" that are putting farm workers and small farmers out of work by enriching agribusiness.

Since migrants are not a stable work force, they are displaced more commonly than other farm workers. As labor costs rise and farm sizes increase, farmers can be expected to place funds increasingly in cost-effective capital investment to substitute for labor investment. Demand will rise for skilled rather than unskilled farm workers, causing another economic fallout that particularly will hurt migrants.

Related to the phenomenon of mechanization is the comparable one of concentration. Small farms, usually family run, may have been the backbone of early American rural life and the agricultural world; but that no longer is the case. Much more vulnerable to national economic dynamics, less able to cope with the inevitable vicissitudes of life, the small farmer's holdings are being absorbed. According to USDA estimates, half of the farms in America had gone out of business by World War II and shutdowns are proceeding at the rate of 2,000 farms each week. As a result, experts have noted that there is both vertical and horizontal integration of farming into the food industry, more frequently dubbed agribusiness. The U.S. Food Marketing Commission reported that in 1958 "about 80 percent of the food industry was under oligopolistic control . . . the trend is to concentration." In California, for example, about 4 percent of the state's farms included 70 percent of the farmland; 7 percent of the farms hired 75 percent of the farm labor force.

To register concern about the phenomenon of mechanization and concentration and its impact on migrants is not to bemoan progress nor to suggest that it inevitably must hurt all farm workers. Not all crops can be harvested mechanically any more than they all can be handled by a nonmigrant labor force. Technical advances should help workers (who may be able to move into more skilled jobs) as well as consumers (who may get price cuts), along with employers who are presumed to be the chief beneficiaries. One study has shown that between 1947 and

1963 the growth in productivity in agriculture increased at twice the annual rates (5.7 percent as compared to 2.4 percent) for nonfarm work.

Mechanization is not a phenomenon unique to farm workers, and it should not be viewed as some particularly devious and inhuman scheme of the growers. However, the general vulnerability of migrants, compounded by their lack of options and political bargaining power, makes them potentially special victims rather than beneficiaries of technological progress. The disparities between rich and poor groups often are widened. As one prestigious report has noted:

Unemployment tends to be concentrated among those workers with little education, not primarily because technological developments are changing the nature of jobs, but because the uneducated are at the "back of the line" in the competition for jobs. Education, in part, determines the employability and productivity of the individual, the adaptability of the labor force, the growth and vitality of the economy, and the quality of the society. But we need not await the slow process of education to solve the problems of unemployment.[9]

NUMBERS AND EARNINGS

It is impossible to do more than estimate the size of the universe of migrant farm workers. The number generally accepted is one-quarter million; however, there are numerous variations, depending on whether one counts illegal aliens, families, and the unemployed; these would inflate the number into the millions.

A 1976 study of migrant farm workers estimated that there were 830,000, including 200,000 defined for programmatic purposes of eligibility for federal programs and 630,000 illegal Mexicans in addition to 10,000 to 20,000 Puerto Ricans.[10] The *New York Times* has reported that there are between 200,000 and 250,000 migrants and 600,000 seasonal laborers among the 2.6 million hired farm workers in the United States. The USDA estimated that in 1974 migrants were 8 percent of all farm wage earners (209,000 out of a total universe of 2.7 million). However, the USDA survey also found 927,000 "seasonal" workers, defined as people (including migrants) who did farm work for 25–149 days. The Department of Labor reported in 1975 that 135,074 migrant and seasonal farm workers used the Employment Service (many do not use this service, which accounts for the low number).

Most data available to the counting agencies of government are supplied by employers and as such, do not include illegal aliens, workers not on official payrolls, and available workers who are not hired. Thus the data describe production demands but not the size of the agricultural work force nor the number of illegal aliens who work on farms.

A 1977 report by Rural America, Inc. analyzed and criticized the standard government data regarding farm workers.[11] Government representatives who collect this data use different definitions of farm workers and the term "migrancy," confusing the statistical picture; various federal programs have different, legally drawn target populations and program eligibility (upon the basis of which $208 million was distributed in 1976).

The Statistical Reporting Service of the USDA reported in January 1977 that in 1976 there was an annual average of 3,229,000 farm workers in the United States (7 percent less than a year earlier). These figures include farm operators and the working members of their families along with local and migrant hired workers. The figures peaked at 5,046,000 in July 1977. The Economic Research Service of the USDA estimates 2.8 million hired seasonal, migrant, and full-time farm workers in 1976, of which 213,000 were migrants.

The USDA 1975 report stated that migrant farm workers earned $3,324 on the average (part-time student workers averaged about $1,000, and full-time migrants averaged $4,700) annually for 155 days of work, an average of $21.40 a day. Year-round nonmigrant farm workers earned $5,821 for 315 work days ($18.50 a day). White farm workers averaged 138 days and earned $2,635 ($19.15 a day), while black farm workers averaged 117 work days and earned $2,105 ($17.95 per day). Hispanics worked 141 days averaging $2,699 ($19.10 a day). The majority of hired farm workers (between 60 and 80 percent) in all the migrant streams worked less than three months a year during the 1960s and 1970s. About 10–15 percent of all migrants worked between three and six months; about 20–25 percent worked more than six months. Whites composed 60–80 percent of the hired farm workers, nonwhites 20–40 percent. Most migrant farm workers were less than 25 years old (40–65 percent); the second largest category was 25–54 years old; between 5 and 15 percent were over 55 years old.[12]

Concentration and mechanization of American farms and the displacement of marginal farm workers are current and ongoing phenomena. Farm employment has declined 22 percent between 1960 and 1970, studies report:

Farming has been and continues to be a rapidly declining sector from the standpoint of use of labor. Total farm employment (demand) has dropped from about 11 million persons in 1940 to some 5.6 million in 1965. Total man-hours dropped more sharply from 20 billion to 8.2 billion. These changes came about quite unevenly among regions and among enterprises. Much of the declining demand for labor in farming occurred in regions where nonfarm employment was not expanding or was actually shrinking relatively. These conditions resulted in reservoirs of unemployed and underemployed population, much of it largely immobile because of its unskilled nature and its extremely limited occupational experience.[13]

Despite these phenomena of the farm labor market, the migrant streams will continue. Mechanization and concentration can only go so far; there will no doubt always be small farms requiring seasonal laborers. All farm workers will not or could not move out of farm work even if they had the choice. It is in the nature of the labor force that since some migrant farm work always will be required, some will want to do it. The migrant streams may shift or become shallower, but they will not disappear. Their sources, flow, and direction need to be discerned, not for historical purposes alone but also to understand them and to be able to assist them as they enrich us all.

2

BOSSES OF THE STREAM

THAT THEIR WORK is hard and their lives especially difficult are realities well known to migrant farm workers. These facts of life are accepted because they are inevitable conditions. Other related problems have also plagued the farm workers' existence and defied government efforts at reform.

One such problem faced by many migrants is neither inherent in their work nor a necessary result of their economic relations with farmers. This is the evolution of crew leaders who occupy a critical role in the navigation of the migrant streams and have caused and exacerbated more problems for the workers than they have solved or mitigated. The crew leader's role as a factor in the agricultural labor marketplace reveals a graphic picture of the enslavement of migrant farm workers.

Some migrants find work on their own or through personal contacts. For years, families will travel to the same small farm in Illinois to assist in harvesting crops; then they will return to Texas to rest. Worker and farmer rely on the relationship and are satisfied with it. Other migrant workers use the U.S. Employment Service, which has an interstate agency that matches farm jobs and workers around the country. But farmer-employers are using the Employment Service less, and a great many workers do not use these free services because they do not know of them or have had bad experiences.

CREW LEADERS' ROLE

Many workers rely on crew leaders to get them their jobs and arrange their lives; sometimes this situation works well. A small crew of family members and friends may make their way together under the supervision of an adept patron who assumes responsibility for all the people in the group. Or an ambitious individual may save his money and organize his life so that he can lift himself out of farm work and become a useful middleman between the farm worker and the farmer. Remembering his experiences as a farm worker, he may be an effective advocate for those he supervises. In this situation, the crew leader is an example of the American dream of enterprise rewarded.

Some commentators believe crew leaders provide an essential and irreplaceable role in the agricultural job and labor markets. At Senate hearings in 1974, one witness put it this way:

Like any other group, labor contractors have their share of bad actors. Unfortunately, the general public has gained the impression that all labor contractors are bad actors and all learned the business of exploiting unfortunate migrant workers.

This image of the labor contractor is not justified. The great majority of these people are responsible businessmen who have made a significant investment in their businesses and who make every effort to abide by the laws, rules and regulations that govern their operation. They are small businessmen who provide an essential service to agriculture.[1]

Congressional committees that have criticized and attempted to regulate crew leaders have proceeded on the assumption that they are an indispensable part of the existing farm labor system:

With all its faults, the crew leader system has served a useful purpose in the farm labor market by helping to bring individuals together into manageable units with which the employers and employment services can more effectively deal.

This government approach—to regulate rather than abrogate the farm labor contractor system—is questionable. Too many crew leaders are predators who, spying a bad system, have found a way to profit from it and in the process to make the system worse than it had been or ever needed to be.

Free-lancing because they have means and know the system or operating under conventional contracts with farm employers, crew leaders recruit farm workers, transport them to jobs,

Paying potato workers in an Oklahoma field. (Library of Congress)

manage their affairs, and return them home—often plundering their hapless clients in the process. Some crew leaders are registered with the government and do their mischief under license. Others, called "coyotes" by Chicano farm workers, operate openly in violation of government regulations. Many are the only employers farm workers ever deal with or see.

Federal laws define crew leaders (formally called farm labor contractors) as anyone who recruits, hires, furnishes, or transports agricultural workers (not members of their own families) for agricultural employment and is paid a fee for these services.[2]

A crew leader may be an individual farm worker who transports other farm workers to a distant job and is paid for that service by the grower; he or she (many are women) may be an employee of a giant agricultural corporation or an individual operator wholly disengaged from any but monetary ties to the workers and the grower. Essentially, a crew leader is an agent between farm workers and their employers, one who effects the functions of the agricultural marketplace: matching people who need jobs with agricultural employers who need workers.

Crew leaders are paid well for this work. The economics of the business as it relates to a tomato harvest has been described:

In 1974, if a crew leader had twenty workers, the grower would pay him $30 daily simply for bringing the workers to the field. If the crew leader supervised the work in the fields, he would earn a day's salary of $25. The crew leader would be paid about $.90 for each box of tomatoes that the crew picked. He would in turn pay each worker $.40 for every box that he picked, so the crew leader would clear $.50 on a box. On a good day, a crew of twenty workers can pick about 1,000 boxes of tomatoes. Each worker would make an average of $20, and the crew leader would pocket $500. Out of that, the crew leader must pay for his truck and his insurance. Of course, such good days are not frequent, either for the crew boss or the pickers; they occur only when the crop is ripe and full.[3]

The typical labor contractor has been described to a Senate committee as "a man with six grades of education but with a high degree of hard knocks, knowledge and personal experiences." He began his life doing hard farm work:

He was exposed to the bitterness of his elders who cussed and drank to forget their own frustrations. He knows what it is like to move from one camp to another and face the rejection of the communities whose interest in him has 100 percent economic connotations.

In early life he came to the realization that, as a migrant, he would be accepted only if he had cash which people could try to wean from him. This translated itself into an intense passion to achieve this cash status, and a passion he was able to satisfy because he was blessed with a little more drive and shrewdness than his fellows. He took a little more interest in learning English so he could talk to farmers and association representatives, so he could persuade the immigration officer to leave him alone, so he could make figures and shuffle them in transactions, so he could write primitive type payrolls, and in short, so he could turn himself into a businessman . . . a leader of his people.

He lives in a home, either in the community or near the camp. He has a television, a washing machine, a refrigerator. He always has a bank account. . . . He is very impressive and insists that you notice it. Of course, he knows what the migrants are experiencing for he was once one of them. . . .

A typical contractor develops instincts to play every angle. Gambling, prostitution, narcotics . . . they are just part of the game.

He performs the recruiting, transporting, and often supervisory service for the farmer or the association but the pay for his service largely derives from his crew.

During his experience as a migrant worker himself, he lived under circumstances where he received a "short end of the stick." . . . In another social setting, he might have become a Main Street businessman, a professional man or a technician. . . . His drive has carried him inevitably to giving the "short end of the stick," instead of receiving it.[4]

Along with negotiating the basic economic relations between farm workers and farmers, crew leaders carry out all the related roles that expand like ripples from their initial and fundamental job-finding role.

First, the crew leader recruits in the home base states where the farm workers live during the winter months. They may approach pickers in the fields, on the streets, or in their winter homes. Crew leaders contact workers they know or others who have been recommended to them. They hire prospects either on the promise that they will find them jobs or for specific employment with definite terms for which they already have contracted.

According to one account, 100,000 farm workers are employed in Florida during the winter months. During the summer only 25,000 agricultural jobs are available.[5] Thus as many as 75 percent of those employed in Florida during the winter months may be available for summer work in the fields along the eastern coast or in some midwestern states. Crew leaders will find many willing recruits among these 75,000 workers. Some are so eager to line up seasonal work elsewhere that they contact the crew leaders. By February, crew leaders will have contacted the growers they regularly supply and will know how many workers are needed and what the terms of the future work contract will be.[6] From this ready and oversized pool they then match people with known jobs.

A critical need of migrant farm workers, one that too often has been filled in a scandalous and tragic way by crew leaders, is transportation. Most migrants need a way to get to their faraway jobs. The crew leader will provide a ride in a car, truck, or old bus. In addition, the crew leader usually is responsible for transporting the crew on a daily basis from camps where they are housed to fields where they work. When one job is done, the crew is taken to the next, often in another state. Eventually, when the opportunities are exhausted, often months later, the leaders transport the crews back to their homes and the migrant process is complete.

ABUSES

Crew leaders have been responsible for horrible accidents costing human lives as well as for property damage caused by the faulty mechanical condition of their vehicles and use of careless drivers. In California during a ten-year period (1951–1961), 112 farm workers were killed and 2,575 were injured while being transported to and from their jobs by crew leaders.[7]

Periodically, newspaper reports describe a ghastly accident that has killed and maimed traveling farm workers. In 1957 a truck crashed in North Carolina, killing 21. In 1963 a bus driven by a crew leader was rammed by a train outside Salinas, Calif., killing 27 farm workers and injuring 30.[8] On January 15, 1974, a bus owned by a labor contractor in Calfornia plunged into a drainage ditch, killing 19 and injuring the remaining 28 workers. The safety violations causing that accident were described to a Senate investigating committee:

The bus was overloaded. The capacity written on the side of the bus was 45 and there were 47 people on the bus. People were sitting on water cans in the front of the bus. The emergency braking system in the bus was inoperative. The voltage regulator was defectively installed. The wiring in the vicinity of the lights and ignition were in very poor condition. . . . The exhausts from the engine were not released from the exhaust pipes underneath the bus behind the bus, so it came up in the passengers' seats. There were holes as large as three or four inches in the fire walls between the engine and the passenger section, right in front of the driver, so carbon monoxide had a chance to come right into the bus. . . . The contractor was transporting workers to and from the fields without requiring permits as required by law. Most seriously, when the bus came to rest in the canal, it was straddling the canal, and only 28 inches of the bus was under water, but in that 28 inches of water, 19 people drowned. You might ask why so many in so little water? At the impact of the bus, as the bus hit into the bank of the canal, every seat of the bus came off the floor, crashed into the front of the bus, and as the bus went onto its side, all went to the left. People were crushed and buried.

The bus seats were held to the floor by screws 2/8ths of an inch wide and 5/16ths of an inch long. California law requires that bus seats be securely fastened. There is a California law against all of these other violations.[9]

A New York newspaper reporter who traveled with migrants reported his experiences:

I rode in a bus with a labor crew of seventeen, including a young couple with a four-month-old infant. The trip from Homestead to Ruskin, Florida covered 125 miles. The driver, in a moment of candor, told me he was subject to violent epileptic seizures.

Our crew traveled 13 hours before the first stop was made. The driver stopped for gas, but not for people. The infant had to use for toilet purposes a filthy rag salvaged from the bus floor. As for the men and women, their experience must go undescribed.

The driver in the ark-like vehicle I rode in admitted his license had been lifted because of a conviction for drunken driving. . . .

On our antique bus, windows were cracked or broken. Floor boards had long since broken away from mountings and been removed. Both rear wheels, with their smooth, worn tires, were visible from inside the bus. The owner admitted to me later that the bus had not been inspected in the five years he had owned it. Baggage and trash [blocked] access to the rear emergency door. And, because the door catch was broken, [the door] had been bound firmly shut with baling wire.[10]

Along with their basic role of finding jobs, many crew leaders exploit their control over the lives of their totally dependent farm workers by cashing in on every necessary function of their lives on the road. A leader will arrange for housing and provide all food and living supplies for a price that is usually outrageously high. He and his wife may prepare and sell meals. They may drive workers to town to find the only relief they can get from their work; they may supply candy, cigarettes, and wine—all for a price. If the workers under their supervision need money for any of this, the crew leader will lend it to them, often at usurious rates that keep them bonded and dependent. Here is how one observer described the system:

Sometimes these leaders are fair and honest. Sometimes they're brutal. Often they go to New York or other cities, and wait around shelters for homeless men, offering work. They promise them money and booze, then to keep them dumb they give them all the drinks they want; but they charge them a dollar for a beer, three dollars for a pint of wine, twenty-five dollars for transportation. Much of this is on credit because that way the crew leader stays in control Often he becomes extremely rich; the migrants become indentured servants, always owing more than they can earn.[11]

Crew leaders have a monopoly on every corner of the farm workers' lives, and they exploit it. It is no wonder then that the crew leader has been described in testimony before the U.S. Senate as the single most important person in the lives of migrant farm workers:

Everything of importance to the farm worker is affected by the labor contractor—how he gets a job, terms of his employment, his transportation to and from work, his housing and that of his family, medical services—the whole gamut of his relationship with the ultimate employer, the grower.[12]

"They're the sheep and I'm their leader," one candid crew leader told the Harvard-based doctor and social critic Robert Coles; that statement seems to sum it up.

When farm labor contractors recruit workers to be members of a crew, they act as if they were the growers' employment agents, and in many cases they may be. But because the worker does not know the actual conditions of the proposed employment, crew leaders may misrepresent the terms and conditions. They may take workers where there are no jobs. They may charge excessive fees for providing housing or other services, while insisting, dishonestly, that they are required by the grower. Crew leaders may fail to inform the migrant about the weather-dependent aspects of the harvest or may not inform them of any labor difficulties existing in the area, such as strikes or layoffs. In short, prospective members of a crew are at the mercy of a contractor who recruits them, and they have no independent way to determine whether the promises are true or false.

Crew leaders also supervise workers in the fields. They hand out the work assignments; prod the workers; keep records of the hours worked or the piece work performed; provide water, sanitation facilities, and food; and decide just about everything that goes on during a work day. They are paid on the basis of

Crew leader's son waits by bus used for migrant farm workers. New Jersey tomato farm. (Robert C. Cosgrove)

what their workers produce; usually, they do not do the work themselves.

The pathetic life and death control over the crews they service is epitomized by the leader's role as banker. Generally, it is the crew leader who pays the workers for the employer; that is, keeps all records, makes all deals. Crew leaders have been known to cheat the employer, the employee, and the government in carrying out this role as migrant bursar.

The unscrupulous labor contractor who extends credit to the crew or is responsible for paying them has the tempting opportunity to cheat. Some contractors underpay their employees, either by misrepresenting the wages that the grower has provided for disbursement, by miscounting the actual amount of work produced, or by lowering the piece-rate wage. Others will overcharge members of the crew for housing, food, transportation, or other items or goods provided. Crew leaders have charged workers for dues to a nonexistent union and have retained Social Security deductions collected from paychecks. In extreme situations, the crew leader may abandon workers without payment or force them to leave their work without receiving pay they have earned.

As one veteran Florida farm worker has reported:

> It is a favorite gimmick to exploit the illiterate, inarticulate migrant workers. Hang him up in a camp or a farm where he can't run and then charge him for his food and lodging. What does a migrant do? . . . They stay on, run up debts to the farmer-grower or contractor and then work off their debts with sweat and toil when the crop comes in. And at the end? They have nothing, and so they move on.

No wonder, then, one crew leader has said, "If they complain it does them no good. I say, 'Well, you can go back home, but how are you going to get there?' "[13]

A United Farm Workers union representative had this judgment to make of crew leaders:

> [F]arm labor contractors all over the country suck sweat, health, money, even life itself out of our people for years. [The] labor contractor traffics in human beings, women, men and children, brown, black and white. He conducts a modern-day slave trade. . . .
>
> The labor contractor's job is to be the middle man between the grower and the worker and his goal is to make as much profit from that task as he can. He does not earn his living by the work of his own hands, but rather by providing cheap, docile labor to the rich and powerful men who control agricultural production in this country. The tools of his trade are his broken-down unsafe trucks and buses, . . . his beer cans and string bean cans contain the tepid water for the workers in the blazing fields; his over-priced cheap wine, soda pop and sandwiches made of one slice of bologna between two of white bread, to sell to the workers, miles away from the nearest store. Sometimes he throws housing into the bargain, and, true to form, it is of the same bad quality."[14]

REGISTRATION AND LICENSING

The government has tried to control the supply of migrant labor through the establishment of the Department of Labor's Employment Service in 1933, through the USDA's Agricultural Extension Service in the 1940s, and under the bracero program during World War II. After the abuses of the crew leader system became publicized in books and articles and eventually in testimony at hearings before the Senate, attempts were made to help migrant farm workers by controlling the suppliers of migrant labor, the crew leaders themselves. These exposés culminated in the Farm Labor Contractor Registration Act of 1963 (FLCRA), which was amended in 1974.

Through the process of registering crew leaders, FLCRA attempted to regulate and eliminate the abuses perpetrated upon migrant and seasonal farm workers by some labor contractors. The Labor Department established two specific requirements crew leaders had to meet before a license would be issued: they must assume the financial responsibility to transport crew members and they must have no character deficiencies (as determined by the Labor Department) or prior criminal record.[15]

In addition, the Labor Department was to police the licensed crew leaders. To keep a license, the crew leader must prove freedom from certain prohibited activities, that is, misrepresentations or false statements in an application for a license; false or misleading information to crews concerning their terms, conditions, or existence of employment; failure to carry out agreements with farm operators. Crew leaders were required to be financially responsible, not to employ illegal aliens, not to have a criminal record, and to abide by set rules.

In addition, the FLCRA required crew leaders to disclose certain important information to each worker at the time of recruitment: the area of employment, the crops to be harvested, the transportation and housing insurance to be provided, the wage rates to be paid, and the charges to be made by the contractor for services rendered. The crew leader also was required to provide fair and honest payroll services, a statement of which was to be provided each migrant worker in the crew. A $500 fine could be assessed against any farm labor contractor who violated the act willfully and knowingly.

Registration under this new law was intended to uncover crew leaders who were unfit, to provide information as to their whereabouts and backgrounds, and to impose penalties for violations. It did not work that way.

Abuses of migrant farm workers by crew leaders continued. A key reason was that the act was not adequately enforced. "The bureaucrats who were given the responsibility to enforce it did not get out of the regional offices to enforce it,"[16] one critic testified. The FLCRA bureaucrats explained that they were understaffed and underfunded. Prior to 1972, 17 people in the Farm Labor Services Division of the Department of Labor concentrated their attention on crew leaders. Six (in the national office) were field investigators responsible for conducting all investigations of violations of the act throughout the country by the approximately 3,000 registered crew leaders as well as apprehending the thousands of others who had not even registered.[17]

In October 1972 responsibility for FLCRA enforcement was transferred to the Employment Standards Administration as a result of a directive from the secretary of labor. The transfer was made partly as a result of Labor Department findings that crew leaders were paying less than minimum wages and were responsible for other violations of law. After October 1972 the 1963 act was enforced by approximately 1,000 compliance officers located in 88 area offices and in more than 200 field stations throughout the country. Nevertheless, abuses by crew leaders continued. In 1973 the Employment Standards Administration conducted 1,100 investigations. About 70 percent of these disclosed violations of the act; yet cases were brought against only four crew leaders.

There were other problems. The 1963 act covered only contractors who crossed state lines, ignoring those in the largest, most active farming states (California and Texas, for example) who did not operate in interstate commerce. In addition, the act did not contain effective sanctions for violations.

As a result, in 1974 Congress amended the FLCRA, making three basic changes: it extended the coverage of the 1963 act, expanded the obligations of those registered under the act, and provided for stronger enforcement.

Coverage is no longer restricted to farm labor contractors who cross state lines, although purely local activities of crew leaders, that is, within a 25-mile radius, are exempt. There is no longer a requirement that crews include ten or more people for the leader to be covered by the act. Furthermore, some new activities (packing and freezing, for example), which were not previously covered, are now included by the 1974 amendments.

The amount of insurance required to remain licensed has been increased, and the exact vehicles of transportation by which the crew leaders intend to transport migrants must be identified. Leaders must supply additional information to the members of their crews: the period of employment, the existence of strikes or other work stoppages or interruptions at the place of contracted employment, and the existence of any arrangement with the grower by which the farm labor contractor receives a commission or other benefit from the work of the migrants supervised.

Most important, the enforcement provisions of the act were

broadened and made more severe, allowing for the imposition of prison terms and increased fines for violations. Migrants were granted legal action against crew leaders who violate the act. Retaliation (intimidation, coercion, threats, blacklisting) by crew leaders was expressly prohibited. Growers were made liable for hiring farm labor contractors who did not have a FLCRA license.

Following the enactment of the 1974 amendments, enforcement activity by the Labor Department seemed to improve. Between December 1974 and September 1975, the Employment Standards Administration conducted 2,010 investigations of complaints against crew leaders. Injunctions were issued in 135 cases; and the secretary of labor refused to issue one license (though there were recommendations that he refuse 17 others). There has been a dramatic increase in the registration of crew leaders, according to Labor Department officials. In fiscal year 1975, 2,500 crew leaders (representing over 80,000 farm workers) registered; in fiscal year 1976, the number of registered crew leaders increased fourfold to 10,900 (representing over 286,000 farm workers).

Despite the apparent increased effectiveness of the FLCRA, some observers still believe that regulation of the activities of crew leaders is not enough to end the abuses that have occurred in the past and still continue. The United Farm Workers union advocates the replacement of the farm labor contractor system by the union hiring hall,[18] a view shared by the California Rural Legal Services.

Reading about the abuses of crew leaders and their virtual immunity from control, one may recall the prophetic tirade of the Ragpicker in Jean Giraudoux's play, *The Madwoman of Chaillot*:

COUNTESS: What work do they do?

THE RAGPICKER: They don't do any work. . . . They don't do anything, but wherever you see them, things are not the same. I remember well the time when a cabbage could sell itself just by being a cabbage. Nowadays it's no good being a cabbage—unless you have an agent and pay him a commission. Nothing is free any more to sell itself or give itself away. These days, Countess, every cabbage has its pimp.

COUNTESS: I can't believe that.

THE RAGPICKER: Countess, little by little, the pimps have taken over the world. They don't do anything, they don't make anything—they just stand there and take their cut. It makes a difference. Look at the shopkeepers. Do you ever see one smiling at a customer any more? Certainly not. Their smiles are strictly for the pimps. The butcher has to smile at the meat-pimp, the florist at the rose-pimp, the grocer at the fresh-fruit-and-vegetable pimp. It's all organized down to the slightest detail. A pimp for bird-seed. A pimp for fish food. That's why the cost of living keeps going up all the time. You buy a glass of beer—it costs twice as much as it used to. Why? 10 percent for the glass-pimp, 10 percent for the beer-pimp, 20 percent for the glass-of-beer-pimp—that's where our money goes. Personally, I prefer the old-fashioned type. Some of those men at least were loved by the women they sold. But what feelings can a pimp arouse in a leg of lamb? Pardon my language, Irma. . . . So now you know, Countess, why the worker is no longer happy. We are the last of the free people of the earth. You saw them looking us over today. Tomorrow, the street-singer will start paying the song-pimp, and the garbage-pimp will be after me. I tell you, countess, we're finished. It's the end of free enterprise in this world! . . .

COUNTESS: They're a lot of fools and so are you! How can you bear to live in a world where there is unhappiness? Where a man is not his own master? Are you cowards? All we have to do is to get rid of these men.

PIERRE: How can we get rid of them? They're too strong. . . . They have all the power. And all the money. And they're greedy for more.[19]

3

HEALTH, HOUSING, AND EDUCATION

MIGRANT FARM WORKERS travel to earn money; to solve that economic problem, they incur many others that concern their welfare. Health, housing, and education pose major special problems for migrants—problems that do not inhere in their work but derive from the extraordinary lives their work requires.

HEALTH

The general problems of life, shared by all people, are especially intense for migrants. The general costs, quality, and availability of good medical and hospital care to the public have been questioned in recent years. This situation is generally worse in rural areas. These problems are exacerbated for migrants who have no funds, community ties, or political power to cope with them. In any situation and for any group the problem of assuring adequate health care would be serious; in the case of migrants, what they endure is shocking.

The problem begins with a dilemma that defines migrants' lives and causes all their problems—lack of power over their own destiny. How this dilemma arises in the context of migrant health becomes clear from one farm worker's conversation with Dr. Robert Coles:

Sometimes we'll be out there in the field. The grower will be on my back, telling me the tomatoes have to be in by the end of the week or he's through, completely destroyed. I'll be pushing on my people to pull those tomatoes in. The sun will be beating down on us. And I'll be looking at my people and thinking to myself that half of them are in real bad trouble, the men and the women and the children. Maybe *all* of them are in trouble, and I should be taking all of them that day to the doctor. But if we don't get the tomatoes in pretty soon, none of us will be eating three meals a day and then we'll *really* need to see a doctor—and he'll tell us to go and eat! And how, I ask you, how will we go and do that except by getting those tomatoes in, right on time?[1]

The United Farm Workers union has alleged that many of the 80,000 children of migrant families have been run over by tractors and poisoned by pesticides. The average life span of a farm worker is 49 years. "There is blood on the grapes," Cesar Chavez has claimed; the facts support his melodramatic charge. The president of the National Association of Farm Worker Organizations, Humberto Fuentes, has spoken out against the harsh death rate of the migrant infant, the reduced life expectancy of the middle-aged adult, the ever-present malnutrition and hunger, the incredible proliferation of turn-of-the-century diseases, and the intolerable environmental conditions endured by migrant farm workers.

Hearings in 1972 before the Senate Subcommittee on Migratory Labor and the House Interstate and Foreign Commerce Committee unearthed the deplorable health conditions that plague migrants.[2,3] On the move and without funds, these workers have limited access to medical care. In 1977 a survey in Indiana revealed that only 8 percent of migrant farm workers there saw a doctor each year (70 percent of the general U.S. population does so). A Virginia Health Department study in 1974 found that 28 percent of the migrants in that state received no medical treatment for their serious and critical health needs.[4]

One knowledgeable medical witness reported to the Senate:

Most of these people live constantly at the brink of medical disaster, hoping that the symptoms they have or the pain they feel will prove transient or can somehow be survived, for they know that no help is available to them.[5]

Health problems run the gamut: malnutrition, visual defects, ear infections, tooth decay, heart and parasitic diseases, skin and respiratory infections, and high rates of mental illness and preventable diseases such as polio and venereal disease. The infection and parasitic disease rates of migrants are 200–500 percent higher than the national averages. Their mortality rate is double the national average; life expectancy is about 30 years lower.[6]

These health problems start with migratory children; they are born premature three times as often as others, 20 percent are born without proper medical assistance, they have a 25 percent higher chance of dying in the first year, and the infant mortality rate is at the 1930 national level. As the migrant child grows and matures, he or she has little if any preventive medical care, and health care is rare when sickness occurs. They are subjected to atrocious, inhuman environmental conditions—water, food, housing, clothing, sanitation—which contribute to poor health.[7] One Department of Health, Education, and Welfare inspection team reported:

As we walked between the rows of dwelling units, many small children played around us, running about barefooted through mud and pools of stagnant, refuse-filled water—the perfect culture for intestinal parasites, polio, and bacteria—causing infectious diarrhea which kills so many children. . . .

There has to be also a very vigorous attack on sanitation, on housing, on water supplies, on sewage disposal, garbage pickup; all these things. Otherwise, you are simply putting a Band-Aid on a horrible wound.[8]

The *New England Journal of Medicine* has reported:

Health problems cannot be solved without addressing other important aspects of the community's health such as housing. . . . Programs that focus on curative medicine without major attention to these traditionally non-medical areas will achieve at best a marginal success. . . .[9]

One health problem that is unique to farm workers is caused by their exposure to pesticides commonly used in farming. A Senate committee reported in 1970 that despite incomplete medical records there was documentation that 800 farm workers are killed each year and over 800,000 are injured as a result of pesticides. In California alone, a Department of Public Health study in 1960 revealed that 3,000 children received emergency or hospital treatment for ingesting pesticides. Who knows how many others were affected but failed to make the record books?

For years, the Occupational Safety and Health Administration (OSHA) and the Environmental Protection Agency (EPA) fought over the question of which had the responsibility to police this problem. A federal court finally determined that OSHA's authority was preempted by EPA in 1974. However, EPA has done little since then to enforce its standards. It does not have the enforcement powers that OSHA has (it cannot enter a farm without permission or a warrant, for example) nor the staff needed to regulate pesticide use (it has 50 inspectors to police pesticide manufacturers and users all over the United States). According to its own officials,

EPA's enforcement program is limited to responding to complaints.

While program administrators at OSHA explain that farm workers are relatively few in number and their occupational hazards are relatively innocuous, statistics show that they suffer disproportionately from job-related injuries. The National Center for Health Statistics reports that in 1975, of 3.6 million farm workers, 200,000 suffered disabling injuries and 2,100 suffered fatalities in the course of their work. Fatalities were almost four times the national average. Though farm workers made up 4.4 percent of the 1971 work force, the National Safety Council reported that they suffered 16 percent of the occupational fatalities and 9 percent of all disabling injuries.

OSHA conducted 47,000 inspections in 1973; only 197 were in agricultural workplaces. Officials in Washington account for this neglect with comparative data. There are 5 million workplaces in the United States and only 2,300 OSHA inspectors. "What more can we do?"

According to Chavez, the health and safety of American farm workers is the single most important issue of the United Farm Workers. It is one that must be resolved in collective bargaining; government controls will not suffice, since government response to health needs of migrants has been inadequate. One critic described government activities in the migrant health field as "slim pickings":

The Environmental Protection Agency hasn't yet worked out specific tolerance levels for pesticide exposure for farmworkers. . . . The Occupational Safety and Health Administration . . . hasn't gotten around to regulating sanitary facilities in the fields. . . . Medicaid regulations . . . usually have a residency requirement so strict as to effectively exclude farmworkers.[10]

Total neglect and hostility by private and local power structures have been exposed by sensational legislative hearings. Laws have been passed; but well-intended bureaucrats have not been able to assure the delivery of services. Much money has been spent, but the problem remains. One medical expert told a Senate subcommittee that migratory medical care "represents a problem that has been handled by strategic neglect."

The failure of the earlier Public Health Act to deal with the health problems of migrant farm workers, having been highlighted in Senate hearings, led to the passage in 1962 of the Migrant Health Act.[11] This was a grant program under which money was given to public and private nonprofit organizations to establish health clinics and to improve health services for migrants. Public health departments, which had been a cause of the problem this program sought to cure, became its beneficiary. Of the initial program budget, 80 percent went to public health departments. But the migrant clientele who were the intended beneficiaries of the program saw few improvements. Later amendments to the act (in 1965, 1968, and 1970) included necessary hospital care, added seasonal farm workers to the coverage, and mandated consumer involvement in recipient organizations.

By 1975 a new Act emerged, the Special Health Revenue Sharing Act.[12] Under this the Department of Health, Education, and Welfare made grants to public and private organizations, which created migrant health clinics in what were called "high impact areas" (where over 6,000 migrants and their families lived for over 2 months) and "low impact areas" (places not meeting the "high impact" criteria). Migrants were to be on the governing boards of these clinics; the inclusion of broad services, training, and facilities was contemplated. A National Advisory Council was to oversee the progress.[13]

Despite being "studied to death" during its first five years in operation, in the words of a Senate subcommittee, and despite significant costs, health services to migrant farm workers were poorly coordinated, lacking in facilities for continuous care, and of questionable quality.

While the lack of preventive care and general medical assistance is pathetic, the serious and emergency medical needs of migrants have been handled in a criminal fashion by some hospitals. The availability of good hospital care depends on money, and those without funds typically do without it.

Since over 90 percent of migrant farm workers are not covered by any hospital care insurance, local hospitals simply will not treat them. Hospital administrators are callous and reluctant to incur unreimbursable expenses, according to one public health expert. Hospitals refuse to accept migrants unless they are referred by a private physician (ordinarily not the case for poor, transient, and alienated groups) or can pay a deposit ($275 in Florida, $150 in Texas). These requirements are not supposed to be enforced in emergency cases; but at hearings, a Senate committee heard about one pregnant woman who died in labor because she was refused admission and about sick infants dying without treatment while their parents were hassled about signing a promissory note. A press report has described the death of an 11-month-old child of migrant parents. A Texas hospital refused to treat the child because the couple did not have $400 and were not residents of the county.

Hospitals receiving Hill-Burton construction funds (as most do) are expected to provide free or low-cost medical services to indigent clientele. Under the Migrant Health Act, provisions are supposed to be made for in-patient care for migrant farm workers. In fact, according to legislative inquiries, only 0.1 percent of the eligible migrant farm worker population has been receiving these hospital services.[14] The experts seem to agree that there are several reasons for this shocking situation. There is hostility to migrants in many local medical communities, for good reasons (doctors are overworked) and for bad reasons (racist notions about migrant farm workers).[15]

One study in Indiana showed that, for no apparent reason, a local optometric group opposed a migrant health project created to provide eye examinations. The director of a California clinic said before a Senate inquiry that his experiences demonstrated that medical societies "do not like us as a matter of philosophy." The director of a clinic in Yakima, Wash., testified that the local medical societies look on "every change from the customary as a threat." In one city, he told a Senate inquiry, doctors who worked for a migrant farm worker clinic were threatened with expulsion from the society. The director of a clinic in Palo Alto, Calif., Dr. Russell Lee, concluded, "The old piety of medicine—it's the principle, not the money—really means: it's the money and the principle doesn't have a damned thing to do with it." A crew leader described this principle to Dr. Robert Coles in blunt language:

Doctors are like growers; they pay attention to money. If you have money, they'll take care of you. If you don't they'll tell you to get the hell out of their office. My sister says the doctors are like the ministers, "God's people," she calls them. I get a laugh out of that. I say to her, "God's people," yes, they're "God's people" if you have "God's dollar bill" for them; and if you don't, then they're the Devil—worse than the Devil, because at least the Devil doesn't pretend to be something other than what he is.[16]

In addition, experts have concluded, there is antagonism in local and state governments to migrant clinics, which is reflected in the press and commerce of the areas. Migrants are viewed as outsiders, as beneficiaries of expensive and unnecessary federal protection, as the cause of federal intrusions on the local establishment, and as temporary necessities who are drains on the overall local economy.

Growers, who should have a selfish if not a humanitarian interest in the well-being of their workers, often are the leaders of opposition to migrant health programs. One might expect employers to feel that productivity and efficiency would improve if their employees were healthy. But one researcher concluded that those most affected by the migrants' poor health are most responsible for delaying and interfering with the effective implementation of migrant health programs.

Some growers have a short-sighted, negative view of their workers, whom they see as "deadbeats" who "live like animals," as one Texas farmer told a federal inspector. Some growers have the attitude that if migrants get something for free, they will not work, that they are temporary employees who are not worth any serious investment, and that do-gooders are duped by migrants' needs and intolerant of the growers' private interests. When one grower learned that the 9-month-old baby of a migrant family he employed was refused admission to a hospital and died of diarrhea and dehydration, he philosophized, "Babies die all the time, why should they get so excited when one dies here?"

If the medical and health services establishment and farm employers are unsympathetic if not hostile, imagine how the crew leaders deal with health needs of their workers. One migrant recently complained to an interviewer:

That nurse who comes here and teaches us how to use pills or get fitted is the best friend we have. No wonder the crew leader wants to get rid of her and her program. He says she's an outsider, that nurse. He says she's white, and she doesn't understand us. But she understands all right—she understands him; that's what has him worried. He keeps asking me when I'm going to have a baby. He looks at me as if to say I'll never be a real slave of his until I come up with that kid! Then I'll be hooked! That's the one big lesson I've learned.[17]

To complete this cynical cycle, farm workers' health problems are held against them. A 1974 report by the Orange County Human Relations Commission concluded:

[I]ll men are ignored or intimidated by threats of being fired . . . laborers have been thrown out of camp for fear their diseases will bring authorities to the camps . . . laborers believe complaints to government officials will result in being "blackballed" . . . farm owners don't like trouble makers.

HOUSING

It is difficult to write about migrant housing without seeming to be melodramatic. One can approach the subject with the most modest expectations and be abashed at the realities. Simply stated, the conditions of migrant housing are grotesque; they can be nightmarish. Public reaction to these conditions has been one of sad tolerance.

It could be expected that a class of people so poor and powerless would live in housing that is minimal in its provisions and its esthetics. But the living conditions of migrants in transit and while working in the migrant streams are scandalous; conditions are often far beneath acceptable, civilized standards. In my travels, invariably the most jarring and disturbing conditions I saw were in the housing projects used by migrant farm workers. These migrant homes commonly are dilapidated, unsanitary, grim warrens unfit for human habitation.

Without funds, without options, and with few protections, migrants, even though they work hard and adhere to traditional American values concerning family and industry, are forced to live like hoboes or the most deprived ghetto inhabitants. While traveling, migrant farm workers often live, eat, and sleep in their cars, trucks, and buses because they do not have the money to stay elsewhere. Frequently, they stop near a park or stream, sleep briefly at the side of the road, and then push on to their destination.

After reaching their place of work, they must find cheap, temporary housing. If they cannot, as is often the case, they are at the mercy of their employer. In farm work, housing is commonly provided by the employers; the situation requires it. In Oregon and Washington, about 80 percent of their housing units are on the farms where the migrants work; in Michigan, 91 percent of the growers provide housing.

It is the rare employer, however, who is prepared to provide good housing to temporary workers, who have little if any bargaining power and inadequate funds to pay more than the most minimal rents. Since most migrant housing areas are on private property in scattered, remote, rural agricultural areas, there can be little policing of conditions even if the appropriate officials wanted to crack down. As a result, most migrant housing is "substandard,"

Housing.

to use a cold euphemism of government language.

In Florida, where 400 private migrant labor camps were surveyed, 40 percent did not meet minimum health and safety standards. Open sewage dumps, unsealed wells, and absence of privies were noted. It is no wonder that there was a typhoid epidemic at one camp and that the labor contractor at another was convicted of peonage and involuntary servitude for the way he treated his workers.

Traveling around the United States and surveying migrant housing conditions, one will witness filthy tar paper shacks; converted chicken coops; broken-down old trailers, cars, and trucks; crude barracks; and abandoned or condemned sheds and enclosures that house large families, single drifters, old people, and babies. A journalist described a migrant housing project he observed in Florida:

The houses . . . are in constant need of repair. [The] smell of backed up toilets . . . [and] odor of urine (is) everywhere. [The] water . . . smells bad, tastes bad and sometimes is not potable. [There is an] absence of lighting. Wiring is exposed. Windows do not have screens. Pests, bugs, and rats are a problem.

Said one foreman, these are homes "congressmen from Washington wouldn't keep their dogs in. . . ."[18]

A doctor recorded his observations of migrant housing:

We saw housing and living conditions horrible and dehumanizing to the point of our disbelief . . . without heat, adequate light or ventilation, and containing no plumbing or refrigeration, each room (no larger than 8×14 feet) is the living space of an entire family, appropriately suggesting slave quarters of earlier days. . . .[19]

Journalists have written occasional articles condemning these conditions. Public service organizations have testified and railed before agencies of government that supposedly are responsible for these situations. But the inhuman conditions continue. As one interested group concluded:

[A study of migrant farm worker housing] is a study of the pieces and scraps used by farm workers for shelter. It is a study of the pieces and scraps, called programs, designed by the government to improve that shelter.[20]

When he was president, Franklin D. Roosevelt promised

that the one-third of all Americans who were ill housed in the 1930s would be helped by government programs. In the almost half a century that has elapsed since his uplifting resolution, several government programs have indeed been created and funded to deal with these problems; but the conditions of migrant housing continue to be deplorable.

It is not as if government officials are unaware of the problem. One Senate committee reported in 1969 that 42 percent of all farm housing was substandard (compared to 14 percent of nonfarm housing). The Farmers Home Administration of the USDA reported in 1972 that about 65 percent of the migrant workers needed new or improved housing. A survey of Colorado migrant housing disclosed unsanitary conditions in 83 percent of all houses: 41 percent had unsafe water, 28 percent had no toilet facilities or unsatisfactory ones, 57 percent had structural problems.[21]

These disgusting housing conditions breed disease and cause death. One Senate report warned that poor housing caused disproportionate cases of tuberculosis and other respiratory diseases, stomach disorders, accidents, and children's diseases (mumps and measles) as well as psychological problems, juvenile delinquency, and mortality.

Employers of migrant farm workers have no practical incentives to provide adequate housing. Decent living quarters cost money, the season is short, and employer risks from maintaining bad housing are minimal. In addition, the laws of economics are perverse: if a farmer improves housing, property taxes go up; yet if migrants are employed, overall real estate values go down and general taxes will rise to cover the social costs of additional poor people in the area.

The dynamics of private enterprise have not worked to assure acceptable housing for migrants, nor have the government programs designed to rectify this situation. Government agencies charged with enforcing housing codes have failed to meet their responsibilities. Lack of staff and enthusiasm results in codes not being enforced. State, local, and federal regulations are sometimes inconsistent; none are enforced adequately.

I visited an ugly migrant barracks in North Carolina at a time when workers were in the fields. With a Labor Department official, I walked around the facility and inspected the conditions. Although my colleague noted a long list of violations of federal housing regulations, a local inspection certificate was nailed to the wall in the common room, stating the place had been inspected that same morning and was considered fine.

Where there is occasional housing law enforcement, it is a waste of time. Petulant farmers will throw up their hands and close their housing, leaving the migrants with no place at all to live. Other farmers will accept the minimal risks of enforcement as a minor and occasional cost of their operations. OSHA, which generally does a poor job of inspecting migrant housing, with minimal effort did find about 5,000 violations in 1976. The fines proposed amounted to about $4 per violation, hardly an amount likely to be an effective deterrent to the continuance of illegal and dangerous housing conditions.

In Florida, according to one study, only 276 of the state's 425 labor camps were licensed. Inspections in one year (1967) uncovered 15,225 violations. Only 41 percent of these violations were corrected. And, pathetically, if these camps had been closed by hard-driving officials, the migrants there would have had no place to go. When housing codes were enforced in Colorado and Washington during one period, migrants were forced to sleep in their cars or in the open fields.

The few law enforcement officials who might press their farmer neighbors, in order to help strangers who are just passing through, face a dilemma. If a labor camp is closed in mid-season, the migrants in effect are put out of work as well as out of a home; and the farmer-employer can be wiped out if the crop cannot be harvested when it is ready.

Whenever a national situation gets very bad and there is some publicity, the federal government can be expected to take programmatic action. In the housing area, this predictable phenomenon occurred; the undesirable but nonetheless equally predictable results also ensued. First, the New Deal's Farm Security Administration; then the 1949 Housing Act and the Department of Housing; then OSHA in 1970 and the Office of Equal Opportunity and the Community Services Administration, all took turns dealing with migrant housing problems.

The problems still exist. The bureaucratic reactions are familiar: not enough money, not enough staff. Critics attribute government failure to inadequate program enforcement, unrealistic eligibility criteria (minimum residence and income requirements, for example), poor coordination between state and local governments, inconsistent regulations (should inspections be made before migrants move into the housing camps provided for them or after they are living there?), and co-option by growers who have become the programs' customers rather than the workers.

Consider OSHA, for example. The federal law allows the

secretary of labor to prescribe and enforce health and safety standards for the benefit of workers in agriculture and industry; OSHA was a major labor law meant "to assure so far as possible every working man and woman in the Nation safe and healthful working conditions."[22] States were encouraged to develop their own programs, which would be 50 percent federally funded if they equaled or surpassed federal standards. Almost half the states already have done so.

OSHA has done very little for farm workers, however. Its competing priorities have required that the agency use its limited resources where the most people are affected. This means that, however demanding the needs of farm workers may be, this program generally will not reach them. A few specific standards have been promulgated to meet their needs, and the general duty clause of the act requires every employer, farmers included, to provide employees with workplaces free from hazards likely to cause death or serious physical harm. However, hazards considered "nonserious" because they are not likely to cause death are not covered. Poor sanitation or dangerous pesticides, for example, are not covered for this reason, although the hazards they create are "serious" in every other sense of that term.

In 1975 when I called upon OSHA officials to do something about the horrible conditions in migrant housing sites around the country, they excused their historic inactivity, blaming overwork and lack of funds. Under pressure, they promised to make a concerted effort to inspect 3,500 migrant housing places that summer, ten times the number they had inspected the year before. They actually conducted only 1,825 inspections of migrant labor camps, claiming inadequate enforcement staff and inability to locate migrant camps in some states (as if they could be hidden). And this was with a court order and a court-appointed committee focusing attention on their efforts.

If one were to consult the most dated muckracking reports about inhuman migrant housing, they could be read as an indictment of present conditions.

EDUCATION

All people want more for their children than they have had in their own lives. For many people, securing a better life for their children is their only accomplishment. Certainly, this fact of life is especially true of farm workers. They are not ashamed of their work; they are proud and hard workers. But they know there are better, easier, richer opportunities they have missed and would like their children to have. For this reason, despite the fact that farm work is family work that often continues through generations, most farm workers want their children to make it out of migrancy, to get out of the stream.

Education is the classic route out of poverty. A painful reality is that the very migrancy of these farm workers often forecloses this route to their children. Inherent in the migrant life is the special problem of educating the young. When always on the move, there can be no stable school life for children. Migrants live in many different places during the school year; their children are constantly in and out of different schools. When they are attending, they are strangers, often marked by language and cultural differences. They usually are without friends and meaningful associations. Migrant children are hungry and without necessary books and supplies; they usually can be found in the worst facilities, in places not conducive to a good educational experience. They have no assistance at home because their parents are away all day and often are without means and abilities to be helpful when they return. These children are strangers in a hard and puzzling world.

For years, generations, either no one who could do anything about this problem knew of it, or no one cared. Most efforts to come to grips with it were made by private organizations with limited agendas and funds. Then in the 1960s, Congress learned about the problem and acted. Funds were made available, first to the Office of Equal Opportunity and later (1966) to Health, Education, and Welfare under the Elementary and Secondary Education Act, to provide programs tailored to the special needs of migrant children. But the future would demonstrate that there is a wide gap between congressional intent and changed realities. One cannot assume that after Congress highlights a problem and legislates a programmatic solution, it will be dealt with properly and be solved. Migrant education is a casebook example of this phenomenon: good laws do not necessarily solve hard social problems.

The problems of education for migrant children have been a special interest of the National Committee on the Education of Migrant Children, whose findings were reported in two startling reports: *Wednesday's Children* in 1971[23] and *Promises to Keep* in 1977.[24] The National Child Labor Committee, a private citizens' organization, that for a half a century has concerned itself with the exploitation of children in industry and agriculture, had a staff of experts analyze the special educational problems faced by migrant children and monitored and assessed government response. Its reports were disheartening.

In its first report, in 1971, the committee noted that poor administration of migrant educational programs undercut the intentions of Congress to deal with this problem:

Late appropriations, inexperienced personnel, uneasiness about federal intervention in the local schools, and the lack of any national leadership or plan for educating the migrant children were ample reasons to fear for the effectiveness of these programs.

The committee's field investigators documented a pathetic situation: the bureaucrats' salaries and overhead consumed the money they were paid to administer for clients who were not served sufficiently to justify the programs. Ultimately, only the bureaucrats survive; the programs and the clients fade away.

Migrant children were found in schools in 47 states during a typical year; most of them live and go to school in two or more states each year, and not always in the same schools in each place. Periods of migration do not coincide with school terms, so study is interrupted and often missed. Thus the children have special personal problems in schools and cause others as a result.

Under the federal government's program, funds are made available to states that administer special migrant education programs. Most states pass the money on to local school districts; although some states use the funds to conduct statewide programs themselves, and others allow private organizations to do it.

The committee's survey showed, however, that all the money was not being used, even though most of the projected clientele were not being served; and, at that, too much of these funds was being consumed by administrators. During three fiscal years surveyed, of the over $90 million that was given to the states for migrant education, about $13 million was not spent; over $4 million appropriated for this program was not allocated to states.

The committee estimated that about 200,000 migrant children were eligible for programs these funds were intended to support. But local schools had neither a sufficient number of bilingual teachers or individualized programs to cope with the special problems and needs of migrant children nor adequate home-school contacts through which migrant parents could play a part in the educational programs. Most special programs were aimed at summer schools for transient migrants; but migrant parents felt that the programs were needed in the home-base states as well.

Teachers and school administrators commonly were hostile and uninterested in the migrants' educational problems. As one investigator reported after touring schools that enrolled migrant children and interviewing many of them:

School authorities have no concern for the children's attendance in the schools. They argue they are entitled to the Migrant Title I funds whether or not the children drop out of school. No checks are made for truancy. One child whose leg was broken and who stayed home for several months was never visited by the truant officer. Other children are forced to drop out of school. The principal of the school was very critical of the dress of one child and required him to drop out unless he changed his clothing style. A similar occurrence took place with another child's hair style. Students are discouraged from going to college by school counselors. One student now attending Pan American University was informed that she did not have the ability to finish high school much less go to college. Many students are unable to graduate from high school because the school will not accept their credits from other schools on the migrant stream. They make it very difficult for the information to be sufficient for them to accept credit. Thus the children become overaged and do not want to stay in school with children much younger than themselves and drop out of school. This is especially unfortunate as they in fact have sufficient credit from their summer school migrant programs to graduate. . . .

In some instances the schools use the older children to babysit for the younger children. In Arizona, one fourteen-year-old girl who did not know English was put into the first grade to work as aide with the Spanish speaking children. She was not paid and she was not taught anything. She was also unable to teach the 1st graders anything of substance as she herself was rather uneducated. Similarly, in Wisconsin the 11-year-old children are used by the schools as teachers' aides for the younger children. They are not provided with any educational program and they are not paid. They take the burden for day care from the teachers in the area. . . .[25]

Though federal migrant education money was earmarked for nutrition, health, and child care services related to primary education—programs crucially important to migrant families—those funds were not used. The committee noted the irony: "While migrant children went hungry, about a million dollars ($954,986) or about 31 percent of the migrant educational funds budgeted for food services were not spent."

The problem had been analyzed. A program was created. Funds were appropriated. Migrant children went hungry, nonetheless. In addition, according to the committee, "The great majority of the migrant children were not receiving the routine, minimal health services. . . . About $686,000 (or 30 percent of the $2.3 million budgeted by the states for health services in fiscal 1969) were spent."

Probably more than any other group of people, migrant families are in need of day care services. The federal government provided funds to meet this need. But the committee found:

Few of the migrant education projects we visited provided all-day programs for migrant children during the hours their parents were working. In many cases, children of all ages were left without supervision in migrant camps for several hours in the morning (between the time their parents left for work and the time the school bus came) and for a large part of the afternoon and early evening.[26]

As a result, it is not surprising that few migrant children (half the national average) stayed in school beyond the sixth grade or that they were found only rarely in high school.

Despite the aspirations of migrant families that their children get good educations and find their way out of the stream and despite government programs and public money aimed at helping families accomplish these hopes, the facts of life remained bleak. Although the government (the legislative arm) finally recognized and provided for the education, health, and welfare needs of migrant children, funds were wasted and went unspent (by the executive arm), while children who were the intended beneficiaries of these programs and funds went uneducated, hungry, and without necessary medical care.

The committee recommended that "immediate changes were required to guarantee that migrant children receive the services they need." It suggested techniques to improve the planning, evaluation, recruitment, training, staffing, and programming in this field—changes calculated to make the migrant education program work in a full and real way. Six years later, the committee conducted a follow-up study to see if any changes had been made. Its findings were depressing.

Repeating its earlier judgment that "the very facts of migrancy and poverty militate against meaningful educational opportunities for migrant children" and lock most of them into failure, and raising its estimation of the number of migrant children from 200,000 to half a million, the committee drew a sorry picture of failed intentions to reform. Despite a larger bureaucracy and greater funds, migrant children still suffered from poor nutrition, poor health, language problems in schools, community prejudices, poor facilities, and erratic school careers—all problems not only bad in themselves but also destructive to the personality.

The committee reported that migrant children are systematically denied their right to equal educational opportunities, and the special compensatory educational programs designed to meet this problem (at public cost which rose from $9 million a year in 1966 to $131 million in 1977) have been improperly implemented or systematically subverted.

The administrative perversions at Health, Education, and Welfare had continued. Masses of paperwork only confused and slowed the federal-state system and added to the costs. State programs were inadequate, but federal officials were unable or unwilling to make them work. A vicious cycle existed. To make the program work, federal administrators needed to collaborate with state administrators. The desire to keep cordial relations with these officials inhibited the federal workers from assuring that the programs were being adequately administered. Worse still, the committee found that "money, earmarked for migrants, is used for equipment, staff, and services for nonmigrant students." The special education needs of migrant students, the very needs that occasioned the special programs and additional funds, continued to be ignored.

In 1972, to help the program along, the federal government invested in a computerized national record transfer system. Located in Little Rock, Ark., the project plugged into 130 terminals around the country, disseminating school and health records of over 450,000 migrant students. The purpose was to develop records to guide the government in allocating funds for schools that enrolled migrant students who traveled around the country with their families.

But simply identifying candidates for federal programs was insufficient; only a fraction of eligible migrant students in fact received special education assistance. Some states never bothered to seek available federal funds for these purposes. Funds specifically targeted for migrant students consistently were used to provide services for nonmigrants. State violations went unnoticed and unchecked. Federal and state officials did not coordinate their activities; state programmers were not made accountable for their delinquencies by federal administrators. Although permitted to do so by the legislation, federal personnel did not seek alternate ways to carry out their programs when states failed.

The 1977 report concluded that a decade after the major attempt of Congress to deal with the problems of migrant children's education, the beneficiaries of the legislation were still being deprived of adequate educational opportunities. The Office of Education was not properly implementing the law.

The human result of this government failure was documented by Dr. Robert Coles. Coles spent long hours with the uprooted children of migrant farm worker parents in what he referred to as the deprived "world of the wanderers." Most migrant children forget even the pretense of school by the time they are ten, Coles reported. These children are stigmatized and disfavored, unwanted and struggling; they are hardened and fatalistic, scarred and psychologically disfigured for life. He concluded:

It is bad enough that thousands of us, thousands of American children, still go hungry and sick and are ignored and spurned—every day and constantly and just about from birth to death. It is quite another thing, a lower order of human degradation, that we also have thousands of boys and girls who live utterly uprooted lives, who wander the American earth, who even as children enable us to eat by harvesting our crops but who never, never can think of anyplace as home, of themselves as anything but homeless. There are moments, and I believe this is one of them, when, whoever we are, observers or no, we have to throw up our hands in heaviness of heart and dismay and disgust and say, in desperation: God save them, those children; and for allowing such a state of affairs to continue, God save us, too.[27]

The uniqueness of the problems of educating migrant children was brought home to me by one poignant, very personal vignette that occurred in an unlikely place. Several years ago I had gone with a friend, a 45-year-old Chicano, for a drink at a wood-paneled grill in a posh hotel near Central Park in New York City. We were joined by a writer friend of mine who happened to arrive while we were there. When my friend left, my companion commented that he enjoyed listening to him talk about his writing.

Then his eyes stared into space, and in a stream-of-consciousness rush of words that he seemed to be reading from some far-off slate out of his past, he reminisced about his early days in elementary school in Colorado. He had been the child of poor, Spanish-speaking, farm worker parents. Despite hard times, this man (who at this time was quite successful) eventually had graduated from college, risen to high rank in the Marine Corps, held high government positions, and earned a graduate degree from Princeton.

But, he told me, it had not always seemed possible. As a child, he had difficulty in school, in great part caused by his poor English. One day his parents were called to the school and told that he would have to leave because he was thought to be retarded. As he related this, tears streamed down his face. As if in a trance, apparently unaware of his present surroundings, he repeated these words, "They said I was retarded and could not stay in school," in disbelief and embarrassment, reliving a humiliation born of misunderstanding, a humiliation from whose wounds few children could survive unscathed.

This highly personal incident conveyed more to me about the dilemma of educating migrant children than all the books and studies I later would read.

4

THE NEGLECTED MINORITY

THIS CHAPTER and the next will deal with a gigantic government system that might have helped migrant farm workers solve many of their fundamental problems but, instead, was administered in such a way as to frustrate them. This federal-state system involved specific programs designed particularly to help migrant farm workers as well as broad programs to help disadvantaged groups generally, including migrants. Pathetically, this system ignored and even discriminated against migrant farm workers in continuing and egregious ways. This story is sad and complex, but it is a revealing case history that needs to be told. It demonstrates the weakness of farm workers; at the same time it reveals the futility of well-intended government programs in righting social wrongs as well as the complicity of government bureaucrats in causing some of the problems their offices were set up to cure.

OFFICE OF EQUAL OPPORTUNITY

In 1964 President Lyndon B. Johnson declared his war on poverty and created a governmentwide task force to develop the program and devise the enabling legislation for what was to become the Office of Economic Opportunity (OEO). As one of four Justice Department representatives on the task force, I can recall that there were no existing government programs designed specifically for farm workers, no pressures at all were put on us by farm worker representatives, and our response to their dire situation was inadequate and wholly fortuitous. No one represented farm workers in any OEO planning, I regret to report; and it is no surprise that after our great governmentwide effort, nothing was in our omnibus poverty package for them when it was sent to Congress.

Assistant Secretary of Agriculture James Sundquist, his department's delegate to the task force, had to promote what rural legislation we did propose to Congress. When he called on Congressman James Roosevelt to seek his support for our legislative package, Roosevelt insisted on adding his own pet provisions that had been around for years. Sundquist found the Roosevelt proposals acceptable and was willing to strike the deal to get his help. Because farm workers have no stable community, no political muscle, and no voice in the nation's capital, this serendipitous experience was an unusual and random happenstance whereby farm workers happened to benefit from covert government deal making.

Senator Harrison Williams of New Jersey, who headed a subcommittee on migrant affairs, was interested in the same bills as Congressman Roosevelt. Their interests covered four areas: housing, education, sanitation, and child care. The OEO planners added these items to their rural agenda. They later would come to be known as the III B programs (from Title III, Section B of the legislative package); as such, they provided the first real, if fortuitous, farm worker program in the federal bureaucracy. No one else in government was doing anything for migrants, so the new agency had a void to fill.

A decade later, the first administrators of these programs reminisced with me about their experience—creating a nationwide farm worker program out of whole cloth. Sargent Shriver, who headed the OEO, wanted action—fast; and he supported his imaginative, activist staff. An office of special programs was set up; it covered Indians, territories, and migrants. But there was no organized constituency "out there" to seek or even to be solicited with this small pot of gold earmarked for migrants.

State agencies were not interested. Some private institutions saw the OEO as an opportune new source for funding and came looking for grants. Agribusiness organizations, for example, would have taken the money to build permanent migrant housing on private land, but that was not what the early administrators wanted. Instead, these unusual Washington bureaucrats traveled around the country, looking for private, nonprofit, charitable organizations that sought social action and happened to have common agendas. Self-help housing, day care, special education, job training: these were the programs the administrators wanted to fund; so they went out and found decent, minority-based organizations to run them. The officials insisted that these groups include farm workers on their boards of directors and come to grips with the workers' problems.

Politically savvy as well as idealistic, these activist officials knew they not only had to create a constituency but also had to fight the established bureaucracy to make their programs work. "We were wild-eyed liberals, who were anathema to the bureaucrats with white socks, car pools and 20-year pins," one of these former OEO activists told me, "and we had to remember that migrants don't vote and growers howl." So they put growers on the boards of the local organizations. This assured conservatives that nothing communistic was happening; at the same time it coopted local representatives of the "natural enemy" into becoming defenders of the national program.

In Washington the OEO administrators acted as the migrants' advocates before other agencies of government, which historically had been dealing with critical problems without farm worker input. By 1967 there was a migrant division of the OEO and a growing network of migrant organizations in 35 states, with developing expertise and growing government-based bankrolls of $30–40 million, administering useful social services to migrant farm workers. Shortly thereafter, administrations changed from a sympathetic Democratic administration under Lyndon B. Johnson to a very unsympathetic Republican administration under the influence of Richard M. Nixon. Naturally hostile to the OEO, President Nixon eventually scuttled the agency after having assigned its administration to an avowed critic who, candidly, was there to stop all the action.

By the early 1970s the cadre of activists in government was burning out. Nixon appointees were keeping up the pressure to the accompaniment of vocal state (Ronald Reagan) and federal (Spiro Agnew) officials who, at best, viewed all of the OEO, especially its effective legal services arm, as leftist social engineers who were radicalizing the free-enterprise system, if not as anarchist revolutionaries to be feared as open enemies of our government.

Eventually, the whole organization was dismantled. Some programs were discarded; some were shifted to a new agency, the Community Services Administration; while others were transferred to standard, old-line agencies such as Health, Education, and Welfare and the Department of Labor. "We were amalgamated into nothing," one bitter former official told me. "Our early OEO programs were helping farm workers, but Nixon was against all programs that might raise the cost of oranges." Migrant education programs went to Health, Education, and Welfare; labor-oriented programs went to a skeptical, suspicious Labor Department, a gigantic old-line agency with a historic record of neglecting migrant farm workers.

CETA

In a few years, the former OEO-based job-training programs for migrants were moved to Labor's Employment and Training Administration—funded by the Comprehensive Employment and Training Act (CETA) of 1973—which then established a migrant division. There were fears that supportive services the OEO had favored would be dropped at Labor because that department was manpower oriented. The OEO staff feared the Labor Department would be, at best, a reluctant home for farm worker programs; they feared it would "manpowerize, regionalize, and pulverize" the OEO farm worker programs, as one staffer who made the move from the OEO to Labor told me. Oldliners at the Labor Department viewed the OEO staff that moved in as "paranoiac zealots"; they perceived the changes under the CETA legislation as a way of centralizing federal manpower programs and initiating President Nixon's program of special revenue sharing with the states.

Farm worker representatives implored Senator Gaylord Nelson—who had a long, proven interest in their problems—to pressure Assistant Secretary of Labor William Kolberg, then Labor's manpower chief, to continue supportive services for farm workers when the change was made from the OEO to Labor.[1] Kolberg eventually went along. Essentially, the same people, programs, and money were moved from one agency to another. One of my clients (who administers a community organization for disadvantaged clientele) remarked to me at the time about CETA, this newest acronymic government creation, "They change the letters every couple of years, but ain't nothin' that really changes."

The CETA program affecting migrants was essentially a grants program; money was distributed to public and private organizations, which developed local projects designed to meet the needs of local migrants. The same was so of the education programs moved to Health, Education, and Welfare. There the federal role was to decide which state and local education programs designed to meet the needs of local migrants were worth funding and then to do so.

EMPLOYMENT SERVICE

The major model for federal-state partnership in solving local labor problems, one of the most pervasive and fundamental attempts at government programmatic problem solving, was the Labor Department's Employment Service. Its failure to fulfill its potential in the agricultural labor market generally (and particularly its failure to serve the interests of farm workers) is a classic example of the great promise and the sad failure of government solutions to solve broad social problems. The revealing story about the Employment Service's neglect of farm workers is worth telling in detail.

Created by the Wagner-Peyser Act of 1933, the National Employment Service was meant to be one of the great, innovative New Deal programs aimed at dealing with the catastrophic unemployment that resulted from the Depression. The breadth of its coverage and the immensity of its challenge were awesome:

As the oldest [1933], largest (2,200 local offices), best equipped (35,000 people, $400 million annual budget), and only nationwide manpower service system, the federal-state employment service is the institution with the greatest potential for becoming the chief instrument for national manpower policy. . . .[2]

Through the years, the Employment Service has accounted for between 10 and 15 percent of all job placements, supplementing the private labor market to this extent rather consistently. As if this task was not a difficult enough assignment, Congress soon added another major program to its jurisdiction. Its original job-finding business was expanded in 1935 by the Social Security Act, which created the unemployment insurance program providing security for workers who lose their jobs. The Employment Service was given responsibility for the administration of both the employment and unemployment services of the government, funding the former with revenues collected from employers under the latter program.

Originally funded on a 50-50 basis by the federal and state governments, by 1946 the whole operation was 100% state run and 100% federally funded (via the unemployment tax on employers). The sheer massive amount of the relatively mechanical unemployment services, however, has overwhelmed the agency's more creative employment responsibilities. I remember seeing a graphic illustration of this problem in an office in the southern Imperial Valley in California near the Mexican border. Here was an active area for farm workers, the site of a busy operation involving masses of Mexican day workers and a natural location for a multiservice Employment Service center. Yet what I saw was a dead-quiet office in the middle of a warren of activity outside on the streets where contractors swept away gangs of

"Shape-up" outside employment agency, California.

workers on behalf of private employers in that area. The only activity inside was from stragglers lined up to collect unemployment insurance. I also saw bigger urban offices where, despite the availability of job banks and manpower program specialists, the greatest part of the hurly-burly activity inside was the long lines of people out of work collecting unemployment insurance.

More serious problems evolved as the Employment Service agency matured. While the organization was created to help *employees,* it evolved into an organization that served *employers.* Because employers were the sole funding source for the Employment Service and their cooperation was needed if jobs were to be found for applicants, the service became overly influenced by employers. An annoyance to employers who resist the inevitable paperwork and bureaucratic controls of any government agency, even a fawning one, and an irrelevance to potential employees who have encountered historic neglect and discrimination in their dealings with it, the Employment Service had developed into an impotent and wasteful government failure in the agricultural labor market.

In addition, while the service was created to place people in jobs, it did not mature with the times, so that years later when the administration of human development programs was added to its charter, there was institutional resistance. Testing, counseling, training, outreach, follow-up, working with especially disadvantaged clientele—all these supportive services were added to the list of Employment Service responsibilities by later social welfare legislation. Many old-line officials viewed these additional chores as "nose wiping" and resisted. As one labor expert told me: "The employment service is and always has been a place where people go to be referred to someplace else where they can get what they need: a job, some training, some education, some food stamps, income support. . . . It has little or no capability, on its own, to give disadvantaged people what they need to change either themselves—or the system—so as to materially affect their employment. The ES is not and never has been the major instrument for the implementation of national manpower policy."

In 1976 the director of the General Accounting Office, Manpower and Welfare Division, testified before a House subcommittee about this change:

Since its establishment in 1933, the Service's focus and the labor market in which it participates have changed. Unlike 1933, the Service now competes with a multitude of other placement activities. From that competition, it emerges as an agency serving a relatively small and specialized segment of the labor market—jobs and persons characterized by low pay.

Originally conceived as a labor-exchange for persons seeking work and employers with job openings to fill, the Service took on a broader range of manpower activities as part of the World War II effort. In the face of acute manpower shortages, it assisted in recruitment and manpower utilization activities.

Another big change in focus occurred in the late 1960s and early 1970s. In line with the legislative emphasis on the disadvantaged, the Service provided intensified and individualized service to people who experienced the most difficulty in getting and holding jobs. This emphasis diverted attention from the job-ready and resulted in a sharp decline in job orders and placements. . . .

After 1971 emphasis turned to increased placement of all people, the job-ready and the disadvantaged. Increased productivity (more placements) as well as placement of individuals in certain target groups was emphasized. . . .

In August 1974 the Bureau of Labor Statistics (BLS) reported . . . that although a third of the job seekers [10 million people in 1972] used the Service, 95 percent of the job placements occurred through other means. The major sources were: applications directly to employers (35 percent), friends and relatives (26 percent), and newspaper ads (14 percent). Private employment agencies and the Service each accounted for about 5 percent of the placements. . . . The Service is primarily a placement service for low-paying jobs. . . .[3]

The Wagner-Peyser Act mandated that certain especially disadvantaged groups should receive special treatment, and one of these was farm workers. In addition, a federal court in 1974 singled out farm workers as one group for which the Labor Department would have to raise all its standards of services. So the grower-oriented agency had to become farm worker oriented, and it had to include all manpower services—not merely job placements—in its repertoire.

The operation of the Employment Service system eventually was challenged in major litigation resulting in a historic case. That case—*NAACP et al. v. Brennan et al.,* it came to be called—which monopolized my life for two years, was the distillate of the historic problems farm workers have had with their lives and with their government.

5

JUDGING THE EMPLOYMENT SERVICE

IF THIS PARTICULAR CASE had a discernible beginning, it was early in 1970. The basic idea for bringing some broad, major litigation to make the Department of Labor responsive to farm workers had germinated in the minds of activist lawyers for several years. But the exact nature of the case—the precise remedies that would be sought, the parties, the timing, all the strategy—evolved in a serendipitous way, which would prove to be both its genius and its undoing.

Migrant Legal Action Program lawyers in Washington, D.C., and California Rural Legal Assistance lawyers were looking for a way to reform the Employment Service.[1] It was well known to them that the service treated farm workers like second class citizens. Employment Service offices were run like segregated schools; there were separate and unequal physical facilities for farm workers in rural areas. Farm workers were aimed only at agricultural jobs—an obvious selection, but one that denied them a chance to get out of farm work and kept them in their ruts of poverty. The Employment Service allowed growers to oversubscribe for farm workers to protect their own needs at harvest time—to the prejudice of the workers who often would travel at great sacrifice, only to find no jobs waiting for them. Limited job information was available at the rural offices. Little if any attention was paid to the wage, health, sanitation, and housing conditions to which farm workers were subjected in the jobs they got through the service. Those who complained to the Employment Service were sometimes blackballed. Placements were the only goal; as long as the number of placements in jobs was high, state offices received their federal funding. The conditions and qualities of their services or of the jobs they secured for clients were not a serious concern to the Labor Department or to the state employment offices.

To some critics, these facts showed that migrant farm workers were being discriminated against on racial grounds. They were predominantly from minority groups; many of them were poor blacks or Chicanos. Other observers analyzed the same facts differently. One activist California lawyer who was on the scene during this time saw the problem as one of economic discrimination more than racial. To this observer, the problems of migrant farm workers seemed to result from the resistance of state employment agencies to the dual labor market; farm workers composed a secondary labor market. Another tactician in the case saw the facts as demonstrating that federalism did not work and that the Employment Service had to be state or federally run and not conducted through a specious pseudopartnership. Whatever the truth, there was little question in the minds of advocates for the migrants that the Employment Service was vulnerable and ripe for reform. The issue was how to bring it about.

BACKGROUND OF THE TEST CASE

A few cases had been brought in California, Florida, and other agricultural states by migrant lawyers specifically questioning the responsibility of the Employment Service to farm workers.[2] Using the class action technique, and relying on the U.S. Constitution, as well as the federal and state statutes that protected farm workers' economic and personal well-being, these lawyers were buoyed by court rulings that some state Employment Service failures to protect farm workers' rights and discriminations against them would not be condoned. They began to envision a broader, dramatic case in Washington, D.C., a national case that would deal with "the system."

The idea was to hold the federal government responsible for meeting the promise of its programs. If government did not succeed in its assignment on behalf of the public constituency to whom it was dedicated, that public needed some remedy. Advocacy groups decided they must attack the failures of the system to deliver services to their impotent clients, and they had to do it in a highly visible case to keep the light and the heat on an otherwise unresponsive government agency. As one of these California lawyers said, "We wanted to get at the umbilical cord which ran from Washington to the state employment services, instead of fighting the system on a state-by-state basis. The lawsuit was intended to be a can opener."

THE MIGRANT LEGAL ACTION PROGRAM CASE

Larry Sherman was the legal director of the Migrant Legal Action Program in Washington, D.C.; this organization was headquarters for the nation's publicly funded migrant law offices around the country. He and his assistants sought tactical advice from the public interest committee of one of Washington's big, commercial law firms. He asked for help in fashioning a legal strategy to attack the Labor Department's failure to require all the states to deliver employment services to migrant farm workers.

In April 1971 Sherman received a long letter from the firm advising the Migrant Legal Action Program that it had the legal right to sue the Labor Department in behalf of aggrieved migrant farm workers and recommending that it first bring an administrative complaint attempting to resolve these grievances within the department. The firm's legal advice was predicated upon what should be a clear and fundamental government fact of life. Federal agencies administering federal programs and providing federal funds to state agencies have the responsibility of assuring interested people and groups who are the public beneficiaries of those programs and funds that the funded states are performing their services according to the law. Such a promise seems so obvious as not to require sophisticated legal analysis; but Sherman preferred careful, sound planning.

The analysis prepared for the Migrant Legal Action Program studied the Wagner-Peyser Act, the Labor Department's regulations under that act, and the general law on the evolving subject of litigation by members of the public against federal departments regarding their administration of federal programs. The very purpose of the act, it concluded, was "to promote the welfare of wage earners in the United States, improve their working conditions, and promote their opportunities for profitable employment." Thus the department has the obligation to develop standards of performance for the states, to regulate use of funds it provides, and to assure efficient state administration of its employment offices. States are required to report to the secretary of labor about their use of Wagner-Peyser funds, and the federal government has the right and responsibility to exercise controls to assure that state programs are carried out properly.

Federal regulations had been passed requiring that state employment offices provide precisely those services that migrant farm workers were complaining they were not receiving: jobs requiring higher skills than farm work; work conditions not in violation of federal, state, or local laws; adequate wages; appropriate counseling; and training services. The Wagner-Peyser Act placed enforceable legal obligations upon states to implement these federal regulations for the benefit of workers and to assure efficient and economic services to farm workers, the advisory letter stated.

The letter then analyzed the law, concluding that the government's failure to enforce appropriate statutes and regulations can be remedied by the courts. When acting in such cases, courts simply are assuring that federal agencies adhere to their own regulations, and they are fulfilling their legal obligations to require state recipients of federal funds to carry out their duties. One who can show that any agency's delinquency caused personal injury, as the farm workers represented by the Migrant Legal Action Program alleged, was within the zone of interest of the laws, regulations, and Constitution to which courts look in permitting a lawsuit against a federal agency.

Sherman was advised to seek administrative relief before going to the courts and, failing to get that relief, to sue. It was not a legislative problem; his advisors said that they did not believe the problem really was that the existing regulations were by definition inadequate, but rather that they were not enforced. Technically, Sherman's group could ultimately bring suit; but, tactically, specific aggrieved farm workers would be more compelling plaintiffs.

That was the advice Sherman needed to assure himself that his instinctive feelings had a sound legal basis. In the spring of 1971, 398 specifically named farm workers and 16 migrant and civil rights organizations, on behalf of themselves and all other farm workers and migrants, filed an official complaint with the Department of Labor. The complaint alleged that the department's Farm Labor Service and later its Rural Manpower Administration, which had been conceived to be a farm workers' service agency, had evolved into a growers' subsidy. The plaintiffs sought to end that state-run, federally funded branch of the Employment Service, which they argued "cycles migrants into poverty." Though it was created to assist farm workers in finding jobs, they argued, the agency had become grower dominated, grower oriented, grower staffed, and totally perverted.

The migrants' complaint read like a passionate documentary, deploring a three-decade Labor Department policy of neglect, which violated workers' civil rights, sent them to bad jobs in deplorable conditions, and punished them for complaining. This government program had been a total failure, they claimed; the funds for 9,000 bureaucratic jobs would have been better used to take that many migrants out of the stream, at half the cost. Government officials were more interested in gathering statistics to justify their existence than in serving their farm worker clients; they were too concerned about growers, crew leaders, and data to adequately service their real clientele, the complainants argued. The complaint even cited a secret government report that candidly stated that migrant program administrators had neither the attitudes nor the capabilities to operate these programs properly.

In a long, documented array of charges, the complaint detailed countless specific abuses, indifferences, discourtesies, and discriminations to which farm workers were subjected in cities and states all over the United States by the very officials who were paid to provide them with services. Claiming that "Steinbeck's Joad is now Jiminez," the complaint noted the bitter irony that in Steinbeck's era the grower exploited the migrant on his own without federal subsidies; today, the exploitation is accomplished with the monetary assistance of the migrants' legal guardian. The civil rights laws, the Wagner-Peyser Act, and related public laws for the benefit of farm workers had been violated, they claimed; and they sought a public hearing and administrative redress from the Department of Labor.

The Subcommittee on Agricultural Labor of the House of Representatives took an interest in the plaintiffs' case and made this known to the department. The bureaucracy reacted typically, although it was to be surprised later by the events its response would generate. The secretary of labor appointed an in-house committee, called the Special Review Staff, to investigate the workers' complaints. Ten months later, in April 1972, the staff submitted a voluminous, documented report.

Special Review Staff Report.

The Special Review Staff analyzed the petition and the 1,500 pages of exhibits submitted along with it. Its investigators went to 11 states, including some complained against as well as others, and they visited 73 local offices. They talked to all concerned parties—farm workers, state and local officials, growers, migrant advocates. The report demonstrated that the staff had taken its assignment seriously. There was no defensive whitewash; it dealt seriously and frankly with the complaint that the multimillion dollar Rural Manpower Service should be discontinued because it had become a farmers' agency.

Changing conditions, traditional grower dominance in economic relations with farm workers, and lack of legal protection and organizational power were noted by the departmental investigators; and the workers' need for new, broad services—counseling, training, job development, for example—was confirmed. The Rural Manpower Service had not reformed the older, more traditional Farm Labor Service it replaced. The changes had been more cosmetic than substantive.

The farm workers' lack of an advocate was noted—a serious need in view of the fact that protective laws usually excluded them from coverage. Thus these workers were peculiarly "susceptible to exploitation" and "afraid to press their complaints because of the strength of the forces working against them." The report also documented the complaint that the Employment Service and the Rural Manpower Service often operated as two distinct systems; the former provided far more and better services than the latter, servicing an essentially white clientele, while the latter served essentially minority groups.

Sex and age discriminations were also uncovered in Employment Service practices toward farm workers. The perversions of the foreign labor certification process were described. Abuses under the Social Security laws, underpayments in violation of minimum wage laws, evasions of the Crew Leader Registration Act, minimum age law violations, failures to enforce immigration laws—all were unearthed and described with detailed examples.

The investigators also reported about problems not covered in the farm workers' administrative complaint—the special problems of freewheelers, for example. Freewheelers migrate looking for farm work without using the Employment Service but do present related problems to the service (housing complaints, for example). They also described vagaries of the interstate clearance order system by which farm workers were recruited in ways that prejudiced them and farmers as well.

Job applications were taken improperly, and facilities for farm worker job applicants were separate from and unequal to other Employment Service offices. Day labor pickup sites were not being operated according to regulations; in fact, they were used to gather placement statistics, not to provide employment services. Offices were recruiting farm workers for growers when no adequate housing was available, possibly attributable to the grower backgrounds and connections of many Employment Service employees. Pesticides and sanitation conditions to which workers were exposed were illegal; men and women workers were forced to urinate in the open fields or behind machinery; and they were sprayed with deadly pesticides while they worked. Some forms of transportation to the fields were scandalously dilapidated and dangerous.

In sum, the Labor Department's in-house survey, bearing its own title and insignia, documented most of the farm workers' complaints in such a way as to condemn across the board this agency's administration of laws intended to protect the workers.

The Secretary's 13 Points

In response to this powerful Special Review Staff report, then Secretary of Labor James D. Hodgson issued a department pronouncement to his assistants, referred to as "the secretary's 13 Points." Rhetorically, these were responsive to the migrants' needs; had they been truly implemented, all the litigation that was to follow could have been avoided.

First, the secretary's memorandum called for the consolidation and integration of all rural employment services in local offices to assure that rural workers would receive the same treatment as all people looking for work. This requirement was aimed at ending the historic practice of running rural Employment Service offices as second class job and service centers for farm workers.

The secretary also called for immediate steps to correct all violations of law: child labor laws, civil rights laws, minimum wage laws, the Immigration and Naturalization Act, Occupational Safety and Health Administration (OSHA) laws (especially those concerning field sanitation and safety), housing and transportation regulations that were of special relevance to farm workers, and the Crew Leader Registration Act.

The secretary's 13 Points also called for the development of mechanisms to handle complaints; for a survey of wage rates to assure that the piece work rates (an amount based on production, for example, $1 a bushel) conformed to traditional minimum wage laws (an amount based on time worked, irrespective of production, for example, $2.10 an hour); for improvement of the interstate clearance system under which Employment Service offices around the country synchronize jobs for migrant workers; for reform of day-haul operations (informal pickup areas where workers congregate to seek jobs early each morning); and for reform of civil service regulations to permit recruitment of more suitable Employment Service administrators.

The document was published on April 21, 1972; it responded to problems that had to be well known to the Labor Department, and it proposed no more than that things be done as Congress always had intended.

The secretary's 13 Points did not change realities, however; and negotiations between representatives of farm worker organizations and the Labor Department (with some probing by the House subcommittee) continued for months. Those negotiations finally lapsed when in July 1972 the department "re-funded in place the entire network of the state Rural Manpower Service and the Employment Service serving farm workers" without taking "any visible action to correct the problems pointed out in the Special Review Staff report."

NAACP ET AL. V. SECRETARY OF LABOR HODGSON ET AL.

In early October 1972 a complaint was filed in the U.S. District Court in the District of Columbia, the federal trial court for the nation's capital, by the Migrant Legal Action Program and other migrant organizations. The formal legal case was based upon their administrative complaints; it asked for an injunction against the secretary of labor, ordering him to end the unlawful and unconstitutional practices of the Employment Service against which plaintiffs had complained administratively and of which the department's staff report had provided ample documentation. The complaint was signed by 88 farm workers (some identified but unnamed for fear of reprisal) from California, Colorado, Florida, Georgia, New Jersey, New York, and Texas and by representatives of 17 national organizations including the National Association for the Advancement of Colored People (NAACP); the American GI Forum; and numerous migrant, Chicano, and farm worker organizations. The case was first formally entitled *NAACP et al. v. Secretary of Labor Hodgson et al.* (Later, under Secretary of Labor Peter J. Brennan, it came to be known as *NAACP v. Brennan.*)

Judge Charles Richey's Opinion

The case was assigned to District Court Judge Charles Richey, a Washington, D.C., and Maryland Republican attorney, who after having been appointed to the bench by Richard Nixon had become noted as an activist humanitarian judge. On May 31, 1973, Judge Richey issued a memorandum opinion that was an extraordinary document. The judge described in damning language the historic misconduct of the Employment Service network and the failure of the Labor Department to use its ample powers to do anything about it: indeed, the opinion noted the department's complicity.

"This is a case of nationwide significance . . . it bears directly on the well-being and social dignity of migrant and seasonal farm workers throughout the U.S., . . ." his opinion intoned in its opening words. Using the department's own reports to support its conclusions, the court found that rural employment agencies denied minority farm workers the full range of services it made available to others; subjected farm workers to discrimination based on race, sex, age, and national origin; provided them with substandard facilities and services; processed improper work orders; referred workers to employers who violated minimum wage and child labor, Social Security, and housing and health laws; condoned illegal crew leaders; failed to assist Immigration and Naturalization Service law enforcement; and was unresponsive to farm workers' complaints. The department had not used its fiscal or regulatory powers over the states to control their activities.

It was illegal and unconstitutional, the court held, for the Labor Department to provide farm workers with services, benefits, and protections in a discriminatory fashion. The Fifth Amendment of the U.S. Constitution, the Wagner-Peyser Act, and Title VI of the 1964 Civil Rights Act all forbid such government activity.The department's defense, that it had issued regulations calling for proper treatment of migrant and seasonal farm workers, was deemed inadequate. The court said the department had the coordinate obligation to enforce its own standards and had failed to use its quite adequate general and specific enforcement powers to do so.

The court noted that the Labor Department's own staff report had documented extensive problems and inequities in the Employment Service, and it found that the department had approved and funded state programs that had violated farm workers' legal rights. All this existed despite the department's directives to the states supposedly implementing the secretary's 13 Points and its appointment of a task force to insure the states' compliance.

The department argued that it was doing all it could to secure voluntary compliance by the states; it was reluctant (then, as it was continuously as the case progressed) to exercise its ample enforcement powers to assure the required reforms. The plaintiffs argued that nothing had changed since they appealed for relief and that the department's steps were inadequate, unenforced, and unmonitored; they asked that the department be enjoined from providing any more money to the violating states.

The court tried to balance its response to the two arguments. The secretary's 13 Point plan sounded good to the court. The department should have some time to implement it, without taking too long to alleviate acknowledged serious problems. The department would be indulged, but not endlessly, while (in the court's words) other secretaries issued fourteen-point and sixteen-point plans.

The court kept its jurisdiction over the case, determined officially that past violations had occurred, and enjoined the Labor Department from perpetuating these unlawful practices, threatening sanctions if compliance was not ensured. The court noted that cutting off state funds at that time could only hurt the very people the plaintiffs were trying to protect. Finally, the court stated that it needed extensive, complex data, which would require hearings and reports to finally judge compliance, indicating that a master or hearing examiner might be appointed at the defendants' expense to gather this information and monitor compliance for the court. The judge solicited the parties' views within one month on this latter proposal.

Second Hearing

Meanwhile, a new secretary of labor, Peter J. Brennan, had been appointed (three more secretaries would arrive and depart in the course of this litigation). The parties negotiated and came back to court one month later (June 1973) as requested by the judge, having agreed to a tentative stipulation. The Labor Department was to advise all the states of the court's order, conduct summer on-site reviews in 50 local Employment Service offices in 15 states, share its information with the plaintiffs, and develop means to institutionalize monitoring and enforcement techniques to ensure future state compliance. The court held in abeyance its decision on the appointment of a special master and continued its jurisdiction over the case for 90 more days. The court issued subsequent supplementary orders requiring the department to take specific steps to coordinate and react to the findings of the summer on-site reviews and allowing additional time to report about its compliance.[3]

Third Hearing

The case came back to the court again in February 1974 on motions by both sides for a summary judgment. The Labor Department argued that it had created procedures aimed at implementing the court's earlier order. The plaintiffs argued that these procedures were inadequate and there was no proof that conditions in the fields actually had changed. Exploitations of farm workers were not being adequately monitored or corrected, the plaintiffs argued.

The department's own report of its on-site reviews in 15 states (filed in court in December 1973) had demonstrated that "an extensive pattern of gross violations of the rights of migrant farm workers and the denial of services to which migrant and seasonal workers are entitled by federal law" continued, even though mentioned in the plaintiffs' administrative complaint and documented in the staff report.

The plaintiffs stated to the court:

Defendants, who have already been found to have committed myriad violations of federal statutory and constitutional law, simply ask that the Court trust them to cure in the future those violations they have not been willing or able to cure in the eight months since the May 31 Order. . . .

Defendants' submission . . . [is] an attempt to sweep under the carpet the duty of the Department of Labor. . . .

The voluntarism and self-policing the Labor Department had asked the court to accept as performance of its obligations under the court order "has not succeeded and more specific affirmative relief must be fashioned," the plaintiffs pressed.

Amicus Curiae

Late in 1973 another participant emerged in this burgeoning litigation. Judge Richey had asked then Antioch Law School Dean Edgar Cahn, an innovative legal educator with a special interest in public controversies concerning the accountability of government agencies, to enter the case as amicus curiae to aid the court in evaluating the growing materials and contentious arguments. Dean Cahn's first report to the court in August 1974 dealt with the Labor Department's compliance with the court's May 31, 1973, order. His conclusion was that, based on his exhaustive study of all the available information, substantial compliance had *not* been achieved despite considerable effort.

Dean Cahn's memorandum to the court stated that there were indications of manipulation of data, continued illegalities, racial discrimination, ritualistic enforcement, and patterns of violations; it concluded that the considerable effort expended by the department could not be equated with actual benefits conferred on farm workers. In effect, Dean Cahn noted early a fundamental difference of mentality, which continued to divide the key participants throughout the case: the department continually limited its chore to exhortations and to the creation of procedures to guide the states, while others later called upon to judge the department looked for changed realities in the lives of farm workers.

Labor Department representatives kept reminding their critics that farm workers were only 1 percent of the universe the department had to serve, and that it was channeling more than 1 percent of its resources to farm workers. That kind of bureaucratic response, that is, looking only to memos, data, and plans instead of the facts of life in appraising department efforts—in government jargon, looking at "input" rather than "output"—characterizes the battles waged during the next two years and in my mind damns the Labor Department as a classic example of an institution that has lost sight of its public consumers and wastes its opportunities by concentrating on devising techniques of administration.

In November 1974 Dean Cahn reported to the court again that the Labor Department's own reports demonstrated its ineffective compliance with the court's order and, indeed, its participation in evasionary and condoning acts as well. The department had told the states they would get no additional funds to perform their remedial obligations, inviting if not encouraging noncompliance. Its monitoring, data-gathering, and enforcement policies were inadequate, Cahn's memorandum to the court stated. The department was "generating an adequate paper record" of compliance, the dean stated; it was merely "going through the motions" of implementation. In six months, a court-appointed review committee had not even been able to recruit a chairman. It was time to deal with the question of court enforcement, he concluded; voluntarism had not worked for 18 months, during which time the court had indulged the department.

The Court Order

Judge Richey was hopeful that by keeping up his pressure and judicial oversight and by exhorting the Labor Department about its high responsibilities and the historic nature of the endeavor it was reluctantly in the middle of, it would work out a mutually acceptable solution with the plaintiffs. He maintained his insistent optimism along with a tough-minded willingness to hang onto the case "until hell freezes over," as he once threatened the parties throughout the years of official and unofficial manipulating, wrangling, negotiating, and even occasional real government efforts on behalf of farm workers. But at this stage, as would happen again later in the proceedings, the plaintiffs bargained away much of what they had gained in their lawsuit by imprudent negotiations with defensive department lawyers who managed to delay and threaten and talk their way out of the corner into which they had been pushed by the court.

How the parties negotiated the consent order Judge Richey signed in August 1974 reflects both the unplanned and inadequately prepared nature of the farm workers' suggested remedies and the general negativism of the Labor Department. Migrant Legal Action Program lawyers with different visions of the case came and left that organization; as one of them stated years later, "MLAP wanted the money to be able to participate in the case, so it became the client instead of the lawyer." Lawyers from another large Washington, D.C., law firm volunteered to work on the case awhile. Labor Department officials and lawyers (with occasional assistance from Justice Department attorneys in the U.S. Attorney's office and in the Civil Division, which represents all executive agencies) were shuffled in and out of the case. The judge's clerks asssigned to this extraordinary case departed after serving their clerkships, and they too were replaced. The professionals involved in this case were as migrant as the farm workers they all professed to be representing.

The court order that both sides eventually signed, which became the bible for the Department of Labor and the state Employment Service network for the next two years, was a classic in vagueness, compromise, and, at the same time, unfulfilled opportunity. When the authors disappeared, like Solon after writing the Greek constitution, leaving other mortals to interpret their grand words, the parties were left to quarrel for years about what each side had meant and what goals this powerful document actually demanded and from whom.

Simply, in its relation to farm workers the whole Employment Service system, along with related agencies of state and federal government, was to be reformed, in spirit and in very explicit detail. The assignment was as pervasive as it was complex; it was a staggeringly ambitious attempt to enforce nationwide the reform of a vast and varied system of programs and services run by federal and state officials for the benefit of hundreds of thousands of needy clients who were on the move. It would turn out to be a quixotic quest to make government work.

The assignment was especially difficult because of the interrelation between federal and state governments, which complicated all views of the defendants' compliance. Conceived as a cohesive national organization, the Employment Service network had become a confederacy of autonomous state agencies, each calling its own tune, in the words of labor experts Stanley Ruttenberg and

Jocelyn Gutchess.[4] That diversity was at the heart of most of the problems faced in evaluating compliance with the court's order. To do what the parties agreed and what the court ordered, it was necessary not only to change the national policies of a vast, old-line federal bureaucracy but also to translate them into realities in 50 separate state organizations, each politically powerful, quite different, and committed more or less to accomplishing (as California was) or ignoring (as was the case in Indiana) the court's order.

The Labor Department had ample powers to force states to comply with the law. Every year, each state submitted an annual plan of service, outlining its programmatic intentions. On the basis of the rationale of its services as described in these plans, the department approved the states' funding. This power could be used to ensure that the states complied with their legal obligations. In addition to these administrative controls, the department also had powers and responsibilities under the Wagner-Peyser Act to police the states it funded. How it used or failed to use these powers could become the confirmation of the department's complicity in the sins of any state that acted illegally toward its farm worker clients.

Special Review Committee. In analyzing the seven parts of the court order and assessing what happened as a result of each of these obligations, one must begin with Section VI; doing so will make the rest of the chapter more understandable and will introduce some of the key players in the drama that unfolded.

Section VI called for the creation of a Special Review Committee to monitor the defendants' compliance with the court order. The committee was to be composed of three representatives of migrant and seasonal farm worker groups to be selected by the plaintiffs, three departmental representatives selected by the secretary of labor (one to be from the office of the secretary or under secretary), and a chairperson to be selected by these six partisan members.

The committee was authorized to meet at least quarterly, file a semiannual report to the court evaluating the defendants' compliance, and make interim recommendations to the secretary of labor for changes or improvements. The Labor Department was ordered to pay all the committee's costs and to cooperate fully by making available all information, documents, facilities, services, and staff.

Regrettably, the six partisan members took half a year to agree on who their chairperson should be. Each side was suspicious of the other's suggested candidates. Both sides had inflated notions about getting a former secretary of labor or Supreme Court justice to take the job. After coming perilously close to failing to agree and after a quarter of its projected life had passed while it fretted over the proverbial shape of the table, the committee decided upon me.

This choice was a surprise. I had no experience in this field. Perhaps this was one reason I was acceptable to both sides: there was no prior involvement to have corrupted me. My background also fitted the hopes on both sides: the Labor Department no doubt saw me as an ex-prosecutor for the Justice Department, presumably neither antigovernment nor unsympathetic with the problems of bureaucrats; the plaintiffs saw me as a practicing public interest lawyer who had fought for the underdog in other situations and as one who was aware of the failures of government and unafraid to fight them. In my mind, both sides were correct if those presumptions indeed motivated them.

The challenge was interesting, and a few experts in the field had encouraged me to take the assignment and had promised to help. Jocelyn Gutchess was my most helpful associate. A bright, savvy, energetic labor specialist who formerly had served in the Department of Labor, she tutored me in the beginning, aided me throughout, and was a constant source of balance and reason as times grew contentious and partisan. Larry Sherman—a young lawyer who had worked on the original complaint for the Migrant Legal Action Program, knew as much as anyone about the field, and was very able—also offered valuable help and advice throughout. Because each had worked earlier for one side in the dispute and was respected by former colleagues, the committee approved both of them as consultants.

By talking to everyone in Washington, D.C., who had expertise in this field, by reading voraciously on all related subjects, by taking advantage of the court's order requiring department cooperation and seeking numerous briefings by department officials, by relying heavily on Jocelyn's and Larry's constant tutelage, and by traveling extensively throughout the migrant streams in the United States, I also gained expertise and confidence. But one-quarter of the committee's tenure had been squandered before I was chosen, and another would fly by before it was fully functioning.

The other members of the Special Review Committee were, on paper, an interesting bunch. Representing the plaintiffs were a young Chicano Legal Defense Fund lawyer who had been a farm worker as a child; a young, idealistic lawyer, formerly a Peace Corps volunteer, who was fluent in Spanish and had been a legal services lawyer in New Jersey and Florida; and a bilingual, former Peace Corps volunteer who had just started a new organization for former volunteers. The latter seemed to be the leader, activist, and spokesman for the plaintiffs' representatives when I first came on the scene. He eventually was replaced by the director of the National Association of Farmworker Organizations, an evolving lobbying arm of farm worker groups around the country.

The defendants also replaced one of their three members early in the committee's tenure. The representative of the under secretary on our committee, presented with a challenging opportunity elsewhere in the Labor Department, moved on to other activities. He was replaced by Fred Romero, a middle-aged Chicano, a self-made professional and a man driven by a passion about his role and opportunities. In my judgment, Fred was the one department representative who always did his job in the public interest and in the farm workers' interest, and for this he paid heavily. The department he served so well would turn on him, charging him with traitorous criticism; his colleagues and former friends pressured him, humiliated him, and eventually isolated him for doing with uncompromising integrity the job he was appointed to do. In an experience marked by government incompetence, misguided purposes, and chilling self-aggrandizement and self-defense, Fred Romero's work was a hallmark of devoted public service in the highest order. He deserves a medal.

The other two Labor Department representatives were long-time employees. Although they occupied high level offices (one administrative, the other policy oriented), they approached their committee assignment with reluctance, skepticism, and a limited, essentially defensive view of our charter and their roles.

This group, created by court-inspired compromise and uniquely able to provide farm workers with needed government attentions, was provided the additional support of a Department of Labor task force. A small group of competent, hard-working, middle-level bureaucrats, the task force, if led properly and supported adequately, could have made a major contribution. Instead, it was headed by an irascible and contentious man who was whipsawed by a Special Review Committee that pushed it to act as the generator of change in the Labor Department and by a departmental hierarchy that was anxious and defensive throughout. He vacillated between trying to do right by his larger lights and needing to do well by his lesser ones.

The Special Review Committee was a compromise agency; in the nature of compromises, it had all the weaknesses and few of the strengths required for the accomplishment of its unique opportunity. The plaintiffs' representatives and the amicus curiae had wanted the court to appoint a master, who would have had independence and quasi-judicial powers to keep the court informed about the case and involved in it. This is exactly what the defendants did not want. The Labor Department had suggested the appointment of either a blue ribbon committee chosen by both sides or a person from the secretary's office who could be trusted to do right by the farm workers. This notion was exactly what the plaintiffs could not accept. The farm workers could not trust the "cat to watch the cream," as one of their lawyers put it. The committee was the inept compromise reached by the negotiators.

The tripartite composition of the Special Review Committee would prove to be its critical flaw. The partisan nature of the members predetermined that the committee's success would be limited. But its very existence provided both sides with a chance to participate in the implementation of the court order they had fashioned and to have a say in the evaluation of Labor's performance. For the plaintiffs, a role on the committee gave them critical access to funds (Labor agreed to pay expenses of the plaintiffs' representatives and the chairman) and the ability to do what they never before were able to do (work on their own problems from the inside). For the defendants, a role on the committee allowed them the fullest opportunity to build or sabotage the implementation process.

The plaintiffs' representatives grappled irregularly with an extraordinarily difficult job; the defendants squandered a unique opportunity to serve a poor constituency. In our final report to the court, we acknowledged that we had done as much as possible under strained circumstances. Ironically, five of us recommended that a master, which the court had suggested at the start but the parties' lawyers had negotiated away, was required to complete the job of implementing the order.

There was no model agency nor were there particular precedents to guide us. Research revealed that courts in recent years had used comparable agencies—masters, monitors, receivers, ombudsmen, special committees, and panels—to carry out quasi-judicial monitoring and implementation roles in cases involving civil rights and civil liberties claims by large classes against government agencies and other large institutions. The closest comparable agency was the three-man group of monitors appointed by the District of Columbia federal court about 20 years earlier to monitor the work and election of the Teamsters' Union.[5] I spoke to the director of that effort, a former Justice Department colleague, but found that our agencies' tasks were different in fundamental ways.

So the Special Review Committee had to design itself out of whole cloth.

Puzzled by the lack of specification of my own powers and the absence of precedents to guide the peculiar entity I was to direct for almost two years, I petitioned the court to specifically appoint me an officer of the court, to officially appoint the six members to our committee (only the secretary of labor had appointed all of us, so far), and to authorize the committee to conduct hearings.[6] These were the key ingredients I viewed to be necessary at that time. The court granted the motion, issuing an order that also reaffirmed the Labor Department's obligation to cooperate fully with us.

I resisted departmental efforts to prepare a book of committee procedures and guidelines, anticipating that each point, however elemental, would embark us on endless metaphysical debates and that such a project would stall us for a year at least. In most situations we were guided by common sense, the court order, and Robert's Rules of Order; eventually, we fashioned some (very few) specific rules of our own when we felt they were needed (how much notice before a meeting could be called, when information had to be exchanged). Good sense and fair play should answer most questions and momentum was necessary; we had to move, to act, to work, and not stand around talking about how.

When the Special Review Committee encountered problems in interpreting the meaning of particular provisions in the court order, which the parties themselves had fashioned and whose implementation we were supposed to be enforcing, we had no available source to help resolve our quandary. I analyzed each part of the court order, studied all the underlying documents, and talked to all the parties and their lawyers to attempt to find a consensus definition of the requirements. Then I prepared an extensive paper listing all ambiguities in the order, suggesting interpretations I hoped all parties would agree to, and sent it to the committee members and their attorneys.

There was no consensus. The plaintiffs were too fearful about being sold out and too imprecise in their notions of what would constitute success in the case to realize that they had much to gain by agreeing on precise standards. The defendants were unwilling to agree to any specific standards for fear they would be held to them. Instead of seeing the case as an opportunity to bring about change, they saw any objective requirement as a challenge to departmental efficiency and a potential basis for its future censure.

Midway through our two-year term, I approached this problem in another way. I was aware that any attempt to judge the

Labor Department by precise standards of performance on the day of reckoning when we made our final report to the court would be frustrated unless the committee agreed in advance on specific standards regarding what performance would constitute adequate implementation of this ambiguous court order. I attempted to define a set of standards the committee could adopt to measure the Labor Department's compliance.

I wrote up one set of compliance standards. The Labor Department eventually submitted a different set. Romero devised one of his own, which attempted to satisfy the concerns of both sides without sacrificing the real needs of the scattered farm workers whose interests he always had in sight. After months of formal and informal meetings on this subject and the exchange of several written proposals, we voted to adopt a composite package of standards proposed by the plaintiffs, Romero, and the chairman, which I then wove into one unified set of requirements. This became our set of guidelines to judge performance of the provisions of the consent order. However, all the parties never fully accepted these standards in a real and complete way.

Once the Special Review Committee came into being, the parties' polarized views were atomized: individual members saw their roles differently from the way others and their clients saw them; and the chairman had a view of his own in addition. One Labor representative argued that our role was a passive, judgmental one. We were simply to review what the department put before us as evidence of its compliance, determine whether it was good enough, and tell the court. Not all his colleagues agreed. Fred Romero joined me in viewing our assignment as a unique opportunity to bring about change, to participate in reforms that would touch real people's lives in real ways.

Occasionally, I wondered just who the parties were in this extraordinary case. The actual named plaintiffs were people and institutions chosen years before by the Migrant Legal Action Program. But that staff turned over rapidly, and there were no adopted game plans or strategic specifications to guide the changing players. This was one reason I hired Larry Sherman, who was the major strategist in the initiation of the case and the only one I found who had substantial knowledge of the background and intentions of the lawsuit.

The plaintiffs' representatives came from different organizations and experiences; they had different goals as well as different skills and styles. They also had different and changing views of who their constituents were, and the lawyers guiding them changed three times during two years.

And then there was the Labor Department. Anyone who has worked in a large agency of government has observed and contributed to a dynamic process. No agency is a monolithic structure having a single opinion on any issue. In this case, two executive agencies (Labor and Justice) of government fought each other over a specific issue raised by the Special Review Committee; agencies within the department disagreed and battled each other; staff members within agencies fought their leaders. Unfortunately, the wrong group of officials defined the department's role in this case by grabbing the power to speak and act for the whole Department of Labor.

Who were "the farm workers" about whom the case was concerned, I wondered? Where were they if we wanted to question them? How do they get real representation? Who decides what is in their interest? How do they make their voices heard? Are they of one voice?

On all my trips, I went out of my way to meet and talk with farm workers at their homes, at work in the fields, in union halls, in and around Employment Service offices, anywhere. Of course, these conversations were episodic and, while personally edifying, I could not purport through them to have a sense of "the farm worker view"—if there was one. At our committee hearings, along with any farm workers called by the parties, I reserved a part of each day's agenda for workers to testify about any relevant matter. This offer was accepted everywhere. But, even so, throughout the two years (and to this day) I had a futile feeling that "the farm workers" out there missed a great and rare opportunity to be heard and to have some influence on matters vitally affecting their lives. This unfortunate fact typifies their basic problem: they are ineffective, not powerful; historically they have not been well represented in events that deeply concern them. It is especially pathetic that the opportunity offered by this unusual case was not exploited in their interest as it might have been. Their ineffectiveness and their profound needs disturbed me throughout this two-year experience; their problems concern me still.

Finally, I had to define my own unique role. Whom did I represent? By what lights was I to be guided? By some undefined personal, moral standard? Some half-baked notion of what was "just" for a group of people I did not know? Was I simply an administrator for the court, only responsible in a ministerial way to see that matters moved as the supposedly consenting parties wished? How could I be nonpartisan? What did that word mean in this context? I took the approach that I must be judicious in conducting all proceedings, evenhanded in dealing with plaintiffs and defendants, and responsible to the court to keep the case moving and away from Judge Richey as much as possible. I would call all shots candidly and forcefully. I would act uncompromisingly in what I viewed to be the interests of farm workers, without capitulating even to compelling, competing interests on any issue. And I had to work with great industry; everyone had a head start on information in this field, the plaintiffs' representatives worked only part-time, the defendants' representatives (except Romero) often worked in a parochial and self-defensive way, and the department's resources required protean efforts of me just to keep up.

Nondiscriminatory Delivery of Services. The key substantive provision to the thirteen-page consent order was the first; under it, the defendants undertook to "take all necessary and appropriate action . . . to ensure the delivery of all Department of Labor manpower services, benefits, and protections . . . to migrant and seasonal farmworkers on a non-discriminatory basis." The defendants agreed to require each state and local office to take specific actions: provide the full range of manpower services to farm workers in ways "qualitatively equivalent and quantitatively proportionate" to nonfarm workers (a standard whose meaning we would debate throughout our tenure), provide job bank information, take complete job applications, develop affirmative action programs, refer all violations to enforcement agencies, improve staffing, and refine job orders.

The qualitatively equivalent, quantitatively proportionate requirement was the most ambiguous, thus elusive, and most subjective requirement of all. Its thrust was to the very nature of manpower services to farm workers; its measurement was our most profound assignment.

The Special Review Committee spent considerable time defining this key requirement and establishing objective indicators upon which to base our judgment of compliance. The elements of this requirement, our standards for judging compliance with it, and fifteen charts illustrating the Labor Department's performance were designed and presented to the court in our third report. Our concluding judgments about compliance in our final report were based on these indicators.

Using the data we gathered nationwide, we compared migrant and seasonal farm workers (MSFWs) to non-MSFWs on national, state, and local bases. States were judged on the basis of their comparative treatment of both groups within their own state and in comparison with the national norms. The committee paid special attention to the 21 states that account for 91 percent of all MSFW activity. We developed quantitative indicators of compliance (how many applicants from each category were referred to any job) and qualitative indicators (were the jobs long or short term, high or low paying, and what were the comparative rates of people counseled). Our findings were not deemed to be the final word, however important we all viewed them. In my mind, the data created rebuttable presumptions that there were problems or successes to note. Data could be explained by such additional sources as personal information gathered on field visits, testimony at our hearings, and observations from on-site reviews.

For over a year, based on the data provided by the Labor Department, the committee compared the experiences of MSFW and non-MSFW applicants who used the Employment Service. The relationships were charted on a comparative basis from cumulative data covering July 1975 through July 1976. Our charts graphically illustrated several facts of life regarding MSFWs in the Employment Service system as compared to non-MSFWs. In referrals to agricultural jobs, MSFWs fared better, and the disparity widened during our tenure. This was an obvious area for growth, and we congratulated the department for this apparent increase in basic services to farm workers. However, in referrals to nonagricultural jobs, MSFWs fared worse than non-MSFWs, and this disparity also increased during our tenure. One quantitative improvement was eclipsed by a comparable qualitative loss.

We also charted the relations between MSFWs and non-MSFWs placed in jobs (not simply referred) and found that MSFWs did slightly better overall and that their situation had improved. This fact showed qualitative improvement. It was diminished, however, by the expectable findings that MSFWs were placed in agricultural jobs more frequently and in nonagricultural jobs less frequently than non-MSFWs. In addition, MSFWs were placed in fewer long-term (150 days or more) jobs and more short-term (3 days or less) jobs than non-MSFWs. Obviously, these were important qualitative elements and MSFWs fared poorly. The same was the case when we compared MSFWs in better paying jobs ($3 an hour and over) and low-paying jobs ($2.10 an hour and less) with non-MSFWs. Here, not only did MSFWs do worse but, despite the Labor Department's protestations and efforts, the gap was widening.

Furthermore, charts demonstrating four key services— counseling, training, job development contacts, and testing—each showed that MSFWs were below parity and that their relative position was declining during 1975–1976. These services are aimed at allowing workers to improve their job potentials and to get out of the stream; thus a majority of the committee attached considerable importance to them. Migrants also were referred to supportive services more frequently than others. This indicated more Employment Service activity, but it also reflected the dire condition of MSFWs who needed more food stamps, medical care, and other emergency relief.

The department's failure to demonstrate improved, if not equal, provision of services to farm workers (as our analysis of the information provided by the states to Labor and by Labor to us showed) informed our judgment that the department had not ensured its services to farm workers on a nondiscriminatory basis. Not only had the department failed to reach ceilings, it had not reached floors. Realities had not changed despite colossal outside pressure and some inside effort.

The department's basic failure here was particularly revealing in light of all its efforts and alleged successes, as it viewed them. It did manage to perform what might be described as the physical and administrative requirements of the court order. It distributed copies of the order to all relevant offices; it ran expensive training conferences and sent out voluminous directory instructions; it placed job banks in more rural offices and ended segregated facilities; it got forms filled out to a fault; and it referred complaints to enforcement agencies. The department's lawyers and the committee representatives (except for Romero) argued that this was all that could be expected of it, all that it could control.

Qualitative services like training, counseling, and better quality jobs remained lacking for farm workers, however; and it was this fundamental failure to change real people's lives in real ways that the plaintiffs and I saw as the department's challenge and failure. Employment Service officials were expected to refer all violations of law to appropriate law enforcement officials. We argued with monitor advocates and other departmental representatives that simply lobbing a complaint in the direction of a wage-and-hour or housing official was insufficient—that was bureaucratic buck-passing. Follow-up, coordination; even imaginative, aggressive use of its own enforcement powers were required to make a failing system work.

A part of Section I required state affirmative action plans designed to get more minority personnel in Employment Service offices. This need was especially important since so many farm workers are black and Hispanic. To make the system work for these clients, staffs needed to be culturally attuned to them; they were not. The Labor Department required states to develop affirmative action plans; the states complied, and the committee recognized this. However, many states did not reach levels of minority staffing necessary to assure that overall staffs were composed of people reflective of the communities they served. There were not enough staff members, for example, who spoke Spanish; this was a critical need in offices serving large numbers of Spanish-speaking workers. Nor were Employment Service offices hiring enough people with farm worker backgrounds, as required by the court order. It was not an adequate answer that state civil service regulations made it difficult to recruit the staffs called for by the court order. There was no evidence that the Labor Department had worked to change these laws or to find and fund imaginative ways to circumvent them. When minority employees were found and used, our hearings demonstrated, they were excellent workers. Indeed, the department pridefully called them as witnesses to show them off at our hearings. But most of them were temporary workers, funded from supplemental budgets; there was no evidence they would be working when the committee functions ceased.

Related to this question was the requirement for outreach staff. To get farm workers back into a system from which they were alienated would take more than intramural changes of attitudes, welcoming posters on the walls, and new hortatory rules. The only way to get many needy farm workers back into the Employment Service system was to reach out to them and demonstrate that they were deemed to be a desirable clientele. To the extent that employment offices hired bilingual staff, some with farm worker backgrounds, they were quite successful in reaching and serving such clients. But to the extent that the Labor Department refused to provide the extra funding this venture required, it failed to assure the performance that was needed. In doing so, a majority of the committee concluded, the department failed to take the affirmative steps required of it. Saying it wanted things to happen was insufficient performance; using all its might and power and money to bring about results was needed, and this the department did not do.

Another indication of the Labor Department's passive approach was the way it responded to the court requirement concerning annual worker plans. Past attempts by the Employment Service to coordinate jobs and workers through plans administered on a nationwide basis had promise. Job openings, special skills, weather conditions, and numerous other variables of the job and labor markets could be coordinated by offices around the country to ensure that the farmers received services they needed and farm workers got available jobs in the most organized and efficient fashion. The department was required to conduct a feasibility study to determine whether experimental projects of this kind could be used to solve problems farm workers faced because of their inevitably moving, changing employment system.

The department never conducted an adequate feasibility study until it was too late to be of use to the Special Review Committee. Then it arranged a survey with a sole source contractor who did other work for the department; its findings were inconclusive. Some committee members' speculations that annual worker plans could be designed to assist farm workers in meaningful ways—a view that might have ripened into one useful reform to have come from our efforts—never saw fruition.

How perverse the department's approach could be is illustrated by its handling of the problem of day-hauls. A day-haul is a place—it could be a street corner, an unused parking lot, a deserted street—where unemployed workers would gather early every morning during the local harvest season to be recruited by farmers and crew leaders for a day's work. People would drift in at 4 to 5 A.M., stand around, be picked up in a farmer's bus or car and driven off for a day's work, and be brought back at 7 or 8 P.M. and dropped off. There were about a dozen or two formal day-hauls and countless unofficial ones around the United States. The Employment Service knew about all these places and actually used some to find day workers for farmers who did not want to come to the day-haul sites and do the recruiting themselves.

We visited day-haul sites in a border town near Mexico in Calexico, Calif.; at a city ghetto in Belle Glade, Fla.; and under a bridge in a deserted, grubby part of Philadelphia, Pa. There we observed a chaotic process of cheap labor recruitment, where Employment Service officials not only let it all happen but also participated in it. Here was a perfect opportunity to reach farm workers and to attempt to provide them with much needed services. But officials failed to do any more than watch it and occasionally use it as a crucible of free marketplace dynamics through which farmers might rummage for occasional laborers they could use and discard with minimal obligations. The farmers set all the terms; the workers scampered for their meager crumbs of work. The whole scene was a deplorable bedlam.

Two New Jersey journalists went to the Philadelphia day-haul early one morning, rented themselves for a day's work, and later described their experiences.[7] According to their report, between 8,000 and 10,000 people participate in this daily ritual to seek work in New Jersey fields during the fruit and vegetable season. When they got jobs, they earned an average of $10 for a day that began at 4 A.M. and ended 16 hours later under conditions that violated the laws then in existence to govern farm labor contracts. Workers were charged for rides and for lunch, so their mosquito-drenched, arduous day's labor netted them merely dismal memories of being what the authors called "human chattels."

The court order required that at official day-haul operations used by the Employment Service, workers were to fill out job applications providing information that might lead to better jobs and alternative opportunities. This whole process was a charade. Day-haul activity was so spontaneous and fiercely competitive that no one wanted to stop to get or give services; workers just wanted the quick one-day jobs that were up for fast bids and would be gone in less than an hour of hectic scrambling.

Instead of attempting to re-create or follow up these day-haul operations to be able to offer real, long-term, useful services to the needy farm workers who used them as job auctions, the Employment Service dropped out completely, fearing the committee would condemn its failure to fill out the forms properly in that chaotic environment. Its answer to this predicament was to do nothing.

When I talked to Cesar Chavez at his union's isolated mountain headquarters in California, he asked if the union could take over the California day-hauls. He would have used these natural convening sites like an outdoor union hiring hall, organizing the workers and seeking more than the scraps farmers were tossing them. His perceptions of and interests in the needs and opportunities of farm workers were obvious and sensible; they made the Labor Department's views and actions all the more censurable. Indeed, I attempted to broker his idea with federal and state officials in California. The offer was not accepted.

These kinds of reactions to farm worker problems typified the different mentalities that symbolized the two sides in this case. The department insisted it should be required to do no more than set things in motion and exhort the states about the direction they should follow; its critics cared most about what actually happened.

This broad example of how institutions work and view their responsibilities reflected a confounding phenomenon—that is, they operate for the convenience of their administrators and often fail to serve the clients or consumers whose interests and needs provide the reason for any institution's existence. Labor Department officials in this case never viewed the failures to improve farm workers' lives as their failures. They judged themselves, promoted themselves, complimented themselves, and rationalized themselves on the basis of abstract processes in which they participated. Images, not realities, of reform were their currency.

Adequate Information. The need for abundant and reliable information was critical. Though it seemed more of an administrative requirement than the other substantive parts of the negotiated order, an adequate information base was a critical element in the case. To measure compliance with the rest of the requirements of the order and to allow proper future planning for programs affecting migrants, a reliable and adequate information gathering system was essential. How else could we fathom the vast situation we had to evaluate? Section II ordered the Labor Department to "modify and refine" its data gathering systems to provide us with specified information about migrants.

We needed a means for measuring the massive facts necessary to assess the desired changes. How does one determine what is happening when events involving hundreds of thousands of migrants are occurring in about 2,700 different offices in 50 different states over a period of two years? The task was mind-boggling. Without a good system to gather information, it was beyond reach.

The department had a computerized information gathering system called the Employment Security Automated Reporting System (ESARS). Its information bank had to be supplemented for us to gain the additional information we sought. Also, a basic question about the fundamental credibility of ESARS had to be resolved before we could rely on it in making judgments. We never did resolve that question.

Early in our work, I met with department officials to work out the necessary changes in ESARS and to devise a way to digest and report the special information the review committee needed. I hired an expert to assist in devising changes in ESARS and relied heavily on Jocelyn Gutchess to analyze and interpret the data eventually cranked out during the next two years. An attempt to recruit the National Academy of Sciences to assist us (as a public service) failed.

The Labor Department made the mechanical changes quickly. The problems arose over the evaluation of information the machinery then ground out during the next year and a half. We were barraged with a continuous snowstorm of paper, most of which was distracting, self-serving, and often unresponsive to our real needs and requests. On the other hand, the data we really wanted and needed to help assess compliance by the thousands of Employment Service offices around the country was late, sometimes fallacious, and interpreted differently by my experts and those of the department.

The committee quickly reported to the court that changes in ESARS were made to provide the new data needed to demonstrate the level and quality of employment services to farm workers. However, we consistently found (and ultimately reported non-

California lettuce fields, 1935. (Dorothea Lange, Library of Congress)

compliance with Section II by the department because of it) that the data generated by the modified ESARS was untimely, incomplete, and inaccurate. We could use the data, but we could not rely on it. Without complete compliance with Section II, there were inadequate means to evaluate compliance with sections I, III, and IV. So Section II was important in itself and, as with dominoes, its failures were compounded in a rippling way.

Each local office supplied specific information about its services to farm workers and other clients; this accumulated information went into state computers and ultimately to coordinated printouts at the Department of Labor. Once the department received, collated, and processed the state data, a "Catch-22" situation occurred between the department and the committee. When we pointed out patent inaccuracies, the department defended that it was being rushed; so we then waited as long as five months to get more accurate monthly data, which we argued was tardy and at that not totally accurate.

The plaintiffs' skepticism about the department's data tables was fueled by a comment in another context by one departmental agent that information gathered by federal officials in the states would be "massaged" by department lawyers. More upsetting were disclosures in the department's own reports and at our hearings indicating that systemic labeling and coding errors were causing major distortions in the images projected by the data we were receiving. For example, some states appeared to be placing large numbers of farm workers in nonagricultural jobs, indicating significant qualitative performance. Yet we found this was not accurate; certain jobs such as corn detasseling were being categorized as nonagricultural jobs. At our hearings in New York and Texas, for example, we uncovered mistakes in the recordation of such important data, which would have led us to draw erroneous conclusions about important elements of compliance efforts in those states.

More profoundly frustrating was our inability to agree about the meaning of the data we received, flawed as it was. Almost a year before our final meeting, anticipating the need to adopt standards well before we made our judgments, we began a long process of developing standards of compliance. Without these, the plaintiffs could unjustly complain that the department failed to meet standards of performance of which it could claim it had no notice.

Neither side really wanted to be pinned down, but both sides had to be. I sent several detailed and analytical memoranda to committee members. The department responded with its own specific proposals, which would have required only that it take steps to create mechanisms and procedures to comply with its obligations, not that it be required to prove results and change realities. The plaintiffs never offered alternative standards until the last moment, when they proposed a general statement saying no more than that everything in the court order should be complied with.

While our intramural arguments over Department of Labor data continued, we were made aware of a 1975 General Accounting Office evaluation of ESARS operations in 15 local Employment Service offices[8] and a 1976 Labor Department audit of the reliability of ESARS placement data in four states. Both reports confirmed our fears about the infirmities and unreliability of ESARS.

These surveys, discounted by the department when it learned the committee had access to them, were corroborated further by a House of Representatives Government Operations Subcommittee report in October 1976. That report, which we received on the eve of our final evaluation and meeting, concluded that federal monitoring of state Employment Service efforts was "spotty and inadequate," and that known inaccuracies in its data-gathering system needed to be evaluated by experts.

I called for regular, independent auditing checks of ESARS. With the plaintiffs' representatives, we tried to find an independent accounting and data analysis organization to analyze the system for the committee and the court and to suggest necessary refinements. This could not be done without funds, and the Labor Department would not underwrite such a project. The department not only resisted all our recommendations about reforming ESARS but also denied our request that it endorse and adopt an experimental and ingenious data-gathering sampling project the California Employment Service had created, and which had been demonstrated to be both accurate and economic. The committee was left with the worst of both worlds in reviewing department compliance with Section II. The system itself was flawed and suspect; at that, the conclusions that could be drawn from the information this imperfect system generated damned the department's purported efforts to change the lot of farm workers in meaningful ways.

Federal-State Monitoring System. Knowing what was happening in what Robert Coles has called the "unwelcoming world" of migrant farm workers was only the beginning to the solution of their difficulties. Doing something about the problems as they became apparent was the next step. An apparatus and procedure to correct them as they were identified was necessary. The consent order provided for this. Section III of the order called for the establishment of a federal-state monitoring system to review the services provided migrant and seasonal workers and to administer the state complaint systems. It enumerated specific features to be included. Section IV required the implementation of a federally supervised complaint resolution system for use in every local Employment Service office, with specified provisions for appeals and timetables for resolution of all complaints. The Labor Department set up a monitoring system under which each state Employment Service agency appointed an experienced employee to be what was called a monitor advocate—a kind of roving inspector general for that state. Eventually, larger states recruited several such staffers.

The system adopted to fulfill the monitoring requirement of Section III was adapted from earlier departmental efforts to cope with Judge Richey's concerns in this case. In May and June 1973 the judge sought some systematic and reliable checks on the state implementation of the 13 Points. To accomplish this task, the department set up a monitoring system in September 1973; it was working in the states by March 1974.[9]

The amicus curiae, Dean Cahn, had urged the court to require federal employees to be the monitors in the states. He feared a conflict of interest inevitably would arise if state employees were asked to monitor a state system. The plaintiffs' negotiators had been pushing for independent monitors, people who were positioned outside the state systems; they submitted a proposed consent order in April 1974 providing for this. But they relented and eventually signed the August 1974 order that adopted the department's existing system.

All Department of Labor materials describing the background and evolution of the monitor advocate system clearly distinguished between the two roles these officials were to carry out. The monitoring role was to scrutinize the operation of the system; the advocacy role was to ferret out complaints and to advocate on behalf of farm workers. The skills, background, disposition, and position required for each of these roles were quite different; the monitor advocates were placed in a schizoid position from the start by mixing both roles into one job description.

The network of monitor advocates was to play a critical role in the course of our case. They ran the complaint system created by Section IV of the court order, and they monitored compliance with what became notoriously known as "the Richey order" to high officials in Washington, D.C., and to every minor clerk in every small Employment Service office in the country. Their duties covered others than farm workers' complaints, but those chores under the Richey court order monopolized most monitor advocates' time. This system was the method by which the Department of Labor purported to police its Employment Service system, one that had been found to be racist and illegal.

The integrity of this system caused a fundamental and revealing debate, which continued throughout our two-year tenure. The idea that a career bureaucrat who was part of a system, relied on it for livelihood and advancement, and often had been part of the system for years while it operated illegally could conceivably have the vision, impartiality, independence, and strength to police colleagues and superiors was untenable from the start. Many of these career employees were asked to watchdog and report on their cronies and superiors in Employment Service offices and to harass farmers in their communities who traditionally had been their social friends and business contacts. How could such a system be effective for the farm workers (often members of another culture or race and speaking a different language) who were its consumers, its clients? Years of distrust and alienation from the system would not be wiped out by the simple announcement of this new program.

In my early travels to Florida, North Carolina, and New Jersey and in all the trips my staff took in the midwest, Texas, Maryland, and Delaware during these first months of our work, we traveled with the state monitor advocates because they were critical to the successful implementation of the court order. If voluntarism was to work, the monitor advocates were the key. Invariably, the state agencies chose experienced, likable people, often members of minority groups—blacks and Chicanos. Rarely did the system work.

In Mississippi on my first trip, for example, I talked with the state monitor advocate. I was quite impressed with the attitude of the Mississippi officials toward the court order and the committee, but the monitor advocate was a dull, desk warmer who viewed this job as a passive, paper-shuffling assignment. I asked him how he accounted for the small number of complaints he had received. Were farm workers in Mississippi without problems or was the complaint system not working? Did he go to organization meetings? Did he travel around the state to local offices to observe operations? What was he doing to learn about realities in the fields? It appeared from his remarks that he opened the mail each day; if he received a complaint, he referred it to some appropriate official. He said he did not view his job as "looking for trouble," which, of course, is exactly what he should have been doing.

My initial skepticism about this system was borne out by numerous encounters like the one in Mississippi, and it was confirmed in the telling testimony of two federal monitor advocates at our committee hearings in May 1976 in Texas and in July in Colorado. These men had been prepared to testify by department representatives and their attorneys; they all knew my views by this time. Yet one regional federal monitor advocate testified that he never had been to some states in his area during two years on the job, that half his time was spent in the federal regional office, that he shuffled complaints to different enforcement agencies and forgot them, that he did not have adequate assistance, and that he believed there was racism in the system. At one point, we had the following revealing colloquy on the subject of his ability to carry out a critic's role while operating within the system he was monitoring:

Chairman: Do you recall making a trip with Mr. Andratti and Mr. Garcia to the Monte Vista office?
Mr. Quintana: Yes.
Chairman: Is it true you got written up after you were there?
Mr. Quintana: Yes. I was. A letter was sent to the regional office because I didn't have a tie on.

His success as an insider fighting against systemic racism was evidenced by the following exchange:

Chairman: What steps have you taken to prove, for example, the claims that Navajo Indians—in one office in this state, at least—are discriminated against?
Mr. Quintana: Well, as far as the Monitor Advocate System is concerned, we have not received complaints referring to specific race issues. But, I have, you know—I was made aware of them. I'm sure that we could either put it through the Monitor Advocate System and make sure it would get to the proper enforcing agency.
Chairman: Was this morning the first time that you had heard of that complaint?
Mr. Quintana: Yes.

The regional monitor advocate whose jurisdiction covered Texas, Louisiana, Arkansas, New Mexico, and Oklahoma was a career Labor Department official. He described how he was recruited:

Mr. Oden: I worked in Texas operations manpower program for about eighteen months prior to that. I've been with the U.S. Department of Labor since 1957. I came in as a compliance officer and stayed with that until its expiration. Then I came on with the crew leader registration. I was the one that administered that program for the region here.

Chairman: How did you become the Monitor-Advocate? How did it happen to be?

Mr. Oden: I was called into the front office and . . . .

Chairman: You volunteered?

Mr. Oden: They said, "You've just volunteered for it," and I've been it. No. Mr. Avilar consulted me and said, "I'm not sure just what it is at this time, but I think you're qualified. Would you take it?" And I said, "I'd be glad to."

During his examination by one plaintiffs' representative, he described the route of one notorious case that came through his office:

Mr. Jones: You are aware of the Agrego case. What's the status of that case in your office?

Mr. Oden: I think I've sent it on to the state office. As far as I'm concerned, we're through with it up there.

Mr. Jones: Have you referred it on to the National Monitor-Advocate?

Mr. Oden: No, it was referred to the National Monitor-Advocate when I first got it. It came up to me and then I sent it up to the Monitor-Advocate in Washington, and, in turn, they, I guess, sent it to Chicago. It went to the Chicago regional office and then, from there, back to my office and back to the state.

He admitted that he rarely visited several states he was expected to oversee and that he did not know the resolution of most complaints after they were referred to enforcement agencies. We talked about housing complaints that were referred to OSHA:

Chairman: As one who is responsible for the referral of these complaints to the enforcement agencies, are you satisfied with the way they are dealt with once they are referred there?

Mr. Oden: No. We can't get any results. . . .

Not all monitor advocates were like this. An active, committed official popped up occasionally. But they were as rare as they were unappreciated by the Department of Labor.

One young man who tried to do the job right and also cooperated with my staff reported that he was severely criticized by his superiors in the state Employment Service and by a department official and was asked to recant critical comments he had made about implementation efforts in his state. When he surreptitiously told me that he had been called on the carpet by officials who were supposed to be encouraging his aggressive, positive efforts, I was outraged and promised to discuss his case at an imminent committee meeting. The next day, he called back begging me not to say anything for fear he would lose his job. I wanted to open his case and end his professional emasculation and that of others, but he implored me to forget what he had said, invoking his family's well-being. He and a few like him would talk privately, endorsing what I was saying about the monitor advocate system; but no one would speak out.

Reviewing these events, it became clear that while the monitor advocate program was central to success, it was fundamentally flawed because it was based within the system. It had to be independent of the Employment Service. In early September, I sent a long memorandum to my colleagues, sharing my travel experiences and analyzing the monitor advocate system. I had conducted extensive research on other ombudsmanlike monitoring mechanisms and had analyzed the need for independence as well as access and the need for credibility among potential constituents. I knew my comments would be controversial, especially to the Labor Department, which was banking on the court's acceptance of the in-system monitor advocate program. I wrote a cool, comprehensive memorandum, and went to individual committee members to explain my feelings and to solicit their consensus.

The plaintiffs' representatives generally approved. The defendants' representatives were defensive of the present program, but at first they did not absolutely refuse to consider my recommendations. My memorandum appealed to one researcher's interests; he speculated about a statewide official who might do what the monitor advocate did and in addition oversee the administration of all federal programs in that state. The idea of the accountability of government programs was gaining general acceptability, and we had a perfect opportunity—with the court order pointed at everyone's head—to experiment with different varieties of officials who would do generally what the order required of the monitor advocates in particular.

This interest was short-lived, however; the Department of Labor consistently defended its monitor advocate plan at first as worthy of a longer, fairer chance to prove itself and later as too established to shelve. The plaintiffs' representatives, however, seized on the position outlined in my fall 1975 memorandum; its thesis became a theme they would repeat in all our reports to the court and in all their subsequent demands upon the Department of Labor.

My idea was that while state officials could and should monitor state activities and state programs—that was the essence of responsible state government—state officials never could be advocates for farm workers at the same time. It was neither in the nature of state employees nor of farm workers to make such a program work. At the time of our committee's report to Judge Richey in October 1975, a majority of us noted our reservations about the validity of the monitor advocate system and its satisfaction of the requirement of Section III of the court order.

In addition, we exercised our right to make recommendations to the Secretary of Labor. I wrote to Secretary Dunlop on behalf of the committee, for the first time specifically testing his commitment to our committee's venture:

In its original conception, described in a report to the Court in October, 1973, the two functions of the Monitor/Advocate were distinguished from each other and their different significances were highlighted. The function of advocacy was to pump into a dispute-resolution system Migrant and Seasonal Farmworker complaints about manpower services they were receiving, or failing to receive, from the State employment services about living and working conditions provided them by employers whom they were referred to by State employment services. The function of monitoring was to resolve complaints filed by Migrant and Seasonal Farmworkers.

Thus, the Monitor/Advocate was to take an aggressive and active posture in his role of Migrant and Seasonal Farmworker advocate and an impartial and judicious posture in his role as complaint resolver.

It was the committee's conclusion (the defendants' representatives disclaiming agreement), I wrote, that state monitor advocates were not independent enough to zealously represent farm workers. This system could not result in the basic structured and systemic changes desired, we urged; the monitor advocates were in an untenable position. We referred to the idea of experimenting with an independent, program-surveying ombudsman and to Dean Cahn's recommendation in his early amicus brief that independent federal employees with proved investigative powers be used to monitor the Employment Service. We recommended that he experiment with different models of farm worker advocates to replace the state-employed monitor advocates. We offered to work with the Labor Department in developing an alternative system, and we set up a committee to do so.

For months, the secretary of labor did not answer; only after I wrote again and pressed departmental representatives did the acting secretary, Robert Aders, deign to respond. Essentially, his answer was dilatory: "In view of the relatively short span of time over which the system has been operational, the Department considers it advisable to evaluate the impact of these recent changes on the system before considering another new system."

However, he also expressed what was and continued to be the department's view about the philosophy of reform, which I viewed as the fundamental difference that separated the majority of the Special Review Committee and the official Department of Labor (though not all its officials) and eventually frustrated our attempts:

There is a basic philosophical difference concerning the independence of ES which you believe is required in the Monitor/Advocate structure. The civil action *NAACP* v. *Brennan* and the resulting consent decree are designed to bring about reform in ES agencies to assure provision of equitable services to farmworkers. For such change to come about, it is essential that there be a commitment within each State agency. A Monitor/Advocate working within the system appears to be the mode in which this kind of commitment can be realized. The crucial issue is not necessarily the vigor of the advocacy, but the effectiveness of services and corrective action where problems are surfaced. To establish an advocacy role outside of ES would not be conducive to comprehensive change inside the agency, and might damage the growing relationship between ES and farmworker groups.

Later that year we learned that the Civil Rights Division of the Department of Justice had done a survey of state Office of Equal Opportunity programs and in doing so had evaluated monitor advocates as well as affirmative action officials around the country. Department of Labor officials refused to provide me a copy of the report, arguing that it was incomplete and unofficial. I was abashed at this intergovernmental obstructionism and suspicious about the reason. Justice Department lawyers who worked on the survey wanted the committee to have it but asked that we go through channels. The Labor Department persistently refused to cooperate; Judge Richey tried to coax the department, but it refused to budge. However, one day, a copy of the Justice Department report arrived at my office "in a plain brown wrapper." The people who had conducted the survey wanted their work to accomplish something and believed the committee should have their report.

The report concluded that local Employment Service offices continued to discriminate, the monitor advocates were inadequately trained and staffed to vigorously enforce the court order, they were not coordinated with Office of Equal Opportunity officials, and the program was detracting attention from the real problems of farm workers. That the conclusions of another branch of government, not a partisan in the lawsuit, supported the intuitive and theoretical judgments and the experiences of committee members was devastating to the Department of Labor.

Later, as we continued to fight under the authority of the Freedom of Information Act for a public copy of the report, the

Department of Justice officially sent a copy. The Department of Labor argued that the Justice Department's findings were out of date and inaccurate and any conclusions based on the report were unfair. The committee heard Labor's defense to the Justice Department report and concluded in our final comments to the court a year later that the key conclusions of the report were valid.

Before our final report to the court, I commissioned the Center for Community Justice to study the monitor advocate system and provide the committee with an opinion of its successes, needs, and reformability. The center is a nonprofit organization of professionals whose expertise is in the design of mechanisms of dispute and grievance settlement. Though its work had centered on correctional and educational systems, it was interested in other innovative models and viewed the monitor advocate system as a classic example to study. Professionals interviewed Labor Department officials in Washington, monitor advocates in the field, and others having relevant information; they compared the system to other comparable agencies and submitted a report to us in September 1976. Its words were balanced and reasoned and sensible.

Their report concluded that the monitor advocate system had too many conflicting functions for one official to be able to carry them out efficiently. It was adequate as an internal administrative monitoring system for the Labor Department, ensuring performance and noting deficiencies of departmental programs. This is a normal activity for any large organization. As an organization for the receipt and handling of complaints against the system, however, the monitor advocates could not and did not do the job. Clients hesitate to complain to representatives of the very agency against which their complaint is aimed. This is especially the case when there is historic mistrust of that agency by a client group, as exists with the farm workers and the Employment Service. All the complaint posters and encouraging announcements in the world will not overcome the credibility gap between estranged Spanish-speaking farm workers and the essentially Anglo Employment Service monitor advocates.

In addition, the monitor advocates who face inevitable peer pressures in dealing with complaints lodged against fellow Employment Service employees are inevitably biased in their responses. A neutral agency is needed to receive and deal with complaints against an institution; it must be able to make final, not advisory, disposition. Employees of the defendant organization never can perform their function as advocates for farm workers.

The center's conclusion was:

The Monitor Advocate is structurally adequate as a component in the DOL's overall internal monitoring system; it is inadequate both as a complaint mechanism and as an advocate, whatever the latter term may mean. The administrative monitoring function of the monitor advocate should not be mingled with a consumer or client advocacy function. The first loyalty of a monitoring system must be to the principal administrator; the monitor provides an evaluation and critique of agency performance so the administrator can effectively control his agency. A client advocate, on the other hand, represents clients and urges the agency to respond to client needs. These functions are not compatible.

A proper system, the center recommended, requires that a citizens' agent be independent of the agency being monitored, a conclusion so obvious that it should have required little elaboration. This point underscored a central division between the Department of Labor and the rest of us in this case. The department insisted, as the secretary did in his letter to me, that the only way to monitor a program is by using people within the system. They alone know it and how to make it change and work. This view reflects the quintessential article of faith in the verity of the bureaucracy, or it is government gamesmanship. It is myopia or it is fraud; but, in any event, it is wrong.

My original memorandum about the monitor advocate system covered varieties of dispute settling and grievance techniques that might have been adapted to meet the challenge we faced. I had talked to experts in this evolving field of arbitration who had found our assignment a challenging opportunity. Various possibilities existed for us to create a responsive agency to generate the official system in behalf of farm workers. The characteristics that all agreed would be required of the monitor advocates were independence, adequate staffing and funding, bilingual abilities, and farm worker backgrounds or experiences. These officials could have come from farm worker organizations, professional arbitration associations, legal services or community action organizations, independent governmental agencies, or even a cadre of court-appointed officials. But this interesting adventure never came to pass. Instead, the Department of Labor steadfastly supported its existing system until the end when five members of our committee voted that the department had not complied with Section III of the court's order. Instead, the department had created a new bureaucracy and spent a fortune on training and generating documentation, but it had not created the effective and necessary agency that the court order contemplated and for which some of us had hoped.

Our final report to the court in October 1976 concluded:

Finding: The SRC finds that DOL implemented and maintained a federal-state monitor/advocate system for two years pursuant to the requirements of Section III. As a monitoring system solely, it complies with the requirements of the court order. As a system advocating on behalf of farm-workers, the monitor/advocate system is inherently inadequate and in fact has been inadequate. The advocacy function of the present monitor/advocate must be performed by persons independent of the ES System. . . .

Five members of the SRC find that the advocacy function of the present monitor-advocates must be transferred to persons outside the ES system, preferably MSFWs or Spanish-speaking persons from farmworker backgrounds, if the system is to be meaningful and workable.

The success of the complaint system was inextricably entwined with that of the monitor advocate system. Without aggressive, activist administrators, it turned out to be little more than paper shuffling. Farm workers we interviewed during our travels and at our hearings confirmed this dim view.

Early in our tenure the department's data indicated that few complaints were being made by farm workers, though comparatively more than by other groups. The department pointed to this data as evidence of the success of the complaint system. Skeptical plaintiffs' representatives saw it as proof that the system was not working; they knew that farm workers had plenty of problems, so the fact that few complaints were being received by the system showed that workers were not using it.

Furthermore, the department view that the whole case and Special Review Committee scrutiny of its performance was limited to the Employment Service meant that even complaints that did surface could only be referred to appropriate enforcement agencies. What happened with them after referral was none of its or our business. And since most complaints were not related to the Employment Service but had to be regulated by other departmental agencies (housing complaints were regulated by OSHA, for example, and wage complaints were regulated by the Employment Standards Administration), the department viewed success by its administration and movement of complaints, not necessarily by their successful resolution.

The Special Review Committee voted at its final meeting that the Labor Department had performed a purely bureaucratic response to its obligations under Section IV; it had not conducted an adequate, real, functioning complaint system but one in name only. We found that the department's system was not accessible to

MSFWs, was too slow and uncoordinated, and failed to resolve farm worker complaints to their satisfaction.

Enforcement of State Compliance. The delicate relationship between the states and the federal government requires careful, balanced interaction. Maintaining that balance calls for exquisite administration. Hard as the task is, it is the essence of the federal system. Unless responsibility is exercised, the division of powers can result in a stalemate, which is what happened. The Department of Labor did not adequately support states like California, which aggressively lived up to the court's edict; at the same time, it failed to push states that defied it. When called to account, the department defended itself on the ground that it could only be responsible for its own actions and not for those of the 50 states.

Section V required the department to do what the Wagner-Peyser Act had required of it all along—to enforce state compliance with the law through all means available, including such severe sanctions as decertification and short-term funding of Employment Service agencies and the transfer of federal personnel to local offices to "assist" in compliance efforts. Enforcement might be viewed as a procedural consideration, but in this case the seemingly technical requirements went to the substantive heart of Labor Department compliance efforts.

The language at the beginning of Section V was general, but it should have been quite clear. The defendants were to "take all the necessary action" to achieve compliance with the court order in the states and to fully enforce the rights of MSFWs. Those words seemed to formally and legally say, "Get it done, period." The rest of Section V reads like a paraphrasing of the Wagner-Peyser Act's requirements regarding state noncompliance. Note violations, investigate, devise adequate corrective action plans, and use sanctions to make sure proper results are reached, even drastic ones if they are called for.

The department, however, read the requirements of the court order as well as those of the Wagner-Peyser Act as requiring merely the issuance of directives, writing of guidelines, monitoring, and placing procedures in motion. In other words, it confined its actions to a bureaucratic response and to assuring change on paper only; the department hesitated to use its sanctions to force states to meet their statutory obligations.

It was this reluctance to take effective action in extraordinary situations that ripened Labor Department culpability for the acts and inactions of some mischievous states. Holding back when it should have taken action created such complicity on the department's part that it became the culprit even more so than the states. This federal complicity arose when the department failed to use its positive powers to assist states in complying with the court order as well as its negative powers to punish states that were failing to comply. Two experiences illustrate these points; one incident occurred in California, the other in Indiana.

California is the biggest state in terms of farm worker activity; thus its reaction to the court order was very important. In view of Governor Jerry Brown's appointment of former California Rural Legal Assistance lawyers to key positions in his government, particularly in the state Employment Service, the bureaucrats here were allies for reform. The Labor Department was proud to point to California experiences as evidence of how things were getting better for farm workers because of its efforts; but the department did not give the state the aid it needed and deserves no credit for the fortuitous appointments made in that state, which were the reason for the changes.

When Fred Romero and I traveled in California for the Special Review Committee in February 1976, state officials asked if we could help solve an administrative problem. The Labor Department doled out Wagner-Peyser money to states on the basis of what was then called a balanced placement formula, which credited states for the number of job placements it could account for. This formula was so rigidly applied, however, that if a given state extended itself to assist farm workers, it got no points, so to speak, for its extra time and efforts; in effect, it was punished financially for taking affirmative action that was necessary to comply with the court's order. A state would do better under the balanced placement formula to forget the farm workers who needed more time and special attention and concentrate on more and easier placements the department would reward with higher budgets.

This result was perverse. We had heard this complaint before and we would hear it again from officials in Colorado, Washington, and elsewhere. This had to be a vagary of the system. The California request provided the perfect opportunity to demonstrate that the committee was not a meddlesome, negative critic of state actions. We would help them solve this problem when we got back to Washington. Or so we thought. When we returned, Fred and I sent a memorandum to the Special Review Committee and to the department pointing out this problem, supporting California's view, and recommending modification of the formula to reward extra effort taken by states to comply with the court order. The department reacted stonily. States did get credits for their special efforts, we were told; and the balanced placement formula had been refined to cover this perversity (it was now dubbed the resource allocation formula).

Nothing was done to deal with our request for encouragement and financial assistance to the states. State officials already had been rebuffed by their federal counterparts when they asked for additional funds earmarked for compliance efforts. The department advised them that everything the states did would have to be done within their existing budgets. The refusal of California's reasonable request to tailor existing budgets could only discourage the imaginative and constructive states that truly wished to use the court order as an opportunity to increase and improve services to farm workers.

The opposite experience occurred in Indiana. The Department of Labor not only demonstrated that it would not reward exemplary conduct in California but also showed in Indiana that misconduct would not be punished. Indiana had significant farm worker activity (for the Midwest) and a reactionary state employment system. When a task force representative visited the state in 1975 to deal with its relatively poor record in improving farm worker services, he was rebuffed by the state Employment Service director. At a briefing covering state failures to comply with the court order (which happened to have been transcribed), the following exchange took place between Hancock (a Labor official) and Coppes (the state Employment Service director):

Mr. Hancock: You are not under a Federal Court Order to do something about claims—alright. But you are to do something about migrants and farm workers.

Mr. Coppes: Yes, but god dammit you have got to take care of claimants and I don't give a damn.

Mr. Hancock: May I go on?

Mr. Coppes: No, not for a little bit, you said we could make comments.

Mr. Hancock: Go ahead.

Mr. Coppes: I get a little sick and tired of a bunch of people coming into Indiana that don't know a god damn thing about Indiana and telling how to do things and I don't give a god damn for Richey's Order.

Mr. Hancock: Well, there is no sense in going on with this.

Mr. Walsh: I would think not.

Mr. Hancock: We'll leave.

Mr. Coppes: Alright fine. Then give us your report written. . . .

Mr. Hancock: Good-by. Let's go Brian.

Mr. Coppes: I'll tell you one thing, there is one gentleman in Washington that is going to hear about this. If I can't make comment when you're making comment, then I don't want any of it. [Hancock, Walsh and Johnson leave.] Good-by.

Labor Department reaction to this episode was defensive, secretive, and puzzlingly tolerant. Its response said a lot to observers who were calculating its true commitment to enforcing the court order and would act accordingly. Surely this incident, involving as it did the deputy director of the task force set up by the department to implement the court order, could have been viewed as a contemptuous reaction to the department's attempt to cajole, persuade, and coax compliance by nonperforming states without using its extraordinary powers. Under the circumstances a strong response would have been both appropriate and a signal that recalcitrance would not be tolerated.

Nothing happened, and Indiana continued to perform below standard in delivering services to farm workers. Word was leaked of the Hancock-Coppes incident. The Labor Department was reminded regularly that Indiana was not performing adequately and was asked what enforcement action it was contemplating. Finally, the Special Review Committee held hearings in Kokomo, Ind., in September 1976; it was to be our last look at the state before our final report to the court. A committee member questioned a federal witness about the Hancock-Coppes incident and placed the transcript of their exchange into the record. Coppes's federal superiors took the position that he was simply expressive, excitable, and cantankerous but that he was really a good man—the aberrational encounter with Hancock and the state's bleak record in complying with the court order and servicing farm workers notwithstanding.

There, as in other situations, department officials justified their reluctance to punish a state agency by arguing that strong sanctions should be avoided, that moderation was more effective. The general principle was indisputable but the absoluteness of its application was self-defeating. No one wanted to see an Employment Service system closed down. That would not help farm workers, in the short run at least. It would be equivalent to dropping an atom bomb when pinpoint, conventional attacks were more appropriate. But in the world of brinkmanship, no state would take the department seriously—especially a recalcitrant state—if there was no indication that it would use its available powers.

Despite monthly analyses of data demonstrating which states were denying farm workers services that were quantitatively and qualitatively equal to those provided nonfarm workers, the department left it to delinquent states to fashion corrective action plans. The committee held hearings clearly establishing noncompliance that warranted sanctions; I met with department officials and exchanged letters and memos with them. But the Department of Labor gave the states time and the benefit of all doubts. In Washington, for example, the department allowed almost a year to go by before the state's inadequate complaint system was corrected satisfactorily.

Finally, in May 1976 I sent the department a long letter stating in detail what I (plaintiffs' counsel agreed with me) viewed to be the requirements of Section V. I asked that these procedures be followed thereafter and that we meet to discuss any areas of disagreement. Neither request was granted.

We debated the adequacy of the department's enforcement efforts a final time at our last committee meeting in October 1976. The Labor Department brought in cartons of paper purporting to show its abundant enforcement efforts. I argued that no proper procedures had even been adopted, adequate sanctions had not been used, and the reality was that noncompliance by numerous states remained uncorrected. Five members of the committee voted that the DOL had not taken all necessary action to achieve and maintain continuing compliance of all state offices with the requirements of the law and to fully enforce the rights of MSFWs.

While the federal government was the defendant in this case, the states' actions were entwined inextricably with the federal response to the court order as well as with its obligations under the Wagner-Peyser Act. Unless the Labor Department ensured state action, the consumers of important federal programs would be whipsawed between irresponsible government entities. State deficiencies, I argued, became the department's transgressions when it failed to invoke enforcement techniques to ensure compliance.

An interesting phenomenon occurred during the course of our case. Initially, the department appeared to be the "good guys" who were trying with difficulty to push and drag reluctant, unsympathetic state officials into compliance with their legal obligations. The department's perception was that it would be an irony to hold *it* responsible for *their* compliance in view of *its* good work in the face of *their* obstinacy.

By the end of two years, I came to feel that, with rare exceptions, which might have been rectified by a more aggressive Department of Labor, the states were trying to perform as the court wished, while the department was not. After our summer of 1976 hearings in the State of Washington, officials there stated that the committee had been pictured to them as the enemy by the Labor Department. The director of the Washington Employment Service told me he wanted to organize the key state agencies to appear before Judge Richey to support his order and to become parties to the case. That did happen at the final formal hearing in court. The department objected; I encouraged their being joined; and the court permitted the states to become an active part of the case.

Administrative Action. Section VII called for certain administrative actions; it gave the defendants 60 days to report their initial efforts at compliance and to describe their complaint and monitoring systems. Copies of the court order were to go to every local office. These requirements were quickly performed. The court maintained its jurisdiction over the case, though it encouraged the parties to resolve their disputes between themselves and their lawyers whenever possible.

Finally, the order ended with some seemingly innocuous language, stating that it did not "affect in any way the continued application or validity of departmental regulations and policies that are consistent with the terms of this order." That final paragraph was to provide the basis for a continuing battle among committee members over a fundamental question: Were the court order and jurisdiction of the Special Review Committee limited to the operations of the Employment Service, or did they apply to other related Labor Department programs like OSHA and the other subjects covered by the secretary's 13 Points, which went far beyond the workings of the Employment Service? That last part of the last section of the court order was interpreted differently by the department and the committee members; at our last meeting that difference finally exploded into a bitter battle.

Throughout our tenure, the committee had viewed these words as incorporating the secretary's 13 Points into the court's August 1974 order, thus giving us a legitimate interest in matters covered by those points even if they were not under the departmental jurisdiction of the Employment Service. I never hid my views on this subject, nor did the plaintiffs' representatives. At one of our first committee meetings, Larry Sherman spoke to us about the need not to view the case solely as an Employment Service case; the under secretary's representative agreed, on the record, as did the department's task force director. Thereafter, in numerous disputatious discussions about the committee's right to look into and act concerning such non–Employment Service issues as wages, pesticides, and housing, the department representatives continuously protested that these were beyond our bailiwick. Yet when pressed, though professing not to be bound by our recommendations, the department sometimes responded as though it was.

For example, my travels had led me to conclude that most migrant housing was atrocious and that something had to be done about it. Everyone agreed. But Labor Department officials in OSHA, which handled housing standards, said it was already overworked and the department's committee representatives argued that we had no right to push OSHA. I disagreed, and I pushed.

As a result, in 1976 OSHA promised to conduct 3,500 inspections of migrant housing, compared to the 350 inspections it had conducted the year before. It also agreed to use the recommendations of migrant organizations we contacted to determine which areas most needed inspections. But this experience was the exception rather than the rule; the department consistently fought our entry into non–Employment Service affairs.

The thrust of the 13 Points was to coordinate and upgrade Labor Department activities by different agencies within the department with respect to farm workers. The points reflected the secretary's judgment that the department's Equal Employment Opportunity office, OSHA, the Employment Standards Administration, the Civil Service Commission, and the Employment and Training Administration (then the Manpower Administration) all played important and integrated roles in serving farm workers, and that only when these roles were coordinated could the Labor Department effectively implement its obligations to farm worker clientele. Indeed, the department created an in-house and an interagency committee to coordinate all such services. Fred Romero was its head.

A majority of the Special Review Committee members consistently maintained that the 13 Points imposed continuing obligations on the Labor Department and that our committee could and should oversee its performance. Historic correspondence between the parties' counsel, the amicus, and the court had made it clear that the intent of everyone involved in the design of the consent order was to include all the protections of the secretary's 13 Points in its coverage.

In its manual of operating procedures, which went to all states as the department's bible on the meaning and interpretation of the court order, this view was confirmed:

U.S. District Court Judge Charles R. Richey ruled in May, 1973, that DOL and state ES officials had violated certain laws and enjoined DOL against permitting or perpetuating discrimination and other unlawful practices against MSFWs. He also directed that DOL be permitted to implement fully the Secretary's "Thirteen Points."

Later, the same document stated that it "consolidates all significant instructions issued since the Secretary of Labor's 13

Points," noting that Labor's "office of the Solicitor has ruled that the court order incorporates the Secretary's 13 Points." At regional training sessions all over the country, which briefed key federal and state officials on the Labor Department's interpretation of the court order, federal and regional officials gave explicit instructions on the continued applicability of the 13 Points.

At the end of its final meeting in October 1976, while considering Section VII, the Special Review Committee again discussed the applicability of the 13 Points. The chairman and plaintiff members again recorded their view that the court order incorporated them. Department members violently objected to this interpretation, repeating their view that only the portions of the 13 Points that concerned employment services were relevant to us.

Because the department had acted officially as if the 13 Points were not incorporated within the order, it never provided the committee with information by which to evaluate its efforts to comply with their requirements. Thus the committee found that the department had not provided information sufficient to determine whether it had complied with significant portions of the 13 Points, and we recommended that Labor Department obligations pursuant to them receive judicial clarification.

The explosion over this question at the close of our last hearing and the damning overall conclusions reached by a majority of the committee (which included one department member, along with all plaintiff representatives and the chairman) left department representatives rancorous and scurrying to write a report of their own. Events aborted my game plan, which was to praise the department for all it had done, replace the committee with a master or hearing examiner, terminate requirements of the court order that no longer made sense or were not needed, and devise a modified consent agreement for the court to adopt, which would have called for fulfillment of the department's remaining obligations. I believed this could be accomplished in a year if the department faced up to realities. I had talked to the parties' lawyers and thought they could be persuaded. A large group of farm worker representatives came to Washington, D.C., at that time; I told them about my proposal and was confident they would accept it.

But the Labor Department's lawyer felt at this time that attacking our report was a preferable course, and he and the lame duck officials (Jimmy Carter was about to be elected president and the department hierarchy was unsettled) decided that their best interest was to rid themselves of me and the plaintiffs.

At a final court hearing an attorney representing several key

State Employment Service organizations asked if the states could join the case, and the court approved. The parties' lawyers were directed to get together and to keep working toward mutually acceptable solutions.

After the Special Review Committee report to the court and the failure of informal negotiations between the parties to come to grips with our findings, the plaintiffs engaged new counsel; for several years still another group of lawyers negotiated with the Department of Labor to correct the inadequacies remaining in performance of its adjudicated obligations to farm workers.

In September 1978, after these negotiations had proved fruitless, the plaintiffs returned to Judge Richey with a motion calling upon the Labor Department to show cause why it should not be found in continuing violation of court orders. The plaintiffs reviewed all the evidence that had preceded their motion, concluding, "This case has a sad history. Defendants have thus far resisted, avoided, or flouted the duties judicially imposed on them to cease discriminating against farmworkers. Unless further injunctive relief is granted, they will continue to do so." They reminded the court of the hollowness of the 13 Point plan and of the department's performance under the existing court orders; they also noted the findings of the review committee. In 1977 and 1978, the plaintiffs concluded, "Defendant's discrimination against farm workers continued unabated." They accused the department of "a concerted strategy of delay, diversion, and broken promises" and stated that Labor's new regulations designed to implement the court order had been inadequate.

The Labor Department's computerized data was used by the plaintiffs to prove its continuing malfeasance in what was described as a pattern—over the course of more than five years—of dilatory tactics, professions of good faith, broken promises, and continued discrimination.

They asked for an ongoing mechanism for monitoring and insuring compliance and recommended the appointment of a special counsel, funded and staffed by department funds, to monitor subsequent compliance efforts. Finally, they asked for clarification of the fundamental question of whether wages and hours, OSHA, the Farm Labor Contractor Registration Act (FLCRA), and certification of foreign workers were indeed issues in the case, as 5 out of 7 members of the committee had decided. The Labor Department accused the plaintiffs of attempting to expand the scope of the litigation by injecting new issues. It argued that the committee's findings were unsubstantiated and anecdotal and that the department was in compliance with the court order. It hoped that the case would go away.

On November 9, 1978, Judge Richey ordered the defendants to explain why they should not be judged in violation of the consent decree. He called on the parties to submit documentation of their arguments and gave them 60 days to question each other. The judge ruled that the issues of wages and hours, OSHA, and FLCRA should remain within the case to the extent necessary to assure full relief to the plaintiffs, reserving any ruling on the question of certification of foreign workers. The Department of Labor appealed the order.

Final Settlement

Finally, in January 1980 the Labor Department and the plaintiffs agreed to a settlement of this historic case; that agreement, including almost 200 pages of exhibits, was approved by the court on June 6, 1980. Judge Richey retained his jurisdiction over the case until December 31, 1983, to assure compliance. Included in the settlement agreement is a thick set of new regulations governing all aspects of farm worker activity affected by the department. The new regulations stress outreach, affirmative action, and improvement and coordination of the enforcement of all programs related to farm worker activity including those of the Employment Standards Administration (minimum wage and age laws), the Employment and Training Administration (the Employment Service) and OSHA (housing).

The settlement included most of the demands made by the majority of the Special Review Committee when it ended its work, except appointment of a master and placement of monitors outside the system. The plaintiff's lawyers attributed the department's change of position to the replacement of its negotiating team by the new department solicitor, Carin Clauss, to periodic inquiries from congressional committees, and to the court's adamant use of its considerable, if limited, coercive powers.

The proper machinery for reform is now in place; it remains to be seen whether it can change the realities of farm workers' lives.

EPILOGUE

What did this prodigious, expensive, painful process accomplish? What did the Special Review Committee experience mean? Was it an innovative technique for judicial administration and social reform in extraordinary situations as the court and we had hoped, or was it just another illusion of progress, another waste of time, money, and opportunity?

It was unlikely from the beginning that we would reform the world and end our work happily. Yet it was disappointing not to have been able to point to a dramatic, unequivocal, clear-cut accomplishment such as a game-ending touchdown or a mathematical solution. The plan I had attempted to persuade the parties to follow was close to what they ultimately agreed to; but the committee was deprived of the opportunity to have been part of the finale.

There were individual small victories along the way and some accomplishments to savour. Our experience was one of major institutional consciousness raising. The public had clearer perceptions of the problems of farm workers and the solutions that could come from government. However attenuated, there had been some accountability; someone out there was watching and counting. The Employment Service will probably never be the same as it was. Perhaps our rejected prodding of the department made the later settlement more possible.

The committee served a special function that had nothing to do with specific projects in which we were interested. Just as a thing observed is changed, our presence perforce changed what we were viewing. Much was accomplished just because, like Mt. Everest, we were there, although some of those achievements would be undone once we were gone. Indeed, after the committee went out of business, the compliance indicators we developed to lend meaning to data the Labor Department was gathering showed that most states were slipping in their relative accomplishments for farm workers, according to insiders.

The Committee's findings were used by the plaintiffs and their counsel in later years as the case matured. Our findings were cited, and the evidence we gathered could be used by the court in its final consideration of the case. Our collective, official imprimatur must have influenced the court and outside observers in their future assessments of the department's performance on behalf of migrant farm workers.

Some useful institutional changes that evolved could not be undone. The department adopted regulations making permanent many of the changes brought about as a result of our work on this case. We also achieved specific successes. When OSHA inspected migrant housing at our coaxing, at least those specific places were checked at those times. Migrant housing was not improved nationwide, however, nor would OSHA be forever receptive to such problems. But at least once an act of public service, limited though it was, took place. That is something.

When the press in a particular locale followed us into groves and migrant housing projects and wrote their stories, at least some public attention, otherwise lacking, was given to the lives of farm workers.

Every frustrated local, state, and federal bureaucrat who was able to seize the momentum caused by our existence to carry out a simple, discrete, parochial improvement helped us bring about some degree of change. Every defensive, reflexive act of the department—like racing ahead into a state to shape things up before a Special Review Committee hearing—at least brought improvement that would not have occurred without our presence.

Though the department maintained the hard line position that no new money would be provided the states to carry out their additional burdens under the court order (its myopic rationale was that the states should already be doing these things so no new money should be allocated), it was persuaded to make one exception. The secretary of labor has the power to distribute discretionary funds under S.301 of the Comprehensive Employment and Training Act. In the summer of 1975 he distributed almost $1.5 million of these funds to 33 states that had submitted proposals for supplemental funds to work on their compliance efforts.

Through that act, other substantial grants were soon made to organizations interested in migrant affairs—both public agencies (the Energy Research and Development Administration received a grant to train farm workers for industrial jobs) and private organizations ($3 million was given to the Rural Housing Alliance to train farm workers to rehabilitate rural houses). The committee cannot claim direct credit for these actions, but one knowledgeable observer speculated that but for our presence and pressures these grants might not have been made.

One of the key participants for the migrants said to me after my job on the committee had ended, "The success of the case was in attaining incremental improvements, along with some institutional restructuring. It was the old OEO, kick-in-the-butt approach. We got judicial, Congressional, and administrative oversight of the ES for a few years. The SRC created issues, caused confrontations, and forced some changes. However imperfect, this is the best that can be done."

This case highlights the weaknesses and the strengths of judicial intervention in the affairs of executive government. Traditionalists would say that a judge had no right or power to attempt to run the Department of Labor, that doing so violates the people's right to representative government. To whom, classicists would ask, are judges accountable? Despite good intentions, the judicial power and presence was overextended and abused in our case, thus our failures were preordained.

Our case was but the latest in a dangerous trend toward over-reaching by what the late Professor Alex Bickel called "the least dangerous," as well as the weakest, branch of government. The role of a judge should be more neutral; he should not take so creative a role in the litigation as Judge Richey did. Lawsuits are designed to settle private disputes between private parties, not to run national programs for needy groups. Courts should fashion remedies carefully, avoiding prospective administration of which they are incapable.

Activists would argue that the rationale for judicial activism in cases like this is not desirability but necessity. If courts do not prevent illegality in government, where else can ordinary people go to protect their rights? Actually, courts are carrying out the purpose of Congress when they enforce the laws; they act all the more in the national interest when constitutional questions are involved. When an agency of the executive government misuses its own power, it has no legitimate right to complain about the defensive uses of power by coordinate branches of government. This indeed is the dynamism of tripartite government and the separation of powers. The courts do not reach out to usurp government power; they react in extraordinary cases in response to complaints by classes of aggrieved citizens, and then only where the abridgement of vital public rights is involved. These complainants have no other recourse than the courts. Judges should not be passive, mechanical eunuchs; there is nothing wrong with being pragmatic, with being concerned about realities. Courts do not want to and never could replace other branches of government; to suggest usurpation is disingenuous hyperbole. The best test of the legitimacy of judicial action, it could be said, is the quality of justice that courts administer; this is the rationale for activism.

So the debate goes. The issue has no answer; it is a dilemma that good and honest people debate regularly and about which different conclusions are reached. As an issue of government and legal theory as much as one of practical power politics, this question historically has confounded scholars and officeholders. But the subject has come under increasing analysis in the 1970s because courts increasingly have been drawn into cases like this. "We are witnessing the emergence of a new model of civil litigation," Professor Abram Chayes recently wrote, and "our traditional conception of adjudication and the assumptions upon which it is based provide an increasingly unhelpful, indeed misleading framework for assessing either the workability or the legitimacy of the roles of judge and court. . . ."[10] Our case was one of the class that Professor Chayes has labeled the new civil litigation; its object was "the vindication of constitutional and statutory policies." *NAACP v. Brennan* fits his characterization of these cases:

The characteristic features of the public law model are very different from those of the traditional model. The party structure is sprawling and amorphous, subject to change over the course of litigation. The traditional adversary relationship is suffused and intermixed with negotiating and mediating processes at every point. The judge is the dominant figure in organizing and guiding the case, and he draws for support not only on the parties and their counsel, but on a wide range of outsiders—masters, experts, and oversight personnel. Most important, the trial judge has increasingly become creator and manager of complex forms of ongoing relief, that had widespread effects on persons not before him and entail the continuing involvement of the court in administration and implementation.

For farm workers, the experience in this historic case was a mixed bag of minor victories, increased attention and public consciousness raising; but ultimately it was a wasted opportunity for major changes to have been made in their lives. As one observer stated, "The system lies exposed; unfortunately, it does not bleed." Farm workers may look to their government for emergency relief; but they will have to look elsewhere for the attainment of basic improvements in their deprived lives.

6

FOREIGN COMPETITION

MIGRANT FARM WORKERS have enough problems coping with the ordinary vicissitudes and deprivations of their lives; it is an unnecessary burden to find themselves pinched by the competition of foreign workers. Because economic conditions are worse in certain countries than they are in the United States, there is a large pool of foreign laborers ready to come to this country—legally or illegally—to cut sugarcane in Florida, pick apples in Virginia and West Virginia or cherries in Washington, or do whatever they can wherever they can.

The presence of this pool of workers creates a classic economic problem for American migrants. Employers can manipulate American wage rates and work conditions by exploiting the availability of foreign workers. In doing so, they give away American jobs and American money at the same time they deprive migrants of even the meager opportunities available to them. Unions have complained that illegal aliens have been used to break strikes by domestic workers. Growers complain that without alien workers they will lose fortunes and consumer food costs will escalate.

The problem arises in two ways. First, farmers use illegal aliens to work in American groves, fields, and ranches. Second, farm employers manipulate a program designed to protect American labor, enabling them to replace significant numbers of Americans by importing foreign workers with temporary legal papers.

The influx of illegal aliens into the American labor force, particularly in agriculture, is a historic and growing domestic problem. For a country settled by immigrants, which always has had a diverse ethnic population and prides itself on domestic policies that are civil libertarian, tough enforcement of immigration laws comes hard. But ideology aside, the fact is that large numbers of aliens are taking jobs away from American workers. There is a perplexing conflict of interests.

We take great pride in posing as the land of opportunity for all the "masses longing to be free," though historians have pointed out that certain classes of individuals always have been excluded from our relatively open immigration policies. In the early 1900s, a national origins quota system established numerical limits on American immigration, depending on what country an applicant came from. In 1952 there was a major statutory redesign of our immigration laws. Three bases for immigration were established: the unification of families; control of alien visitors; and, more to the present point, protection of domestic jobs.

In 1965 our laws were amended again to replace certain hemispheric ceilings (now Asian and Latin countries have preferences over Eastern European countries) and to provide asylum for political refugees from certain countries for humanitarian reasons. The 1965 laws were designed specifically "to protect the American economy from job competition and from adverse working standards as a consequence of immigrant workers entering the labor market."[1]

Immigration policies pertain to aliens who come legally and stay legally, pursuant to our national laws. In addition to these assimilating immigrants, illegal aliens come here in great numbers from all countries. This population is composed of two groups: first, those who legally enter the United States and then stay illegally and, second, those who enter illegally in the first place and either stay or come and go. Presently, Mexico is the country from which the overwhelmingly largest number of illegal aliens comes.

THE BRACERO PROGRAM

For centuries we have commingled with Mexicans; no wonder, since we share a 2,000-mile border that is almost impossible to police. Much of Texas, California, and the southwestern United States was owned by Mexico as late as the mid-nineteenth century; and the cultural ties between our two countries remain strong. Indeed, to meet a labor shortage during World War II, the United States made special arrangements with the government of Mexico to import temporary workers. This bracero program began in 1942 and continued until 1964. Mexicans were given jobs in the United States as laborers and farm workers under special arrangements between the two governments.

Braceros (meaning "strong-armed men") were imported to the United States from Mexico to meet the acute labor shortage caused by the war effort. In 1944 the U.S. government spent $24 million to bring in 62,170 braceros. These workers, along with prisoners of war and convicts, filled a short-term, legitimate gap in our labor market. During this extraordinary period the federal government even condoned and encouraged the so-called wetback traffic. Once apprehended, wetbacks were given identification slips by the Immigration and Naturalization Service (INS), which legalized their presence.[2]

Under various international agreements between the United States and Mexico, the responsibility for recruiting, transporting, housing, and feeding the braceros passed from one federal agency to another—the Farm Security Administration and the Production and Marketing Division of the Department of Agriculture, the War Manpower Commission of the Labor Department's Employment Service, and the War Food Administration each had a role at one time. The bracero program had the powerful support of the Farm Bureau Federation and numerous farm labor recruitment organizations as well as the mild support of the Grange. Opposition came from unions and a variety of civic groups. The secretary of labor was authorized by federal law to recruit workers; establish and operate reception centers and provide transportation, subsistence, and medical care there; assist in contract negotiations; and guarantee that employers fulfilled their contracts.[3]

Employers paid a minor charge (not more than $15) into a revolving fund as a fee for each worker they received. This fund made the program almost entirely self-supporting. Those who had employed illegal aliens were denied access to the program. Workers were exempted from paying Social Security and income taxes.[4]

Specific operating conditions for the bracero program were listed in the law. The worker paid a maximum of $1.75 per day for food and paid for medical insurance, Mexican Social Security payments, and any purchases. The employer provided transportation to and from the reception centers and the work sites, contracting fees, tools and equipment, standardized housing, occupational risk insurance, wages, and adequate food at a specified cost.[5]

The bracero program survived the war that spawned it, reaching a peak in 1956 when it covered 445,000 workers. By

1964 only 178,000 were recruited for work in 21 states (primarily in California and Texas).[6] The number of braceros dropped for various reasons. A stricter assessment of the need for foreign labor was made by some officials. Regulations governing working conditions were strengthened and enforced more rigorously. Wages rose, and mechanization of agriculture progressed. The deficiencies of the program were noted. Despite rigid specifications, there were great variations in living and working conditions. Neither state nor federal agencies had adequate staff to enforce compliance with regulations. Farmers tended to overestimate their labor needs because they feared losses of their perishable crops if they did not have enough workers on hand. Their estimates also depended on unpredictable variables such as weather and prices.[7]

Nonetheless, numerous arguments were advanced in support of the continuation of the bracero program.[8] It was said that the program supplied farmers with workers not available in the domestic labor force. Growers preferred braceros for several reasons: they were uninformed about their rights and in a weak position to assert them in any event; they worked for less money and under poorer conditions; housing and transportation were simpler because growers only had to deal with single males;[9] they could be obtained in large numbers on short notice and sent home as soon as the harvest was completed; and finally, braceros were skilled, highly motivated workers who obeyed orders, worked quickly, and did not complain. Over 98 percent of all braceros completed their contracts.

By contrast, farmers say American workers do not want to do the dirty work essential in farming, no matter what the wage scale is.[10] Thousands of jobs in related industries (such as canning) were said to depend on continuation of the bracero program. In addition, it was argued that the program solved the problem of wetbacks. If open jobs were filled with braceros, the growers claimed Mexicans would have no incentive to enter the United States illegally. Proponents also argued that elimination of the program would increase consumer prices, which would escalate without the benefit of low bracero wages. From their perspective, Mexican workers clearly benefited from the program.[11]

Braceros' annual earnings totaled about $100–110 million through 1964. It has been estimated that between $30–60 million of these earnings reached Mexico. During the life of Public Law 78, it has been reported that over $1.2 billion went to Mexico.[12] Loss of this source of foreign exchange, second only to the tourist trade, would have been a serious problem for Mexico.[13] The money these farm workers sent back to Mexico amounted to 2% of the annual national revenue, according to one report, and provided at the same time a "safety valve on an extremely grave socioeconomic problem in Mexico."[14]

Opponents of the bracero program presented four arguments against its continuation. First, they argued that the presence of the large number of braceros kept conditions for domestic migrant workers from improving. The normal forces of labor supply and demand would not work with a large influx of poorly paid foreign workers.[15] Critics decried the situation of our own poor being pitted against the poor of a foreign country. They argued that the bracero program lowered the already low level of sanitation and health in areas where migrants are employed.[16] Second, opponents argued that there was a large supply of U.S. labor willing to do the stoop labor if given adequate wages and conditions. Secretary of Labor Willard Wirtz noted in 1964:

A good deal of this work is unquestionably hard and unpleasant. . . . But there has been accumulating evidence that U.S. workers will be available to do this work if decent working conditions are provided and if it is paid for on terms in line with other work that is equally hard and unpleasant.[17] If they're [U.S. workers] paid decent wages, . . . it won't be impossible to get the workers who are needed.[18]

One union leader suggested that any labor "crisis" caused by the termination of the bracero program was "a rigged crisis, a deliberately deceptive publicity campaign to force Government to acquiesce to growers' demands for cheap farm labor."[19] Third, the program was said to constitute an indirect subsidy for growers by guaranteeing them low-priced labor. Finally, opponents argued that prices would increase insignificantly if the bracero program were terminated.[20] There were threats that farms would be moved to Mexico or consolidated after the bracero program ended. California Senator George Murphy stated at the time that it was a matter either of bringing braceros here or the farmers would go to Mexico. A trend to larger farms was also threatened.

For obvious reasons, the Mexican government favored continuation of the program. The bracero program had solved the problem of wetbacks. The government worried that termination would harm the Mexican economy. However, despite Mexico's pressure and that of farm organizations favoring continuation of the program, the U.S. government finally acceded to the arguments of organized labor and Secretary Wirtz terminated the bracero program in 1964. As a result, mechanization of agriculture was accelerated. A shortage of skilled U.S. workers (for cutting asparagus spears, for example) caused a drop in some production and exports.[21] Some prices did rise following expiration of the program. The aggregate value of imported crops (mostly from Mexico) rose by $33 million (53 percent) in 1965. Agricultural production in Mexico showed significant increases as the number of braceros going to the United States declined.

Aside from a few crops (strawberries and asparagus), however, it is difficult to link the end of the bracero program with changes in U.S. agricultural production. The Economic Research Service (ERS) of the Department of Agriculture reported in 1967:

> It is difficult to establish conclusive causal relationships between the termination of the bracero program and changes in acreage, production, and foreign trade of bracero-worked crops. The determination of causal relationships between the termination of the bracero program and general economic developments such as changes in the balance of payments is still more difficult, if not impossible.[22]

In 1967 the Department of Agriculture conducted a study of these effects. It noted that a period of less than two years was too short for any conclusive evaluation. The ERS did conclude, however, that there was no lasting, fundamental, or substantial benefit (or detriment) to the United States–Mexican balance of payments. Any labor shortage caused by the program's termination was transitory.[23]

COMMUTERS AND GREEN CARDERS

Though the bracero program has ended, the habit of Mexicans coming here to work has continued. Related to the bracero program and to the two major subjects in this chapter—illegal aliens and certified foreign labor—is the category of laborers known as "commuters" and "green carders."[24] These workers live in Mexico and work in the United States (Texas, New Mexico, Arizona, and California). They may be Mexican nationals or United States citizens; they have been called this generation's braceros.[25]

After fulfilling certain minimal health and morals requirements in Mexico, they can obtain an American visa from the INS (a green card called Form 151). Our immigration regulations entitle the cardholder to commute to the United States daily, work here, return home periodically (it could be and often is daily), and act as a resident immigrant. An early 1970 study estimated that there were 650,000 holders of green cards, about 70,000 of whom come into the United States daily to work, predominantly as farm laborers. Data from 1978, according to the INS, shows the annual number at 601,442.

The tremendous push of poverty and pull of work is manifested in the arduous and problem-filled lives of these green-card commuters. I saw them caravan across the bridge connecting Calexico, Calif., and Mexicali, Mex., before sunrise one morning on their way to pickup trucks and buses that would transport them miles into the California fields to labor all day. Then they would return to Calexico and walk back across the bridge to their homes in Mexico, arriving so late that same evening that all they could do was collapse into sleep so they could muster the strength to rise again at 3 A.M. to repeat this dreary cycle.

These commuter laborers are eligible for public benefits of social welfare programs in this country and, while subject to public obligations (taxes and the draft, for example), they pay less than their share of the costs. In addition, their families automatically become eligible for green cards. They depress wages and increase unemployment here, force local farm workers out of jobs and into the migrant streams, slow unionization efforts, and are abused by employers. One commentator reported that these green carders create what could be called the equivalent of an international trade agreement allowing Mexico to export unemployment and import wages in return for our indirect subsidy to American farm employers in the form of what one critic has called an "elastic supply of labor."[26]

This category of special visas should be eliminated. These people are not residents; it is a fiction that they are residents because they work here. Its continuation is as unwise an immigration and work force policy as it is a cynical manipulation of these poor foreign workers.

ILLEGAL ALIENS

Men seeking work sneak into this country looking for jobs they find easy to get. In many cases they are sought out by growers and their representatives and are brought surreptitiously into the United States to jobs waiting for them. Since our present laws do not make it a crime for employers to hire illegal aliens, there is no practical way to stem the tide. The problem is ironic, and it says something cynical about the nature of power politics in this country; that is, while it is illegal for an alien to accept employment in this country, it is not illegal for an employer to hire such a person.

Because of practical problems precluding adequate enforcement of immigration laws, there is very little that the INS can do about this phenomenon; even what the service has done has caused occasional problems. Raids in which Chicanos are picked up in the middle of the night, searched, and whisked away have caused complaints from Mexican-American organizations. Proposals for identifying documents, which would allow for checks of Chicanos' citizenship, are opposed by members of Mexican-American organizations who feel that this is an improper form of discrimination on racial grounds and reflective of a second-class citizenship. Enforcement agencies are criticized, then, for not doing enough and for overdoing what they do.

The fundamental problem lies in the profound causes of illegal immigration, not in the inadequacy of the stopgap of enforcement. In the parlance of those who analyze our country's immigration policies, illegal aliens in the agricultural labor market pose a "push-pull" problem of international policies. The push aspect is that most illegal aliens come from countries with high populations, a very poor economy, and historic links with the United States. The pull is that American farmers like to use foreign farm workers: they complain less, work hard, are tied to their employers because they lack mobility, are easy to exploit, and work for less money.

Illegal aliens essentially are workers with low skills who compete with the least employable American workers. Because aliens will work for less money, they depress American wages at the same time that they increase the earnings of the employers. It is argued that illegal aliens create local unemployment by taking away jobs from low-skilled American workers. It is also said that illegal aliens deplete the general social service system by taking more benefits than they contribute in taxes. Because illegal aliens are poor, send their money home to their native countries, and are unlikely to pay taxes here, it is presumed that they are taking a lot of public money and contributing little to the public pot.

There undoubtedly are social costs attributable to the presence of illegal aliens, though public perceptions of these may be exaggerated. The INS estimates that the annual cost of social services for illegal aliens is $13 billion, no small sum. There are

limits to the problem, however. Most public assistance programs require proof of citizenship status. In addition, most illegal aliens are young (70 percent are under 30), employed, and not interested in being on the dole. Several studies have contradicted the supposition that illegal aliens produce a drain on public services such as welfare, food stamps, education, and medical care. They indicate that illegal aliens make minimal use of public service and do pay sales taxes; in fact, many pay income and Social Security taxes. Few seek unemployment benefits.

Because many illegal aliens stay here for a long time

"Immigration control." (Stephanie Maze)

(sometimes for several generations), our policymakers are faced with several complicated social problems. As young people come and stay and then bring others from their family or marry into the local society, a low visibility, large-scale illegal class evolves—one with no real, long-term stake in the society, which contributes little to society and lives in a constantly precarious state.

One researcher has noted an evolving immigration phenomenon in the eastern United States which, he suggested, challenges prevailing presumptions about our social policies.[27] Millions of illegal aliens (about 8 percent of the labor force in 1974, the year he conducted his studies) are in the work force, and their numbers are growing. Their historic concentration in southwestern agricultural areas is moving to urban areas all over the United States. They come as visitors or tourists from Haiti, the Dominican Republic, and Caribbean and Latin American countries and then stay. They work at poor, unstable jobs unpopular now with domestic workers who themselves came from the South (in the 1940s and 1950s) seeking those same jobs, in turn replacing earlier immigrants who became assimilated and moved up in society. As an illegal underclass, afraid and unable to use social services, they are not beneficiaries of progressive social programs. Living essentially underground, their progeny are likely to grow into a rebellious and explosive generation.

No one knows exacty how many illegal aliens there are in the United States, nor how many are taking jobs away from American farm workers. It is in the nature of the problem that illegal aliens are hidden from public view; thus their census figures are unknown. It has been reported that twice as many undocumented aliens are apprehended and returned to Mexico each year as the total number of people who enter the United States legally from all other countries. Of course, those illegals who are apprehended are only a percentage of those who are present here. Almost everyone who knows anything about the farm labor situation in the United States concedes that extraordinary numbers of illegal aliens are working for American agricultural employers. Most of them come from Mexico and work in the Southwest. They come mostly from the five poor, rural Mexican states bordering the United States, swimming across unguarded parts of the Rio Grande River, climbing fences, or walking across stretches of uninhabited desert. Others (about one-third, according to a leading report) are smuggled in by labor contractors called "coyotes."

The economic pull drawing illegals here is great and the relative risks are small. To deal with these complicated problems, President Gerald Ford created a Domestic Council Committee on Illegal Aliens in 1975. It was composed of six cabinet members and representatives of major government policymaking agencies such as the Office of Management and Budget and the Domestic Council and was chaired by the attorney general. It conducted an exhaustive study of the situation of illegal aliens in this country and issued a preliminary report in December 1976 (from which the data here are drawn).[28]

The report pointed out that there were 766,600 known illegal

Illegal aliens.
(Stephanie Maze)

aliens in the United States in 1975, almost twice the number of aliens entering legally (approximately 400,000). President Jimmy Carter reported that in 1976, 875,000 undocumented workers were apprehended by immigration officials and estimates are that only one out of three coming into our country is caught. The true number of illegals residing and working in the United States is in the millions. In December 1978 the Environmental Fund reported that the U.S. population was growing faster than all other industrialized countries, chiefly because of a rapidly accelerating pace of illegal immigration. It estimated the number of illegal aliens in 1977 to be 2 million, two-thirds of whom came from Mexico where population growth diminished as a result. Experts guess that the total is over 8 million, though many illegals stay only temporarily. One report stated that 10 percent of the entire Mexican population is living in the United States.

A 1978 Department of Justice report concluded that the most reliable estimate of the number of illegal aliens in the United States, used for policy and planning purposes by the Carter administration, was 3–5 million. That number is growing by half a million each year. About 60% are Mexicans, and a third stay permanently.[29]

A large percentage of illegal aliens come to do farm work; in doing so, they replace American farm workers who desperately need these jobs. The AFL–CIO told Congress that the problem is acute and growing and is having an adverse impact on our domestic labor force. In 1977 the flow increased sharply because of Mexico's recession and 45 percent devaluation of the peso, according to the Justice Department.

Our immigration policies cannot cope with this problem, which is rooted in what the Domestic Council report called conflicting philosophies of economics, sociology, politics, compassion, and prejudice. As early as 1885 Congress passed laws aimed at curbing the importation of cheap foreign labor that would adversely affect our domestic labor markets. This country's interest in and tolerance of alien workers depends on the economic and political status of affairs at home. When the economy is lagging, there is a natural tendency to want to preserve jobs for American workers. If the times are isolationist, there is less tolerance for the importation of alien workers. On the other hand, when our economy was booming during World War II and there was a need for workers, our country sought a foreign supply.

Foreign workers come to the United States for several fundamental reasons. The countries from which they come are invariably very poor. Jobs are few. The people have minimal skills and little education and almost no resources. Whatever they find when they come to the United States in terms of pay and working conditions is better than they had at home. In addition, population growth rates are high in their country. Thus increasingly large numbers of people are seeking employment in a sparse labor market. Finally, there usually are historical and cultural links between the United States and these source countries. Reports come home from family members and friends who have gone to the United States and are able to send back money; their situation sounds attractive to those who remain behind in bleak situations. Experts point out, however, that the average earnings of a temporary Mexican worker are $800 a trip, and expenses at these times are greater than usual.

Little is known about the sociological background of illegal aliens. Some studies were surveyed in the Domestic Council report, however. Farm workers who migrate illegally usually are not criminal types; as a matter of fact, they generally are highly motivated and energetic people, willing to work hard and take risks to be able to work and earn a living. These factors make their subterranean, illegal lives all the more pathetic. Most illegal aliens are men (90 percent). The group is predominantly young, meaning that it will be in the work force for 30 years or more. They have minimal education (averaging 6.7 years). Most do not speak English.

The Domestic Council Committee concluded that the principal impact of illegal aliens is not as a drain on general social services but rather as an interference with the labor market. The standard hypothesis is that the large growers who employ illegal aliens and the consumers who use the products these workers pick and pack have the most to gain from their employment. The employers' profits are higher and the consumers' prices are lower. If this is so, it is unlikely that realities will change. They seldom do when the greater number of people do better at the expense of the few, especially when the greater number are people with more power and influence and the few are relatively powerless.

According to the Domestic Council report, studies conducted after the demise of the bracero program showed that American workers did fill the void when the braceros were no longer allowed to come into the country to work. Employers of alien labor did not want the migration stopped because replacing foreign workers raised their labor costs. The reported lack of interest that U.S. workers have for certain kinds of jobs that alien laborers are willing to take changes if those aliens are not around because the wages and working conditions improve when they leave. As Secretary of Labor Ray Marshall stated at a press conference:

[L]ook at what is happening in the country, that the long-run increase in the work force is about 2 million people a year net. Now, assume that a low estimate would be half a million net increase in undocumented workers. That is one-fourth of the growth. It might be as much as a million, nobody really knows. Now that means that it could be that between a fourth and a half of the net growth in our work force is made up of undocumented workers coming into the country. Now, obviously, that puts pressure on our unemployment.

However, one can exaggerate the adverse effect of alien workers on the domestic job market; one simply cannot assume that removing an alien from a job necessarily means that there is a job available for and taken by a domestic worker. One study of wage differentials between border areas heavily affected by Mexican migration and nonborder areas concluded that the extent that wages were depressed was small and marginal.[30] Nevertheless, the presence of illegals must have some impact, lowering wage rates and working conditions in the low-skilled jobs such as agricultural work, and having a direct impact on domestic workers.

The best evidence of this fact of life, and an example of the touchiness of this whole question, was provided during our Special Review Committee hearings in Colorado. I sent a lawyer-investigator to Colorado before the hearings to talk with people who were familiar with the local scene, especially farm workers. We wanted an assessment of the problems peculiar to that region. He reported that the presence of large numbers of illegal aliens had created a major impact on the Colorado job market and that this was a central problem to American farm workers in that area. Having corroborated this view through knowledgeable public officials in the area, we planned to highlight this subject at our hearings.

Witness lists were exchanged by Labor Department and farm worker representatives and the chairman shortly before the hearings. On the night before, after my staff assistant had briefed representatives of both sides about what subjects we planned to present, I received a late call in my room from two Chicano activists involved in our case. They had heard we intended to get into the question of illegal aliens, and they implored me not to do this. It would only do harm to the people we wanted to help, they argued.

I could not understand this viewpoint. "It will be used to fan prejudice against brown people," they urged, "and it would lead to more violations of Chicanos' rights." We meant well but we were about to cause more problems than we would solve, they pleaded. I promised to think about their views.

I was perplexed and troubled. Surely these men, who knew more about these problems than I and came from backgrounds that should have made their opinions more realistic than mine, had to know they were burying a problem that plagued American farm workers. If they were worried about civil liberty abuses of Hispanic people, surely the answer was not to ignore one serious problem for fear that any attention to it would generate others. Were they forgetting the American farm workers (many of whom were Chicanos) they were there to help because they had higher priorities on their organizational agendas? I decided to leave the decision of whether to expose this problem to the workers themselves, and called several as witnesses. Here is some of their testimony:

Chairman: I have one other question I would like to ask. . . . The argument is made by many growers and others that . . . illegal aliens who go into farm work are not displacing domestic workers, because "Those people don't want to do those jobs. . . ." I would like to know what this family feels, and what they perceive their colleagues and others like them feel about this question, whether or not, in fact, domestic farm workers are kept from jobs. . . .

Mr. Jaramillo (a translator): Undoubtedly yes, the illegal aliens do displace workers in the areas. And it's not because they don't want to do the work. It's because the farmers can get away with paying lower wages to illegal aliens. And therefore they pay . . . lower wages to illegal aliens, and even if the family was willing to work for those lower wages, the farmer would still hire illegal aliens instead.

On August 18 and 19, 1976, our committee held hearings in Yakima, Wash. There we called Anthony Provenzo as a witness. Mr. Provenzo was assistant district director for investigation in the Seattle office of the INS. We had the following colloquy on the subject of illegal aliens and their local impact:

Chairman: We have heard testimony already yesterday from a farm worker that there is apparently a significant number of illegal aliens in this state, and that it was at least in her mind a problem in this area. Would you agree?

Mr. Provenzo: Yes, completely.

Chairman: Would you briefly, succinctly state what the problem is, what the extent of it is?

Mr. Provenzo: Surely. If I may project just for a second here, . . . we apprehended 3,900 illegal aliens in the State of Washington in 1973; in 1974, the figure went up to 4,500; in 1975, to 5,600; the first six months of this year there were over 4,500 already. These are predominantly illegal aliens of Mexican nationality who are in the United States, of course, to seek employment in the State of Washington, primarily in the agricultural related fields. . . .

Chairman: Now, is there some yardstick or ratio? You were giving us numbers of illegals that have been apprehended. Obviously, you don't apprehend everybody. Is there some yardstick that you can extrapolate from, where if you apprehend one you make a general rule that there might be two or four, or whatever?

Mr. Provenzo: We estimate conservatively that we, for every one we catch, we miss three.

Chairman: And what percentage did you say of illegals work in the agricultural fields?

Mr. Provenzo: Close to 90 percent in the agricultural fields.
Chairman: Are illegals brought into this area from Canada or Mexico or any place else by contractors as a general rule?
Mr. Provenzo: Primarily, the illegals that come out of Mexico are smuggled on up, and they usually are smuggled across the border. . . .

I asked one state official at our committee hearing in Yakima about this problem:[31]

Chairman: Are illegal aliens in this state a problem?
Mr. Rowland: Yes, the illegal aliens are a problem. I would estimate that the formalized complaints that I have at the state level would indicate that probably 25 percent of those complaints that involved MSFWs are because of them being replaced or misplaced by the illegal alien worker that is presently in the State of Washington.
Chairman: How extensive are the illegal aliens working in agriculture here?
Mr. Rowland: The number that I have received from the Immigration Application Service runs from ten to twelve thousand, with about 60 to 70 percent of those in agriculture and 30 percent in nonagricultural employment.
Chairman: What effect do they have on wages for migrant and seasonal farmworkers?
Mr. Rowland: They can't help but depress the wages, in my opinion, in agriculture.

The fact is that illegal aliens do pose a problem, one that experts agree is significant and growing. In 1971, INS Commissioner Farrell told a House Judiciary Committee hearing that illegal aliens "are taking jobs away from a lot of people, particularly in the areas where there is the greatest unemployment."[32] The Domestic Council Committee pointed out that it is far more desirable to prevent illegal entry and to screen out potential illegals before the fact than it is to locate and apprehend them after they are in the United States.

The Carter Administration picked up on the themes and recommendations of the Domestic Council report. Influenced by the new secretary of labor, who was knowledgeable about and sympathetic to the problems of farm workers, the White House placed the problems of illegal aliens high on its agenda. During his first year in office, at an August 1977 press conference, President Carter announced his administration's new policy toward illegal aliens. Accompanying the president were Secretary of Labor Ray Marshall, Attorney General Griffin Bell, and Director of the INS Leonel Castillo. The president proposed a series of laws predicated on three assumptions about illegal aliens: they have violated our laws, increased the costs of local government, and displaced citizens from good jobs.

Under the Carter proposals, aliens who have been in the country since 1970 would be eligible for a new and legal permanent residence status, and later for citizenship. That humanitarian provision was designed to demonstrate fairness to what the president described as an "underclass" of people who had invested significant portions of their lives in working here and who could claim an equitable right to exemption from future invigorated enforcement policies. In five years, a policy was to be developed to deal finally with their permanent citizenship status.

The attorney general took pains to make it clear when the program was announced that amnesty was not being offered but a respite from illegal status and an opportunity for future change. We are "freeing them from the fear of being deported for the next 5 years, and no more," he said. Until it is determined how many people are in this class—estimates run from 6 to 12 million—the administration refused to commit itself on a final position. One skeptic pointed out that while amnesty forgives a crime, this new policy rewards it. A press critic reminded the attorney general that one law breaker gets prosecuted, but mass law breakers get rewarded.

The second part of the Carter proposals involved passing and enforcing laws against employers who commonly hire undocumented workers. Carter rejected earlier bills that would have provided criminal sanctions against employers for violations; he recommended $1,000 civil fines instead. A worker's Social Security card would be deemed adequate proof of legal status. The attorney general added, no doubt to assuage concerned Hispanic groups, that the Social Security card would not be a work permit, and it also would not be a national identification card. In the context of farm work, it is hard to understand how it could be otherwise, necessary as it might be. In shifting from criminal to civil penalties for violations, however, the Carter proposals were insufficient to deter wealthy employers who wish to use illegal farm workers. Any solution to the problem lies with the employers.

Third, existing laws pertaining to abusing and recruiting illegal aliens would be enforced more rigorously, and more border control was promised. As Secretary of Labor Marshall acknowledged at the time the administration disclosed its proposed program, "Many employers prefer foreign workers because these workers work scared and hard, are unable to protect themselves, work for less than the minimum wage. Most of our labor force is not self-enforcing. We have to rely on complaints. These undocumented workers cannot complain. . . .'' Better and fuller enforcement of existing laws is necessary; its promise is salutary.

Finally, the president said that he would increase foreign economic and technical assistance to source countries like Mexico to increase employment opportunities in those home base countries so that their workers would have less inducement to flee to the United States for jobs.

The Carter proposals were criticized by Professor Wayne Cornelius, a Massachusetts Institute of Technology political scientist who has studied the illegal alien question and written on the subject.[33] Professor Cornelius pointed out that the Mexican component of the overall flow of illegal immigrants is 60–65% (of those apprehended, 90 percent); therefore, the Carter program's application to Mexico is critical. He stated that twice before during the last half-century the United States has attempted unsuccessfully to limit the employment of Mexicans. While the present program is not a mass roundup or deportation, it is equally inappropriate, he argued. Doubling the border patrols and passing legislation that prohibits U.S. employers from hiring illegals will not accomplish our goals.[34]

Professor Cornelius suggested a much greater emphasis on providing development assistance to the countries of origin, making it less necessary for the natives of those countries to emigrate to the United States. The estimated $3 billion that Mexican workers send home each year is crucial to the Mexican economy. If that economy collapses and political conditions disintegrate in Mexico, some officials have argued, our problems will compound. To talk about breaking the smuggling rings that import illegals is to presume that we will be able to do in the future what we have not been able to do in the past, Cornelius said. And, without what he calls a huge and incredibly costly enforcement apparatus, there is no way to curb the flow of illegal aliens or to keep employers from finding it worthwhile to bring them into the United States. The businesses that would be subject to the Carter enforcement proposals are only those that have shown a "pattern or practice" of using illegal aliens. Since "small businesses" with 25 or less employees hire more than half the illegal immigrants from Mexico, this kind of statute will do little to solve the problem, Cornelius argued.

The big employers can handle thousand-dollar fines; they can write off small fines as a cost of business that can be passed on the illegal aliens themselves. The small businesses are too small and scattered to be policed; and they would not be guilty of patterns or practices in any event. Professor Cornelius speculates that American small businesses would be hurt and American laborers and employers would suffer if these laws were enforced.[35]

Finally, Professor Cornelius is concerned that Hispanic citizens will suffer discrimination because, to avoid conflicts with these laws, conscientious employers will simply not hire Spanish-Americans. With these laws, in his opinion, there is always going to be a significant flow of illegal Mexican workers until there are adequate alternatives in their home countries to keep them from migrating to the United States. There is no way the administration can freeze an ongoing social process, he argued, especially one that has been operating since the 1880s and often involves two or three generations of workers within families.

His theory that investing heavily in Mexican society is the answer to our labor problem may be farsighted, but it also is unrealistic. First, it is presumptuous to believe that with our relatively minor attention we would be able to do for the Mexican economy what the Mexican government has not ever been able to do for itself. Second, there is a serious question whether we should be investing so much in solving Mexico's economic problems while we have such a significant and deplorable poverty class in our own country. However, he is correct in questioning a billion-dollar investment (his estimate of the cost of President Carter's program) that does not get at the roots of a problem.

Another observer, Jonathan Power, has urged that clandestine migration be legalized because it is a reality of the marketplace; declaring this reality illegal only leads to black markets. In addition, he recommended taxing employers to help pay the extra social costs of migrants' families, encouraging employers to migrate to the labor sources (a step some California growers have threatened to take), and systematically creating a corps of American workers to fill these jobs.

The Carter proposals ran into opposition in Congress, and no new laws were passed in 1978. Near the end of that year, the president announced that he would resubmit his legislative package to the next session. Congress responded by creating a Select Commission on Immigration and Refugee Policy to study the problem and issue a report by 1981. Meanwhile, the problem continues, and migrant workers are the chief victims.

CERTIFIED FOREIGN WORKERS

The widespread hiring of illegal aliens by American employers is only one part of the problem posed to domestic farm workers by "off-shore" laborers. American farmers have brought to American farms tens of thousands of aliens under programs intended for the temporary employment of special foreign workers such as visiting artists or performers. How they have managed this importation is a scandalous perversion of a law designed to do just the opposite for American workers.

The unemployed farm workers in other, poorer countries compose a vast and hungry labor force as appealing to American farmers as American jobs are to these workers. A Mexican or West Indian laborer is more dependent upon his employer and more vulnerable to exploitation. In addition, some foreign workers are better at doing certain jobs. Basque sheepherders are considered to be the best in the world and are said to be more desirable than domestic workers; so, too, are Jamaican sugarcane cutters.

The law is designed to deny this foreign labor to American farmers on the grounds that our domestic labor market should come first in the disposition of American jobs and that the use of cheap foreign workers, for good or bad purposes, adversely affects this country's wage rates. An exception is made only to alleviate labor shortages at times of intensified production, usually for the harvesting of perishable and unique commodities.

Our laws are aimed specifically at drastically curtailing the employment of what is called off-shore labor, except in special circumstances. In fact, these laws are circumvented regularly by farmers who are abetted in their devious schemes by bureaucrats in the Department of Labor who each year conduct a ritualistic minuet with some growers and their government satraps at the expense of American farm workers.

Each spring, the secretary of labor blesses this cynical process and, in doing so, perverts his office. With his hands over his eyes and a good deal of bureaucratic fancy footwork, the secretary manages to sidestep his clear legal obligations by certifying the special hiring of tens of thousands of foreign agricultural laborers by American farmers. At any time, this practice would be condemnable; at times of exceptionally high unemployment in this country (highest in agricultural areas), it is a scandal.

A rural legal services lawyer has argued:

It is no less than folly when national policy permits a poor Texas farm worker to stand waiting in the unemployment or welfare line while at that same moment a well-fed, well-housed Jamaican farm worker stands in line at a New York post office to send his wages from picking New York apples to Jamaica via international money orders.

Each year, approximately 6 million aliens come temporarily to the

United States for a variety of reasons, including, in the case of about 60,000, temporary employment in the U.S. labor market. Agricultural workers are one of the major categories of temporary, legal employees from abroad.

Here is how the process works. Under the immigration and naturalization laws,[36] aliens may be admitted temporarily to work in the United States on two conditions: if domestic workers are not available to do the same work and if their employment does not have an adverse effect on domestic wage rates or working conditions. The attorney general is given the authority by law to determine when such off-shore employment is appropriate. He has delegated his power to make this determination to the secretary of labor.

Before a foreign worker can be admitted as a temporary laborer in this special status, the secretary of labor has to certify that qualified American workers are not available to do the work and that the employment of off-shore laborers will not adversely affect the wages and working conditions of those workers. If the secretary certifies foreign workers, the attorney general, through the commissioner of the INS, gives them temporary visas. The network of laws and regulations was passed in 1952; these resulted from a report to the president of a Special Commission on Migratory Labor in 1951, which concluded that the use of temporary foreign labor was displacing American labor and depressing domestic wages and working conditions. This problem is not new; during the last two centuries there have been comparable alien labor laws to deal with it.[37]

The present law is purely and simply an "American first" provision, seeking to protect the job security of domestic workers, keep American money here, and lower our welfare costs. One federal court directly stated that the immigration policy behind this law is "to set up a presumption that aliens should not be permitted to enter the United States for the purpose of performing labor because of the likely harmful impact of their admission on American workers."[38] The basic idea, then, was to use the American economy to employ American workers.

It has not happened that way in agricultural work. In 1976, 15,230 foreign workers were certified to work on American farms despite extraordinarily high unemployment in this country; in 1975, 16,499 were certified; in 1974, 20,634; in 1973, 20,138. The figures between 1966 and 1972 were comparable, never going over 23,000 nor under 12,000. Most of the foreign farm workers who have been certified to work here have been British West Indians; they were imported to cut sugarcane and pick apples. Basques from Spain have been brought here to be sheepherders; Canadians were brought to pick apples and work in the wood industries. They all have been certified to work in the United States despite what one Labor Department official described to me as "no shortage of bodies" here to handle these jobs and despite protests from farm worker groups that the approved wage rate formulas are unrealistic. As a result, millions of dollars of American wages are going to foreign workers each year.

Growers have learned to manipulate the system, and secretaries of labor have allowed themselves to be manipulated. Many of the big employers prefer foreign workers. To get the secretary's certification to hire off-shore labor, these employers play a game with the Department of Labor. Departmental regulations require employers to seek American laborers through the state Employment Service network thirty days in advance of the work date. The owner of a big, East Coast apple orchard, for example, knows that he will need a specific number of workers to pick a predictable crop of apples at a certain time of the year. He waits until the last minute and then goes to the local Employment Service office and asks for a flock of workers, knowing that they will not be available there at that late date. The state Employment Service (fully funded by the Department of Labor) is required to find local workers first, then to solicit workers elsewhere in the state, and finally to put the grower's order into the interstate clearance system in the hope of finding workers in other states. This requirement is in recognition of the fact that agricultural work in large part is done by migrants in the immediate area and other areas of labor supply.

When workers are not available, the regional representative of the secretary of labor can certify foreign workers. State and local officials go through a frantic, expensive search for domestic farm workers; but this late in the growing season most migrants are already in the stream or are either employed or unreachable. Much to everyone's surprise, once this fruitless charade is completed, the growers are able to find a band of, say, Jamaican workers who happen to be at the airport with their visas and toothbrushes and ready to work. Since the growers are not required to request the workers sufficiently in advance of the season, those who really want foreign workers play a waiting game knowing that if they wait long enough and complicate their job orders, the state Employment Service and the Department of Labor will not find domestic workers and will have to certify foreigners.

At our Special Review Committee hearings in San Antonio, Tex., in May 1976, Bruno Abrego, who worked in the Laredo,

Tex., Employment Commission office, told us that if East Coast growers provided plane tickets for American farm workers in Texas as they do for foreign workers he could find them an adequate local labor supply.

One obvious solution to this problem is to require that all interstate clearance orders be in phase with the historic timing of migrant farm worker activity. As our committee advised the Department of Labor:

The basic problem is that the department's certification process, including use of the interstate clearance order system, is out of phase with the need of growers and farm workers and the timetable of commitments necessary to link American workers with American jobs.

If employers were not allowed to wait until what everyone knew was the last minute but were required to submit their orders sufficiently in advance to assure that interested workers were available, the need for certifying temporary foreign workers would diminish to the vanishing point. Off-shore labor would be the occasional, legitimate exception rather than the common, perverse rule.

Several years ago, the Florida state Employment Service tried to get crews of Florida-based migrants placed in jobs with East Coast growers. The service contacted 144 crew leaders representing 4,000 migrant farm workers wanting to pick apples in Virginia, West Virginia, and New England where growers regularly need 2,500 workers. The growers refused to make their plans early enough, knowing the Florida workers would be in the migrant stream when the orders were placed. A frustrated and outspoken director of the Florida Employment Service described to our committee and to the Department of Labor just how the system is exploited by growers:

We had not even seen the first order when, on June 9, 1975, the growers' representatives and their attorney came to Tallahassee to discuss recruitment. We told them that it was late but that we would try to help. We also told them the conditions necessary in order to be successful in recruiting. Our advice was unheeded. The orders which we received later in the summer contained almost exactly what we told them would not work: unreasonable and nonprevailing task requirements; "negotiable" crew leader compensation; requirements for personal applications from each member of the crew; on-site interviews prior to selection; unspecified transportation arrangements; a wonderful new contract for the crew leader to sign, with all of the ominous overtones of a law suit if he breached even a clause; and other matters which cast doubt upon their enthusiasm for finding domestic workers. . . .

The apple growers, with the collusion of the Department of Labor, have deliberately attempted to subvert the laws and regulations dealing with interstate clearance and certification of foreign workers.[39]

His message to the Labor Department was repeated by Florida's secretary of commerce, lest there be any misunderstanding about this phony process:

Recruiters representing the apple industry were utterly unfamiliar with the concept of positive recruitment, frequently had no authority to hire for other than a few growers, objected to the notion of travel advances, and approached negotiations with crew leaders, a major issue deferred from earlier job order disputes, with rigidity or indifference. In view of the numerous reports filed by monitors observing this process, it is not surprising that so few crews were enlisted.

The U.S. Department of Labor certified to the immigration service that there were not sufficient numbers of domestic workers to harvest the apple crop and that more than 4,000 foreign workers were necessary for that purpose.

The narrative of events set forth above raises serious questions in our minds as to whether the intent of Congress regarding the importation of foreign workers has been fulfilled. . . . The fact remains, however, that during a period of rampant unemployment, especially among agricultural workers, no one could be found to pluck apples from a tree.[40]

If growers in the demand states were required to submit their harvest plans to supply states when the migrants are around and looking for work, they would get American workers. Instead, the players engage in a cynical game. I wrote to former secretaries John Dunlop and William Usery about this problem on behalf of our court-appointed committee, describing the problem and seeking reform of the Labor Department system. Dunlop sent us a dilatory and defensive response; Usery never even responded.

A second solution is to devise a more realistic adverse-effect wage rate. The Secretary of Labor has promulgated regulations requiring the department to certify that the temporary use of foreign workers will not adversely affect the wages and working conditions of domestic laborers.[41] The wage rate is calculated on the basis of the average wage in a given state the preceding year. It then becomes the prevailing rate of wages for all crops in that state the next year, creating a perverse outcome for domestic workers who lose their modest bargaining power when foreign workers are ready and willing to work for the relatively low rates of the year before. The federal government, then, through its administration of a program designed to attract and protect American workers, is driving the wages down and drawing in foreign workers.

An example of how this procedure should work was reported at a Florida hearing by Dave Williams, Labor Department expert on the foreign certification question. He explained how the Florida citrus industry converted from foreign to domestic labor (almost 6,000 workers were involved) within several years by adoption of an attractive but reasonable wage rate.

Our committee recommended that the secretary of labor administer this aspect of the certification process differently. We recommended that wage rate data from the busiest quarter in the preceding year in each state be used (not just the crop in question) and that this figure be raised according to the cost of living increases reported in the Consumer Price Index. This would use peak labor wage standards and would consider realistic changes that come with time. The new figure could be expected to attract domestic workers. Piece rates would be used, since this is a chief method of payment for field workers. We also pushed the department to add 25 percent to the figure reached in computing the adverse-effect wage rate, which was a requirement under existing regulations. Finally, we asked that the determination of this rate be made after public hearings in which farm worker organizations would be heard. None of our recommendations were adopted.

Another answer is to coordinate the American labor policy favoring domestic workers with the desire of the Puerto Rican government to expand its contract labor system. There is a special program between the government of Puerto Rico and numerous farmers and farmer organizations in the United States whereby large numbers of workers are contracted for through the Puerto Rican Department of Labor. Since Puerto Ricans are American citizens and the Puerto Rican government is interested in solving its extreme unemployment problem by sending workers to the mainland, theoretically no American farmers should need to have temporary alien workers.

A report to the Special Review Committee by one of our members, David Lillesand, a plaintiffs' representative and attorney who directed rural legal service programs in New Jersey and Florida, noted that in 1973 New York failed to recruit any Puerto Ricans to work in the apple harvest. Though unemployment in Puerto Rico was quite high, over 1,000 foreign workers were certified to work that year in New York. And, Lillesand pointed out, thousands of Puerto Ricans were hired to work in New Jersey and Connecticut at lower wage rates than those paid foreign workers in New York.

After World War II, the Puerto Rican government determined that many of its workers had been drifting to the United

States mainland in search of work. Word came back to officials that many were being exploited. Furthermore, whenever workers encountered problems on the mainland, the government of Puerto Rico was called upon to bail them out, to deal with their problems at long distance and great expense. As a result, the Puerto Rican government decided to control the employment of those who went to the mainland for work.

At a meeting in his office in San Juan, Puerto Rico's secretary of labor, Louis Silva Recio, described to me how this program worked. Growers in the United States who wish to hire Puerto Ricans must sign contracts designed and administered by the Puerto Rican government for the benefit of its farm workers. Grower organizations have contracted to hire large members of Puerto Rican workers. These contracts were all administered under what is known as Public Law 87, under which the conditions that mainland employers had to meet to recruit Puerto Rican workers were standardized.

The Puerto Rican government faced one dilemma. On one hand, extraordinarily high unemployment rates prevailed on the island. Workers who were anxious to have jobs in the United States were less than finicky about the terms and conditions of employment. On the other hand, while the secretary of labor had the obligation to reduce the island's high unemployment rates, he also had humanitarian motives not to collaborate with employers who would place workers in job situations that were unfair or inequitable. He described his painful choice to me at our meeting. How, he asked, could he relieve extraordinary unemployment rates on the island without bartering away the employment rights of workers whose interests he was in office to protect?

The Commonwealth revised its contracts, imposing stronger obligations upon growers who wished to hire Puerto Rican farm workers. As a result, the number of contract workers declined from a high of 23,000 in 1968 to a low of 5,000 in 1975. This resulting drop aggravated the already serious economic situation on the island.

The quandary continues. There is a substantial need for migrant and seasonal farm workers in the United States, and a large number are available in Puerto Rico. The agricultural work force there has proven to be especially good with certain crops. Because of the economic situation on the island, the workers are ready and willing to work in the United States, with or without contracts. Puerto Rican employment service officials estimated for our committee that three times the number of contract workers were migrating to the mainland United States in the mid-1970s during harvest seasons under individual arrangements with American growers. Their needs led them to circumvent the beneficent contract program set up by the government. The fact of life is that these workers want jobs and are willing to take them under any situation.

If the growers are reluctant to accede to the demands of the Puerto Rican government or find they can get the workers without doing so, the government program is undercut, even though it is a good one that should benefit everyone concerned. The standards required by the Puerto Rican government are higher than those the U.S. government demands of American growers when they hire mainland American workers.

Fred Romero, a Labor Department representative on our committee, went with me to Puerto Rico to see how officials administered the program. David Lillesand went with me to New Jersey where large-scale employer organizations hire the greatest number of Puerto Rican contract laborers. We saw the promise of the program at one end and its frustrations and imperfections at the other.

Romero and I spent a day at an employment service office in Bayamon, P. R., observing the island recruitment system. There we saw large numbers of workers who had been notified that on a given day growers from the states would be present to sign contracts for a season of work. Prior to the actual recruitment process, the workers were shown a film prepared by the Puerto Rican Department of Labor, describing the history and operation of the contract labor system. The workers were given a description of the contracting process and an explanation of their rights and obligations. Workers who were interested filled out appropriate forms and then were interviewed individually by representatives of the growers. The growers' agents ultimately decided who would be hired. Workers who were signed up left for work within a day or two.

At Glassboro, N. J., the headquarters of the largest growers association contracting for Puerto Rican farmworkers, Lillesand and I saw where large numbers of farm workers were housed, assigned to jobs, and shipped off for work each day. The grounds and facilities were neat and clean. But workers complained to us that they had been abused and had no redress of their grievances, despite their protests to the resident Puerto Rican government official who was their liaison with the growers. Their complaint was that he was a captive of the employers organization and was an ineffective advocate.

If the relevant U.S. government officials collaborated with

Puerto Rican government officials, the needs of Puerto Rican workers and American farmers could be addressed and the need to certify foreign workers could be reduced drastically.

When our committee held hearings in Rochester, N.Y., in September 1976, I questioned the state Employment Service director as to why New York had certified over 1,000 foreign farm workers for its apple harvest each year since 1970. He offered excuses for this practice but assured the committee that the next year (1977) there would be no foreign labor certifications. I later learned that his answer to the problem would be to contract with Puerto Rico for its laborers instead of certifying the use of foreign labor.

A court case in the summer of 1977 frustrated a Labor Department attempt to phase the foreign labor certification process with the Puerto Rican contract labor system.[42] The case concerned the two-month apple harvest in Virginia and the question of who was to do the picking of millions of bushels of apples.

East Coast growers prefer Jamaican workers to Puerto Ricans. Under the government-run contract program, employers of Puerto Ricans are required to pay travel costs in advance. Growers found that Puerto Rican workers frequently failed to come to work after arriving in the United States, or they worked awhile and then left. So the growers negotiated an agreement with the Jamaican Regional Labor Board, which advanced travel costs to the Jamaican workers, who would be reimbursed by the growers after completion of 15 days of labor.

The Labor Department had rejected the growers' job orders that did not contain the transportation advances the Puerto Rican government contract required. The department ruled that these orders could not be the basis for growers' claims that foreign workers were needed because domestic workers were unavailable. The growers argued that advance payment of transportation expenses was not required by Labor Department regulations; therefore, the department was required to approve the job orders. They pointed to prior financial losses resulting from department refusal to permit certification of foreign workers.

The specific regulations at issue in the Virginia case required that growers provide out-of-state workers "the same terms [of] transportation [as] is commonly provided by employers in the area of intended employment to agricultural workers recruited from the same area of supply."[43] The court held that the relevant "area" referred to in the law was the State of Virginia. Since the normal practice among *all* apple growers in Virginia—not merely those in the plaintiff growers association—was to pay crew leaders after they arrived with workers and not to advance transportation costs, the growers could not be forced to acquiesce in the Puerto Rican government demands.

The court held that advance payment was not required.[44] The decision to consider the practice of all Virginia growers was the key. Most members of the plaintiff association were growers who regularly relied on foreign workers; in the past, they had regularly advanced transportation money to West Indian farm workers. If the court had focused on the practices of the growers association alone, it would have had to meet the Puerto Rican contract requirement for transportation advances. Instead, it allowed American farmers to work out a deal with the Jamaican government, which was willing to help in order to cut its 30 percent unemployment rate.

On July 29, 1977, the court issued a preliminary injunction requiring that the job orders in question not be rejected for failing to provide transportation advances. The court ordered the Labor Department to immediately certify the growers' request for temporary foreign workers. Months later, the appellate court dismissed the government's appeals as moot because the harvest season had ended.[45]

The growers had made it virtually impossible for domestic and Puerto Rican workers to work in Virginia orchards. Because the growers did not advance funds directly to the foreign workers, they technically complied with the requirement that foreign workers not be given greater benefits than domestic workers. This round in the Caribbean chess game was lost by Puerto Rico. The Jamaicans also won a round the next year when the Department of Labor contracted with the Puerto Rican government for hundreds of farm workers to be employed in the East Coast apple orchards. But the growers claimed that they were permitted to hire Jamaicans instead because the Puerto Ricans' contracts were made with the U.S. government, not the American growers. They claimed they were not covered by an exemption from the law the two governments negotiated in order to be able to place more Puerto Ricans in farm work here. Hundreds of workers were brought here by our government only to find their jobs taken by Jamaicans.[46] Others were given work for a few days, fired for incompetence, and replaced by Jamaicans.[47] As one Puerto Rican farm worker spokesman said, "As citizens, it looks like we can die for this country, but we're not good enough to make a living here."

The courts have not helped critics of the certification system, but attacks on its perversities continue. In October 1979, for example, federal and state agencies were sued by American farm workers who argued that the New York apple growers and the Jamaican government were forcing American workers out of jobs in the orchards of the Hudson and Champlain valleys by recruiting Jamaican workers. Farmers are not required to contribute to Social Security and unemployment insurance programs when they use offshore labor, and they can impose fixed salary scales on their workers as well. As a result, the lawsuit charged, low-income American workers were losing their limited job market.

Secretary of Labor Ray Marshall, because of his extensive experience and a special interest in rural labor problems, could have been expected to change all this. The certification problem, unlike that of illegal aliens, is solvable. In the late 1960s, California and Arizona imported over 200,000 foreign workers annually, 83 percent of the nation's total. A special unit was created on the West Coast by Secretary of Labor Wirtz to stop this practice, and within two years it was ended. According to one department official, there is no reason why that West Coast effort cannot be repeated nationwide:

The worker demands in harvesting perishable crops alone in the single State of California dwarfs labor requirements for the entire East Coast. Imagine, for example, 190,000 acres of tomatoes; a single grower with 2,000 acres of strawberries and an 11-month harvest season.
I don't think anyone could ever convince me that fast harvesting of apples and sugarcane (perishability) is more necessary than strawberries and tomatoes. Or that it is more difficult to find workers to climb ladders on orange trees than to hang suspended 8 or 10 hours from a 60-foot date palm in Coachella or spend all day in 120° heat in the Yuma melon harvest.

Secretary Marshall would have to resist departmental undertows and strong pressures from interested senators and powerful farm groups to avoid repeating the transgressions of his predecessors.

The National Association of Farmworker Organizations (NAFO) reported in October 1978 that requests for temporary foreign labor certifications were on the rise. Arizona growers requested permission to hire 658 citrus pickers from Costa Rica. A Colorado growers association requested permission to hire 340 apple pickers. Jamaicans were approved by the Department of Labor to pick pears in Oregon. All this, despite the fact of life reported by NAFO that "with 150,000 unemployed farm workers in this country, farm workers will obviously be available for work *if* the wages and working conditions are decent and *if* growers and the employment service make genuine efforts to locate United States workers."

An example of the relative impotence of farm workers in contrast to organized grower groups in political battles generally and of the political pressures on the secretary of labor in this particular situation was provided in the summer of 1977. For years, growers in the sparsely populated Presidio Valley in southernmost Texas had relied heavily on illegal aliens from Mexico to provide their seasonal labor. During the season, Mexican farm workers crossed the Rio Grande regularly each morning, worked in the fields all day, and returned to Mexico at night. In early 1977 increased border enforcement by the INS severely reduced the number of illegal aliens who entered Texas to work in the valley.

In March 1977 local onion growers requested official certification of their temporary foreign workers. Their request was denied. The Labor Department found that the growers had never offered the jobs to domestic workers through the Employment Service recruitment system, and the growers had failed to provide proper housing for their laborers as required by federal regulations.

After local political pressures did not result in certification or the visas, the growers went to Washington. A group of Texas congressmen led by Richard C. White persuaded President Carter that dire consequences would result from Secretary of Labor Marshall's decision not to certify these foreign onion pickers. Their argument, that without intervention crops would spoil in the fields, was a contention Labor Department officials had considered and rejected. President Carter told Secretary Marshall to resolve the matter with Attorney General Bell. Bell circumvented Marshall's refusal to certify the workers by ordering the INS to issue temporary visas.

The Migrant Legal Action Program sued the attorney general on behalf of a group of local farm workers, arguing that the INS ignored its own regulations in granting these 800 temporary visas to uncertified workers when they had been denied earlier.

The episode is revealing. When one secretary of labor finally enforced the law, grower pressures on Congress and congressional pressures on the President forced a capitulation. The temporary certifications of foreign laborers have been criticized by farm worker organizations as a reincarnation of the bracero programs in a new disguise. This H-2 program, as it is now called,[48] has been used to reduce wages and to break strikes, according to the National Farmworker Ministry.

The problem of foreign competition for American farm jobs will not disappear. Not until domestic farm workers are organized and powerful enough to pressure farm employers and responsible American government officials to protect their special interests will they be secure in their jobs and not jeopardized by the constant allure of cheap and available foreign competition.

7

EXCLUSION FROM SOCIAL BENEFITS

IT IS OFTEN SAID that a disadvantaged group of people is powerless. What precisely does this term mean? Surely it must apply to migrant farm workers, many of whom are members of minority racial and ethnic groups; some of whom are or were illegal aliens; almost all of whom are very poor, alienated from the power structure of American society, without place or connections, and disorganized. For these reasons, many government social welfare programs are inept. But there is a story of farm worker powerlessness that is even more telling. It is the case of a minority that has been systematically excluded from society's emergency care.

Perhaps the clearest illustration of the meaning of true impotence is when a situation has become so grave for a large group of people that society determines to take extraordinary remedial or protective measures in its behalf yet also determines to exclude one segment within that group from the benefits of its charity.

Since the 1940s, American society has recognized, if not adequately confronted, the extraordinary problem of the extremely poor people in its midst. In the post-Depression, New Deal era of Franklin D. Roosevelt and more recently in the "war on poverty" years of Lyndon B. Johnson's administration, broad social welfare programs were conceived to alleviate some of the excessive poverty and its progeny of related social problems that had become the undesirable results of the free enterprise system.

There are several major examples. Workmen's compensation laws were passed to spread the risks of work-related injuries and to assure that workers were compensated without regard to legalistic questions concerning fault if their injuries arose out of their employment. The idea was that workers should have basic protection from the inevitable injuries resulting from their industry and that any burdens arising from their work should be shared directly by their employers and indirectly by the consumers they serve.

The idea still makes good sense. But in most places farm workers either are not covered by workmen's compensation laws or get inadequate coverage. Only about 20% of state workmen's compensation laws cover migrant farm workers in the same way as they cover all others.

Key parts of Roosevelt's economic recovery program were the laws assuring a minimum wage and a minimum age for workers. These two fundamental reforms were designed to insulate the working weak from exploitation by the economic strong in the unequal play of the marketplace. Aimed at establishing minimum standards for all work conditions, these laws excluded agricultural workers, perhaps the hardest working yet most vulnerable group in the labor force.

Unemployment insurance first was established in the original Social Security Act. Its purpose was to protect workers from vicissitudes of the labor market that were beyond their control. The motivating idea was that a worker should be protected from the hardships of job loss if not at fault for the condition resulting in unemployment. All employers contribute to a fund insuring some income for any employees who lose jobs for causes beyond their control. Farm workers traditionally have been excluded from unemployment insurance coverage.

Another glaring example of prejudicial exclusion is the exemption of farm workers from basic federal laws allowing workers to unionize and bargain collectively. This is not giveaway legislation; it is not special protective legislation; it is legal assurance of the basic right of people with common problems to associate so that they can advance their common interests in a more powerful fashion than individuals can acting alone. This is the heart of the labor movement's power. It is the right of a worker to join others in the constant struggle for economic survival and the pursuit of his or her economic destiny. Farm workers have been excluded from this vital social movement from its beginning.

The rationales for these exclusions from major and fundamental social welfare benefits, some of the most progressive measures in a half-century, have been specious. The reality is that farm workers are politically silent, unsophisticated, and impotent. Even in times of emergency when the dire needs of other poor and disenfranchised groups have been recognized, farm workers were forgotten. Consider the following sad stories of exclusion.

WORKMEN'S COMPENSATION LAWS

At 7:00 A.M. on September 17, 1970, a sunny day in McFarland, Calif., 20 migrant laborers were sent into a field to pick oranges. By 9:00 A.M., several workers had collapsed and all were suffering from difficulty with breathing, nausea, burning eyes, headaches, and weakness in their limbs. Twelve workers were taken to the hospital and released the next day after being told nothing was wrong with them. Their symptoms persisted from six months to a year, but all the men returned to work within a few days because they had families to support. Their employer, Paramount Growers, did not pay for their medical bills nor for the wages lost, although their symptoms reportedly were due to the pesticide sprayed on that field the day before.[1]

In August 1967 in Michigan, two migrant agricultural workers fell and injured themselves at their employer's packing company. Frank Gallegos fractured his wrist and Mary Gutierrez hurt her left leg and back. Both missed time at work. Medical benefits were paid under a voluntary arrangement with their employer, but no weekly disability payments were provided. The loss of wages was a hardship; both workers supported several dependents.[2] If these migrant farm workers had been employed in a nonagricultural occupation, their medical bills and lost wages would have been paid under their state workmen's compensation law.

Workmen's compensation is a statutory system that treats work-related injuries and diseases as a cost of production. It places the financial burden on the employer, who is expected to add it to his costs and thus transfer it to the consumer. A broad scheme of compulsory liability insurance equalizes a single employer's burden over an entire industry.

Benefits to workers are paid by the employer (irrespective of who is at fault), who either self-insures, buys private insurance, or participates in the state insurance plan. Under these programs, employers furnish medical care, usually unlimited in time and amount; vocational or medical rehabilitation services; and weekly disability benefits under a state-prescribed rate schedule. This coverage provides injured workers with some wages while they are absent for work-related injuries. While states supervise claims and benefit rates and adjudicate disputes on eligibility for benefits and the extent of disability, workmen's compensation essentially is a program administered and funded privately. Once these programs have been set up, states generally do little to monitor their administration.[3]

As of 1972, 85 percent of the nation's work force was covered by compulsory workmen's compensation insurance.[4] Because of amendments to coverage by several states, about 86 percent of American labor is now protected.

Although every state has a workmen's compensation law, only in 11 states and Puerto Rico are migrant farm workers covered on the same basis as other workers. Eighteen states and the District of Columbia provide farm workers no coverage at all, although in five of these states employers may elect coverage. The remaining 21 states provide partial coverage that excludes migrants in a variety of ways.[5] Some states exempt employers with fewer than a certain number of employees or with less than a specified annual payroll. Some states exclude certain kinds of jobs such as in agriculture or nonhazardous occupations (in which category farming is inexplicably included). Other states cover only workers using machinery or even a particular type of machinery (threshing and hulling, for example). Still other states cover only farm employees who work 35 or more hours a week for a period of 13 weeks or more per year for one employer. Some of these states exclude seasonal or casual workers.[6] Others exclude agricultural workers by making their compensation coverage elective and not compulsory on the part of the employer.

Though farm workers have special needs for protection, only 3 of the 12 major farming states extend total coverage to farm workers (California, Wisconsin, and Ohio); in 7 of these 12, the laws provide no coverage at all for agricultural employees.[7] Additionally, some employers who are covered by these laws fail to meet their legal obligation to provide coverage.[8]

Despite wide national coverage of the general American work force by workmen's compensation laws, farm workers remain in a second-class position. Farm workers are particularly vulnerable and are especially in need of the protections offered by workmen's compensation.

A worker has to be in good physical condition to pick enough fruit or vegetables to earn $10 to $20 a day. This work is so hard that only the young and strong can really do well. Even a trivial injury makes a big difference. . . . The loss of income for one day can mean children go hungry. The loss of income for a week or two weeks is a disaster. We know that many farm workers rely on the money they earn today to buy food for tonight. In many families there is never money left over for the next day, let alone to pay debts incurred the day before.[9]

Though they are covered by workmen's compensation in less than a third of the states, farm workers' needs for protection are clear. Agriculture is one of the most hazardous of occupations. According to National Safety Council statistics, farming is ranked sixth in the frequency of industrial accidents; it is second only to mining in the severity of accidents.[10] Another survey disclosed that only mining and construction have higher death rates and that the risks in farming are on the rise.[11] Since the 1960s the number of fatalities on farms has more than doubled. In addition, occupational diseases from pesticides and chemical fertilizers have increased.[12] With increased mechanization and other forms of industrialization and technology on farms and with a noted rise in the average age of farm workers, which heightens susceptibility to injury, this upward trend can be expected to continue.[13]

Several government and private groups have recommended changes in workmen's compensation laws. In differing degrees, they all have suggested extensions of coverage to farm workers.

The Occupational Safety and Health Act (OSHA) of 1970 created a blue ribbon committee of academics, labor leaders, and state administrators of workmen's compensation boards. In 1972 the committee issued a report of the National Commission on State Workmen's Compensation Laws surveying their status and making recommendations. Although it advised that mandatory protection be provided for all employees then excluded, it suggested a two-stage approach for farm workers. First, it recommended that coverage be extended to agricultural workers whose employers' annual payrolls exceed $1,000. Second, it suggested that two-year coverage be extended to all farm laborers. Additionally, it suggested that an injured itinerant farm employee be given the choice of filing a claim for workmen's compensation in the state where he was hired, where he was employed, or where he was injured.

Since Congress received this committee's report, there have been hearings almost every year on workmen's compensation reform. However, according to Senate Labor Committee staff, little attention has been paid to reforming the specific coverage of migrant workers under state or federal laws.

The Department of Labor has compiled 16 standards for improved workmen's compensation laws, which have been endorsed by various interested organizations and agencies such as the International Association of Industrial Accident Boards and Commissions and the American Medical Association. These standards propose the inclusion of farm laborers under the coverage of workmen's compensation laws on the same basis as other employees. In 1963 the Council of State Governments also endorsed the principle of compulsory coverage of farm workers (except for farmers with fewer than three employees). In 1973 the OSHA council issued a report, "Workmen's Compensation, A Challenge to the States, " updating its suggested model act by providing for a different two-stage approach. For the first year after enactment, all agricultural workers except those whose employer has an annual payroll of less than $1,000 would be covered. The following year that exemption would terminate.

Although it is deplorable that farm workers are ignored by organized industry and the general public they serve, their situation does cause special administrative problems. Many work for several employers, often in several states. In the event of recurring or chronic disability, more than one employer could be held responsible. Farms are geographically dispersed and migrants often have no permanent address; as a result, claims are overlooked and the delivery of more than short-term benefits is difficult. But these are the kind of problems for which program administrators are paid to find solutions.

Indeed, experts have suggested several answers. Each migrant worker could be insured individually by the employer, and each payment would go into a national fund to be used to identify particular workers wherever they happened to be. This plan would solve the problem of migrants on the move who have to establish eligibility anew in every state.

Publicly funded care of injured migrants could be assumed as a method of risk redistribution by the federal system; this could be considered no more than a small element of the public cost of bringing food from field to table.

Dealing with the difficulties of solving these problems is part of the responsibility of public administration professionals dealing with workmen's compensation laws. These problems should not remain an excuse for ignoring the legitimate problems of one group of vulnerable workers.[14]

MINIMUM WAGE LAWS

In the early, active years of the New Deal, major reform and recovery legislation dealing with industry, agriculture, finance, monetary policy, and labor organization was passed. Once these enactments had stabilized the economy and the work force, it was time to consider the conditions under which laborers worked as well as the quality of their lives. One of these conditions was the control of work for those paid by the hour.

Thus in 1938, born of the plight of working men and women who labored under unhealthy conditions for unlimited numbers of hours, the Fair Labor Standards Act (FLSA) was passed by the Seventy-fifth Congress. Its intentions were to prevent a complete wage collapse if another economic depression should occur and to eliminate poverty among workers by establishing a minimum wage; to discourage excessively long hours of work and encourage the employment of more people by imposing an overtime rate (time and a half) for all work over 40 hours a week; and to alleviate oppressive child labor practices.[15] It was hoped that the act would discourage employers from resorting to substandard wages and excessively long hours. The control was expected to add to the nation's buying power by broadening the base of people with money to spend, thus benefiting business and the economy as well as the individual workers involved.[16]

Despite President Roosevelt's good intentions to "help those who toil in the factory and on the farm"[17] the coverage of the act was denied farm workers. One reason advanced in support of their exclusion was that agriculture was not considered to be hard labor, at least not in the same way that industrial labor was viewed. The principal argument was that a minimum hourly wage (as opposed to piece work wages based on the amount of work produced) would destroy a worker's incentive to produce at a maximum level (why this theory should apply more to farm workers than to factory workers is mystifying). The attendant administrative difficulties and inconveniences of the farmer were other rationales cited by opponents. Finally, it was proclaimed to be a protection for farm workers, since coverage by the minimum wage would end piece work pay and thus decrease some wages.[18]

Actually, it should have come as no surprise that farm workers were excluded from the FLSA; they were never given serious consideration. Farm workers were neither very visible nor very vocal in the halls of Congress or anywhere in government; as a result they were politically weak.[19] The general and prevailing view was that farm workers were not exploited. One commentator has suggested:

In part this [exclusion] has been a result of the tradition which portrayed the American agricultural laborer as the son of a farmer, working for another farmer so as to gain the experience and capital necessary to help him rise. . . . He was the social equal of his employer, he ate at the same table with him and slept under the same roof. . . . It is easy to see why most social legislation—even that of the New Deal—excluded the farm worker.[20]

Even the courts of this period reflected the belief that farm work was idyllic when compared to the oppressive conditions of industrial work. According to one judge: "[A]gricultural labor was not subject to the   usual evils of sweat-shop conditions of long hours indoors at low wages."[21] The myth still exists that working in the fields is wholesome and worthwhile in comparison to working indoors and that long hours and low wages somehow should be more acceptable to field workers no matter how back-breaking their work or how despicable their work conditions.

Thirty years after the original FLSA was passed, Congress finally provided some agricultural workers with minimum wage protections. Why it took 30 years is another chapter in the farm workers' story of neglect at the hands of the national legislature. The 1938 act had set the minimum wage at 25 cents an hour and provided for a two-step increase that would raise it to 40 cents an hour by 1945.

By 1949 there were pressures to increase the minimum wage. The war was over, the economy was returning to a peacetime upswing, and returning soldiers wanted higher wages. Bills were introduced to increase the minimum wage and extend the coverage of the law.

However, at that time it was believed that it would not be feasible to simultaneously increase the minimum wage and expand coverage. Although there was considerable evidence that both were essential if the act was to accomplish its basic purposes, the Congress opted for an increase in the level of the minimum wage, leaving large numbers of low-wage workers outside the act. In 1955, spurred by a booming economy caused in some part by the Korean War, the act was amended again. While the minimum wage was increased to $1 an hour, the coverage provisions were left untouched. In 1961, amendments to the act finally recognized that both an increase in the minimum wage and an extension of coverage were essential if substandard living conditions were to be eliminated. Thus the minimum wage was increased to $1.25 an hour and 3.5 million workers were covered for the first time. Unfortunately, farm workers still did not have the ear of Congress; the newly covered workers were principally in the retail and construction industries.[22]

The Department of Labor studied the effects of this broadened coverage. A department report emphasized that the extension was critically important in reducing poverty among the retail and construction workers, and that it did not exert an upward pressure on the country's overall wage structure. This finding helped to counteract employer opposition to broadening the act's coverage for fear that it would set off a nationwide inflationary spiral with each million workers newly covered by a minimum wage.

The Labor Department study was used effectively during the hearings on the 1966 amendments, which finally enabled the FLSA to come closer than at any time in its history to achieving its basic goal.[23] The act not only raised the minimum wage (to $1.60 an hour) but also extended coverage to 12 million additional workers. With others, farm workers were covered if they labored on large farms—those using more than 500 work days in any quarter of the preceding year, which translates to seven full-time employees.

The 1966 amendments were passed in the context of President Johnson's War on Poverty, when social legislation and programs for the poor were receiving priority attention from the administration and Congress. In his message to Congress recommending extending FLSA coverage, the president said:

Many American workers whose employment is clearly within the reach of this law have never enjoyed its benefits. Unfortunately, these workers are generally in the lowest wage groups and are most in need of wage and hour protection. We must extend wage and overtime protection to them.[24]

In leading off the testimony at the hearings on this bill, then Secretary of Labor Willard Wirtz emphasized that Title VII of the Civil Rights Act—affording equal employment to all workers, regardless of race, sex, religion, or national origin—had just become effective. To demand equal hiring and promotion opportunities while continuing to deny large numbers of workers minimum wage protection, he argued, was anomalous. Wirtz also compared the public interests that existed in 1938 with those of 1965:

The pressures behind the enactment of the FLSA of 1938 were the pressures of economic desperation. The force behind its enlargement now is the force of hard headed idealism. . . . The FLSA was a commitment to improve living standards by eliminating substandard working conditions in employment subject to Federal authority over interstate commerce. That commitment, incomplete when it was made, has become less complete with the passage of time. The law has not kept in line with the advancing economy; and some of its guarantees mean less, comparatively, than they did 27 years ago.[25]

The director of the AFL-CIO legislation department testified that in 1965 30 percent of all poor families included a full-time worker whose pay clearly was not sufficient to keep a family above the poverty line. He urged the extension of the FLSA to farm workers, who represented 2 million of the nation's 17.5 million unprotected workers in dire need of special legislation to provide them with an adequate federal minimum wage. The Amalgamated Meatcutters and Butchers Workmen of North America also supported the coverage of farm workers, urging that there was no reason why the "open air sweatshops" should not be brought under full coverage.[26]

The American Farm Bureau presented the opposition's circuitous arguments:

[T]he weight of the evidence is that an extension of minimum wage coverage, or an increase in minimum rates, would harmfully affect employment and particularly the employment of these segments of our population most needing employment opportunities.[27]

It cited a detailed economic analysis showing that every 1 percent increase in wages would reduce by 2 percent the total work days of employment on farms. Characterizing the harvest work force as virtually anyone who is available—including the infirm, the elderly, and the mentally and physically handicapped—the Farm Bureau witness stated that because such workers are slow they are compensated fairly by piece-rate pay. Any extension of a minimum hourly wage to field laborers would compel farmers to pay many workers more than was warranted by their productivity. The act would leave the least capable workers totally unemployed, force farmers to mechanize faster, and force small and marginal farmers out of business.[28] In other words, the farmers rationalized the denial of a minimum wage for farm workers on the need for hiring the old and the handicapped!

The committee that held the hearings also saw Department of Labor studies of the results of the 1961 broadened coverage. The National Farmers Union, a group representing small farms testified:

[T]he corporate farm [is] not more efficient than the family farm but [is] able to do better only by the use of cheap labor, better credit, and financial tie-ins with agribusiness and the food giants and chains. The family farmer and his family must compete with the hired hands and migrant laborers on the corporate farm. When farm labor is paid 35 cents and 50 cents an hour, then the farmer, his wife and children must also sweat at 35 cents and 50 cents an hour. Most family farmers could successfully compete, if the corporate farm had to pay a decent wage to their help. For the sake of the family farm and rural America, if not for the sake of the poor who are hired for the fields, we plead with you not to turn your backs on the poor in rural America by passing a separate minimum wage, and leave the farm laborer to flounder in the backwater of congressional action.[29]

The 1966 amendments covered only agricultural laborers on large farms. This requirement alone excluded 65 percent of all farm workers. Local hand-harvest employees working less than 13 weeks a year and those paid on a piece-rate basis were also excluded. Together, these requirements meant that barely 30 percent of all farm workers were covered.[30]

Eligible farm workers were not covered on the same terms as others in the labor market who worked in stores, offices, and factories. Thus the 1966 amendments denied coverage to many farm workers and established a double standard.[31] The FLSA set a minimum wage for farm workers that was lower than for all others covered by the act. Additionally, covered farm workers were excluded from the time-and-a-half overtime provision.

The FLSA was amended again in 1974. Changes in the technical requirements for the coverage of farm workers increased by almost 10 percent the number of farms that would be included. Somehow, this slight extension was justified by the intention to preserve the historical exemption of the family owned and operated farm.[32] Unfortunately, there are farm workers other than those on family-operated farms, and they remained outside the coverage of the act.

The 1974 amendments did legislate parity for farm workers who were covered. The typical worker, who, according to the Labor Department, averages 1,500 work hours per year could not even rise to the poverty level ($3,643 in 1972 for a farm family of four) at the prevailing minimum wage rate. Statistics from the Department of Agriculture showed that in 1971 wages paid to hired farm workers represented about 8 percent of the farmer's total cash receipts, compared to 14 percent for 1950. Thus the farmer's labor costs as a percentage of his gross earnings were decreasing despite the inclusion of more farm workers under the minimum wage law. The Employment Standards Administration of the Labor Department estimated that the changes from the 1974 amendments would result in a net rise of only 0.2

of 1 cent on each food dollar—no remarkable burden on the consumer.[33]

The most recent FLSA law assured minimum wage parity for covered farm workers by 1978 (when the minimum wage rate went to $2.30 an hour) and phased out all the overtime exemptions by 1977. However, the majority of the farm workers left out of the 1966 amendments are still unprotected; when they will achieve wage equality with the rest of the American labor force is unknown.

CHILD LABOR

In all my travels visiting migrant farm workers, it was a common fact of life that children were working or idling in the fields with their working parents. Families of orange pickers working in Florida groves divided their labors to assure a higher piece rate and daily wage: fathers climbed long ladders to shake loose the oranges while their children crawled under the trees to gather the fallen fruit, which their mothers would package. Families of blacks in the Carolinas and Chicanos in Colorado crawled along miles of lanes of vegetables, pulling, trimming, and gathering during 12-hour workdays. Children worked beside their parents; infants waited nearby until the early day in their lives when their turn would come to work. Children of all ages could and did perform farm work until 1966, when the FLSA was amended to bring agricultural laborers under its child labor provisions.

The original FLSA prohibited full-time employment of children under age 16, and prohibited youngsters between 16 and 18 from working in occupations deemed "particularly hazardous." The 1966 amendments covered farm employers but applied different, less restrictive standards to children employed in agriculture. While the employment of children under 16 is prohibited during school hours, children of any age can do farm work after school and during vacations, almost without restriction. Children under 12 can work on a farm owned or operated by their parents and can hand-harvest with their parents' consent on smaller farms exempt from FLSA minimum wage protection. Since many of the nation's farms are small, use only a few farm workers, and thus are exempt, most children doing farm work are unprotected. Additionally, children between 16 and 18 now may perform "particularly hazardous" work in agriculture.

A 1970 study by the Department of Agriculture estimated that 800,000 children under 16 were employed as farm workers.

Of these, 375,000 were between 10 and 13 years old. These children represented between one-quarter and one-half of all hired farm workers (excluding children who worked on their parents' farms).[34]

Enforcement of the basic school-hour restriction is negligible. In 1970 the Wage and Hour Division of the Labor Department inspected only 1,000 of the approximately 3 million farms in the United States to detect child labor violations. What it found on these farms probably is typical of those it did not inspect; at over half the places, employers had violated some child labor provisions, and more than 90 percent of the infractions involved children working while school was in session.

Since all farm workers were excluded from the original FLSA in 1938, farm workers' children never were covered by the original child labor provisions. The reason for this shocking neglect was the continuing misconception that agriculture was not hard, difficult, or dangerous labor.[35]

At the time of the first child labor laws it was assumed that [oppressive child labor] did not exist in agriculture. Most people raised in rural areas remember the hard work of farm life, but they also remember the strength and the good health that that work seemed to bring them. No one thought that children helping with the seasonal harvest, which was an event that involved virtually the entire community, was a form of exploitation. It was a simple necessity, especially in locations which had no other source to meet enormous short-term labor needs.[36]

More recently, child labor on farms has been recognized to be as oppressive as the child labor in factories that was prohibited in 1938. In a National Safety Council's annual publication, "Accident Facts, 1970," statistics revealed that out of 14,200 occupational deaths in 1969 in a total work force of 79 million people, agriculture, which employed only 3.8 million workers, accounted for 2,500 deaths (as well as 210,000 disabling injuries). Manufacturing (with 20 million workers) accounted for only 1,900 occupational fatalities.[37]

Children doing farm work had more than their share of these agricultural accidents. The Department of Labor analyzed fatal farm tractor accidents in one state over a 10-year period and reported that 19 percent of the victims were under 16 years of age. Commenting on the tragedy that is not sensed in these statistics, a Senate labor committee noted:

Many of the horror stories over the last few years involve fatal or near fatal accidents involving very young children. Typically these accident statistics are tabulated and the totals tend to obscure rather than disclose such tragedies as the 8-year old boy suffocated when he was sucked into and buried under two feet of grain in a wheat bin while helping his cousins load wheat, or the 13-year old boy who lost his left arm just below the shoulder in a potato harvester.[38]

Children doing farm work suffered ill health atypical of their age group. In 1970 an investigating committee of pediatricians in Texas found that almost every child agricultural laborer examined had some physical defect. The children were undersized, thin, anemic, and apathetic. The doctors uncovered in these children many cases of back, hip, and lower extremity pain, which resembled degenerative osteoarthritis usually found in older people.[39]

Farm workers' children also suffer educationally. In 1970 the Department of Labor found that over half (57 percent) of those children found to have been employed illegally on farms were below normal school grade level. For migrants, 68 percent of such children were below average, with 86 percent of the 14-year-olds and 91 percent of the 15-year-olds below proper grade level (from one to three grades behind).[40]

In a Senate committee report on the 1966 FLSA amendments, senators Jacob Javits and Harrison Williams expressed support for tougher child farm labor restrictions:

[W]hat we condemned with indignation over a generation ago in the textile mills and industrial plants of this Nation we continue to accept in an often equally oppressive form—agricultural child labor. There are the long hours, the same negligible pay, the same backbreaking work, the same exposure to the elements, the lack of educational opportunity despite the nominal restrictions on working "during school hours"—all the same practices which deprive the child of a real childhood.

Recent hearings by the Senate Migratory Labor Subcommittee revealed case after case of children employed under circumstances closely resembling the textile mill conditions we outlawed so long ago.[41]

Arguing that the Senate committee bill was not strong enough, these senators described the youngsters who would be affected by a weak law:

Nor can it be said that we are dealing with a few middle-class children gamboling in the fields, eating strawberries as they go, perhaps to pick up a few dollars for a Fourth of July weekend at the beach.

On the contrary, the child we seek to protect is among the most oppressed and deprived of our citizens—the child of a Mexican-American family living far below the poverty level, whose parents, for lack of a permanent residence, cannot even vote and therefore exert no political influence, whose parents have no legal right to collective bargaining. In sum, this is a child who desperately needs to be brought in from the fields and made a part of the society which the rest of our children take for granted.[42]

In 1974 when further amendments were proposed to strengthen the child labor provisions of the FLSA, the Senate committee said:

Thirty-five years ago, Congress reacted to a national outcry by banning industrial child labor. However, since 1938 the nation has permitted in the fields what it has prohibited in the factories—oppressive and scandalous child labor. The committee once again urges that this shameful double standard be no longer tolerated.[43]

The committee pinpointed the reasons for expanding this protective legislation:

Basically there emerged three reasons; each are sufficient by and of itself, as to why child labor in agriculture in its present form must be ended: (1) It is physically and mentally detrimental to the health and well-being of the children; (2) it is a social depressant, stunting the intellectual growth and opportunity of those subject to the vicious cycle; and (3) it is, as was industrial child labor years before, economic exploitation of human resources.[44]

Despite these humanitarian protestations, the child labor provisions of FLSA were left unchanged.

Another chapter in this shameful saga took place in 1974 when the strawberry farmers in Oregon (supported by the potato growers in Maine) asked Congress to allow children under 12 to pick strawberries during summer vacation. The Oregon senators, Mark Hatfield and Robert Packwood, introduced a bill to allow children under the age of 12 to work if the pay was piece rate and the secretary of labor found four conditions: (1) employment was not for more than 13 weeks in any calendar year, (2) the child commuted to his or her permanent residence each day; (3) the child was not employed during school hours, and (4) the nature of the work was not deleterious to the health or well-being of the child.

The Oregon strawberry industry felt imperiled by the growth of Mexico's strawberry crop, and the Maine potato farmers were worried about their source of cheap labor; both groups testified in favor of this legislation. The Oregon senators testified that as children they picked strawberries and that this work, which occurs during the summer, would not be deleterious to a child's health. Yet one Oregon state legislator stated that Oregon's high unemployment rolls would fill the gap left by the children and that the abuse of restrictions on hours worked made such labor oppressive for young children.[45] A representative of the Oregon State Chicano Council also testified that adult migrant workers needed these jobs. He hoped that the requests of a few thousand children would not be used as a predicate to overturn a good law:

[I am] surprised at how 2,000 letters from children make our congressional delegation get very concerned about seasonal farm work when in the past 56,000 seasonal farm workers and 2 million farm workers nationally have not influenced them. . . .[46]

At the hearing held in Presque Isle, Maine, on this proposed change most of the witnesses supported the amendment.

The bill died in subcommittee. Unknown to the witnesses, the committee had made a deal with the Oregon and Maine senators. In return for holding hearings in the home states of the interested senators, it was agreed that the committee would not take action on the bill, according to a Senate staffer.

While further amendments will be proposed to coordinate the FLSA requirements with current economic changes, it remains questionable whether a more equitable minimum wage or age bill will be passed. The strong farm bloc is likely to go to the barricades over minimum wage changes. Since age and wage regulations tend to be treated together, both are likely to meet strong opposition. Thus the more appealing pleas of liberal congressional advocates for minimum age laws may get lost in the more continuous fight to limit coverage of the minimum wage laws.

UNEMPLOYMENT INSURANCE

Unemployment insurance provides partial income maintenance, as a matter of right, to workers who are unemployed involuntarily. This humanistic program aims to preserve purchasing power, enable a worker to meet nondeferrable expenses, and stabilize the economy.[47] Under the current program, all employers of eligible employees must pay a federal unemployment tax, which is a percentage of a set figure (based on wages) established by statute. Unlike Social Security taxes, employees do not pay a portion of the unemployment insurance tax. Employers contributing to federally approved state unemployment compensation programs receive a credit of up to 90 percent against the federal tax.[48] State-held monies are deposited in a federal unemployment insurance trust fund from which distributions are made to eligible employees.

From 1935, when agricultural labor originally was excluded

from the first unemployment insurance coverage, until the Unemployment Compensation Amendments of 1976, when coverage was extended to agricultural labor on a limited basis, there has been continuing resistance by farm employers and congressional representatives to provide farm workers with benefits that routinely are available to the majority of the nation's workers.

The original legislation establishing the unemployment compensation program was part of the Social Security Act of 1935. At the beginning of the Depression in the early 1930s, no state or federal provision existed for unemployment compensation. Relief, such as it was, came from public charities, which were poorly organized and offered inadequate assistance. Not until the country experienced the extensive unemployment of the Depression were the limitations of local soup kitchens and community chests understood.[49] Although legislation was passed in Wisconsin in 1932, the nearly uniform failure of other state legislatures to enact unemployment laws led to pressure for federal action.[50]

In a message to Congress in 1934, President Franklin D. Roosevelt stated that he sought "a sound means to provide at once security against several of the great disturbing factors in life—especially those which relate to unemployment and old age."[51] The president created a Committee on Economic Security, chaired by Secretary of Labor Frances Perkins.[52] After debating whether the nationwide system mandated by federal law should be administered on the federal or state level, a state-administered system, favored by the president, was adopted.[53]

The committee did not recommend the exclusion of any specified industries from unemployment compensation coverage.[54] Nonetheless, the bill passed by Congress excluded agricultural employers from the definition of those who were required to pay the federal unemployment tax. The difficulty of maintaining records on numerous small farms and migrant farm workers as well as the experimental nature of the entire Social Security package were offered as reasons for the exclusion.[55]

In 1939 the Social Security Board recommended that unemployment insurance coverage be extended to at least the large agricultural employers. Instead, Congress broadened the original exclusion of "agricultural labor" to include related activities concerning the processing of agricultural commodities (storage, transportation, and handling). It also extended the definition of "farm," and defined agriculture more inclusively.[56] The expansion was largely a product of pressure exerted by agricultural employer groups. This broad exemption of agricultural employees remained for a decade.

In 1950 the definition of agricultural labor in the Old Age,

Survivors, and Disability Insurance (OASDI) program was amended to include coverage for most agricultural laborers. The definition of agricultural labor in the related unemployment compensation program was unchanged, however, until 1970 when the Senate Finance Committee proposed extending unemployment insurance coverage to a large number of farm workers. The Senate report suggested that an initial extension of coverage to some larger farm employers would provide the unemployment insurance program with the experience to assess the administrative and cost impact.[57] Instead, the definition was altered to conform with the applicable OASDI provisions.[58] That definition of agricultural labor, as applied to unemployment compensation, provided coverage for several processing functions performed in the course of preparing food for delivery to market. The intent was to continue to exclude from coverage employees involved in processing services that were an integral part of farm operations and to extend coverage to employees engaged in processing as a separate off-the-farm activity for several farm operators.

The rejection of the Senate proposal in the conference committee probably stemmed from recurrent fears of enormous financial burdens and administrative red tape that would be imposed on farm owners if agricultural laborers were eligible for unemployment insurance. The 1970 amendments also exclude from "agricultural labor" services performed in connection with production and harvesting.[59] In addition to promoting statutory uniformity, the new definition provided coverage for approximately 190,000 off-the-farm agricultural workers. The majority of the nation's farm workers, however, remained outside the coverage of the federal unemployment compensation law.

The first significant breakthrough for farm workers did not come until 1974 with the advent of special unemployment assistance benefits. In response to alarmingly high unemployment, Congress passed an act providing temporary unemployment benefits to workers not previously eligible under state or federal law. Over a million farm workers were included in this coverage.[60] Although special unemployment assistance was extended in 1975, it expired at the close of 1976.

By 1975 the cumulative experience with coverage of agricultural labor under special unemployment assistance and OASDI, with some unemployment insurance under state programs, and a growing recognition of the inequitable position imposed on farm workers prompted consideration of a permanent extension of unemployment compensation to them.[61] One bill proposed by the House Ways and Means Committee provided that employers

Field packing, California.

meeting minimal standards involving the use of farm labor would be subject to the federal unemployment tax. Doubts about the impact of this coverage weighed on the minds of the drafters, and they did not adopt the broader definition of ''employer'' that applies to nonfarm labor.[62]

In support of an evolutionary approach, the House report noted that many nonfarm laborers of large agricultural businesses already were covered by unemployment compensation programs. It also cited Labor Department studies indicating that the potential cost of providing unemployment compensation benefits to farm workers would have little or no impact on the overall rates for unemployment insurance.[63]

The bill proposed by the Senate Finance Committee reflected the continuing fears of farm operators. It contained no proposal for extending coverage to farm workers. During Senate hearings, concern was voiced by an American Farm Bureau Federation representative that family-owned farming operations would suffer financially; that migrants would cease to follow crops, preferring simply to collect unemployment benefits; and that the seasonal employment of farm workers made it impossible to maintain accurate records.[64] These sentiments, particularly the fear of rising costs, were echoed by other witnesses.

A telling comment on the Senate position is the fact that in two days of hearings on the bill, none of the testimony or statements submitted to the committee came from farm workers or their organizations. According to a staff member who worked on the Senate proposal, opposition to coverage stemmed from the beliefs of senators that, because of its seasonal nature, agricultural labor is different from other types of employment for which unemployment compensation is available. They assumed that rather than being characterized by steady, permanent employment, agriculture is typified by periodic hiring and layoffs. They envisioned a parade of seasonal employees routinely out of work and collecting unemployment benefits. Their fear was that workers would work on one crop and then proceed to collect unemployment insurance for the remainder of the year. Their continuing concern with protecting small farmers from exorbitant costs also was influential.

The AFL-CIO argued to the Senate Finance Committee that farm workers should receive the same protection as other workers:

> Extending coverage to all farm workers would benefit farm workers, farm employers, and agricultural communities. It would help stabilize the farm work force; it would reduce the labor turnover cost and recruitment cost. Farm workers, who now work in both covered and uncovered employment, would be more apt to remain in the farm work force if their total employment was covered and used to determine eligibility for benefits. The worker would then be able to maintain his home and family without seeking demeaning public assistance, as he must now do all too often. Farm workers are entitled to the same legislative protection as all other workers.[65]

On the House floor, the relatively inclusive quarterly wage figure in the House bill was changed (from $5,000 to $10,000) to appease farmers.[66] The compromise bill that emerged from the conference committee provided that the more sizable agricultural employers be subject to federal unemployment compensation taxes.[67] In contrast to the original House proposal, which would have provided federal coverage for 710,000 farm jobs, the Labor Department bill that passed extended the coverage to approximately 459,000 farm jobs.[68] Although a major advance had been attained, the inevitable whittling process made its mark on the controversial provision.

Agricultural labor originally was excluded from unemployment coverage because of the fear that it would not be feasible administratively to maintain records of small farmers or migrant workers who moved from state to state.[69] The difficulty of defining when a migrant farm worker became unemployed and of calculating the amount of wages earned on different farms seemed, and still seems to many observers, an insuperable obstacle to coverage. At the time of the original Unemployment Insurance Act, comparable legislation had covered few farm employees; that fact, combined with the experimental nature of the Social Security and unemployment compensation programs, contributed to congressional concern.[70]

The question of the administrative feasibility of including farm workers was compounded by the confusion over whether a crew leader or farm operator should be considered a worker's employer. The fear was that the responsibility for maintaining records would be hard to pinpoint.[71] Since the 1940s the administrative issue consistently has been raised in support of continued exclusion. In addition, fears of a shrinking labor supply due to farm workers opting to receive unemployment insurance, rather than traveling to find work, have fueled skeptics' arguments.

A 1972 Labor Department study surveyed the New England and mid-Atlantic states, Ohio, Florida, and Texas in an effort to determine the validity of these recurring questions. The study found that the mobility of farm workers would not make record keeping impossible. Ninety-five percent of migratory employees worked in three or fewer states, and 75 percent worked for only one or two employers.[72] As to the likelihood of their shirking work if unemployment compensation were made available, the study speculated that average annual wages were so low ($3,534) that it was improbable workers would sacrifice even a small portion of their meager salaries for the possibility of remaining in their home state and collecting unemployment insurance.[73]

Unemployment compensation benefits are computed as a percentage of an employee's regular salary. Although rates vary from state to state, maximum benefits generally approximate 50 percent of a worker's average weekly salary. To the extent that a migratory laborer chose not to follow the crops, his already modest regular income would be reduced. In addition, state laws require a minimum number of weeks to be worked by employees in order to be eligible for any unemployment benefits.

While costs would vary from state to state, the rate among the states surveyed would average 3 percent of employers' taxable payrolls,[74] certainly not a prohibitive rate. The House committee estimated the cost for coverage of agricultural employers under the 1976 amendments to be $19 million.

The question of administrative feasibility has been answered by several experiences. The few states that have provided unemployment insurance coverage,[75] the voluntary coverage elected by some farmers under several state programs, and the successful coverage of farm workers under special unemployment assistance and Social Security programs have demonstrated that coverage of farm workers can be accomplished without special difficulties.

To eliminate uncertainty about employer responsibility for record keeping, the 1976 amendments provide that the crew leader is to be deemed the employer if he is registered under the Farm Labor Contractor Registration Act or if he uses mechanized equipment. In all other cases, the farm operator is to be considered the employer for record keeping purposes.

The 1976 amendments resulted from pressures exerted by the vigorous farm lobby. In 1976, as in the past, the small farmer was portrayed as threatened with extinction if agricultural labor was covered. The original proposal would have eliminated the smaller farms from coverage. Surprisingly, in view of the historic arguments about coverage of farm workers generally, the present provision extends benefits to larger farms, which though fewer in number, are the employers of significant numbers of migrants.[76] The medium-sized dairy farm, for example, with one or two permanent, stable employees, remains uncovered.

The new federal law undoubtedly will result in comparable state coverage because of the federal tax credit available to employers who pay state unemployment compensation. The present amendments are a significant step in achieving coverage of agricultural labor. But the persistent opposition to insuring farm workers generally, which has endured for almost a half-century since unemployment first was recognized as a recurring national problem, reflects again the dreary reality of the farm workers' continuing lack of political power.

THE NATIONAL LABOR RELATIONS ACT

The National Labor Relations Act (NLRA), originally called

the Wagner Act, was passed in 1935. It was amended by the Taft-Hartley amendments in 1947 and the Landrum-Griffin amendments in 1959. Together they constitute the basic statutory framework governing labor-management relations in the United States. As the act originally was passed and as it continues today, agricultural workers are excluded from coverage. The reasons for this omission derive from arguments made at the time other New Deal legislation was debated; this exclusion of farm workers was barely discussed in the legislative history of the momentous Wagner Act.

The precedent of excluding farm workers was established with the passage of the various New Deal recovery programs.[77] There were two broad programs for economic recovery presented during the early 1930s, one for agriculture—the Agricultural Adjustment Act (AAA)—and one for industry—the National Industrial Recovery Act (NIRA). Convinced that the programs needed voluntary employer acceptance to be successful, Congress tried to adapt each program to the separate needs of the larger management groups whose support was deemed to be essential.

The process of accommodation accounts for the difference between the labor relations provisions of agricultural and industrial programs. The industrial bill was responsive to the demands and influence of organized labor, while the agricultural bill lacked any provisions for labor.

There are several reasons for the exclusion of agricultural members. First, the agricultural interests (meaning farmers, not the farm workers who were their employees) were adamantly opposed to the concepts of unionism and collective bargaining. One observer, writing of agriculture's opposition to the NIRA labor codes stated:

Farmers as a class are opposed to any form of labor organization. Attempts of the I.W.W. [International Workers of the World] in the past to organize migratory harvest hands have helped to give farmers a distaste for unionization of farm labor, a sentiment which deepened into hostility because of the tactics of the I.W.W. group in pulling strikes at critical times during the harvest season.[78]

This hostile attitude toward farm workers and the protective attitude toward farmers was shared by the Department of Agriculture, which administered the AAA.[79] The department's patronizing policy was that the interests of agricultural workers would be amply safeguarded as a consequence of benefits to be enjoyed (under the AAA) by the farmers who employed them.[80] The idea that benefits enjoyed by employers are passed on to their employees is a noble notion, but one that happens to undermine the essential rationale for laborers to organize for their own well-being.

The second reason for ignoring labor in the AAA was that the extent of unionization among agricultural workers at that time was negligible. What unions did exist were weak and ineffective and were not organized nationally. Therefore, whether farm workers opposed or supported the AAA was of little or no concern to the bill's sponsors, who did not hear from any farm labor groups. Farm worker attitudes were not considered; no witnesses testified in behalf of farm workers.

Thus the hostility of organized agricultural interests to unionism, the general public indifference to the problems of agricultural labor, and government (both Congress and the executive branch) policy of placating dominant political and economic interests combined to assure that farm workers received no protections in the package of New Deal recovery legislation.

The NIRA, however, did address the needs of workers. Under this act, a representative group from each industry could write a "code of fair competition" covering minimum wage, length of the work week, abolition of child labor, and other conditions of employment. Upon approval of the national recovery administrator, these regulations had the force of law.

Despite the lack of an explicit exclusion of farm workers in its language, in practice, agricultural workers had no rights under the NIRA.[81] The exact basis for their exclusion is unclear. There was one reference in the *Congressional Record* regarding the exclusion of agriculture from the NIRA administrative codes. Senator Robert Wagner of New York, who was the author of the basic act, testified before the House Ways and Means Committee and was asked if *all* individuals would come under the NIRA codes regarding hours, wages, and employment conditions. His reply was "yes." When asked whether agricultural workers were included, without explanation, he replied "no."[82]

Despite this single reference in the hearing, an argument can be made that the administrators of the act were the ones who excluded farm workers from coverage by the NIRA. The act was broad enough in principle and language to include farm workers. Indeed, the legal division of the AAA believed that the NIRA authorized a code for farm workers.[83]

Irrespective of the actual intentions of Congress, farm workers were likely to have been excluded because Section 3 (a) of the NIRA required, as a condition for code approval, a nationwide sponsoring body that was truly representative of the industry seeking the code. Since no nationally representative group of farm workers but only individuals or small associations submitted codes, farm workers could not be covered.[84]

Soon after their organization, the AAA and the NIRA debated the meaning of agricultural labor. Though the NIRA defined agricultural workers in terms of what they did rather than where they worked ("within the area of production" instead of "on the farm") the AAA ignored that definition and proceeded to deal with farm workers without reference to the NIRA labor codes. Faced with this fact, the NIRA adopted the AAA-preferred definition.[85] Thus the AAA was able to impose upon NIRA an artificial definition of agricultural labor—the classification would depend entirely on the location of the work and not on its nature.[86] According to Professor Austin P. Morris, who made a thorough analysis of the legislative history of the Wagner Act, "The basic policy of accommodation of dominant interests to obtain their voluntary support and cooperation in recovery programs is plainly evident here."[87] Different agencies and departments within agencies still disagree about the definition of farm workers.

While the political power of organized agricultural interests was the obvious influence on this decision, organized labor failed to object. "The same failure to speak out contributed to the ease with which agricultural labor was excluded from the NLRA."[88] The legislative history of this key act demonstrates that no one really represented the needs of agricultural labor.[89]

Senator Wagner's original bill applied to employees generally;[90] it did not exclude agricultural laborers. However, when the bill emerged from the Senate Committee on Education and Labor two months later, "employee" had been redefined to exclude agricultural workers, domestic servants, and those employed by a parent or spouse.[91] During the hearings, only one witness recommended excluding small farmers from coverage; but he had explicitly recommended coverage of large farms such as those operating in California's Imperial Valley.[92] Because of the controversial nature of the bill and the lack of administration support, Congress did not act in 1934.

In 1935, hearings were held on the reintroduced Wagner Bill. Again the needs of agricultural laborers were ignored and the agricultural exclusion was not discussed in the Senate hearings or debate. The Senate committee report noted only that it was administratively wise to exclude farm workers, domestic servants, and persons employed by a parent or spouse.[93] Years later, when Norman Thomas appeared as a witness before the Senate Subcommittee on Migratory Labor, he testified that Senator Wagner had written to him saying that the opposition of the farm bloc made coverage of agricultural labor under his bill out of the question.[94]

Although not discussed in the House committee hearings, the minority report of the House Committee on Labor urged the inclusion of farm labor, a plea repeated on the House floor by New York City Congressman Vito Marcantonio:

[T]here is not a single solitary reason why agricultural workers should not be included under the provisions of this bill. The same reasons urged for the adoption of this bill on behalf of industrial workers are equally applicable in the case of agricultural workers, in fact more so, as their plight calls for immediate and prompt action.[95]

Congressman Marcantonio's amendment striking out the farm worker exclusion was easily defeated when Congressman William Connery of Massachusetts, the bill's sponsor and chairman of the labor committee, argued the specious case for exclusion:[96]

[T]he committee discussed the matter carefully in executive session and decided not to include agricultural workers. We hope that the agricultural workers will be taken care of. . . . I am in favor of giving agricultural workers every protection, but just now I believe in biting off one mouthful at a time. If we can get this bill through and get it working properly, there will be opportunity later, and I hope soon, to take care of the agricultural workers.[97]

The political realities of getting the bill passed eclipsed the needs of one weak constituency despite its natural claims for inclusion.

Agricultural workers were excluded in that same session from benefits of the Social Security Act; again, administrative difficulties were the announced rationale.[98] The decision to exclude farm workers was made during executive sessions of the House Ways and Means Committee. One of the staff draftsmen candidly stated, ''The committee was influenced far less by the difficulties of administration than by the fact that it was felt that farmers would object to being taxed for the old age insurance protection for their employees.''[99] Without political muscle or sophistication of their own, farm workers succumbed to the power of the farm bloc, which wanted farm workers excluded from the Wagner Act and other New Deal legislation.

After reviewing this sorry treatment of the farm worker in the Wagner Act legislative history, Professor Morris concluded:

The exclusion of agricultural labor from the NLRA without public hearing, discussion or debate on the merits is not extraordinary considering the sensitivity of Congress to agricultural sentiment—which was well known to be solidly opposed to unionism—and the failure of anyone, in or out of Congress, to force a dialogue on the issues involved. There was therefore no need for agricultural interests to justify their opposition before the public with any kind of reasoned argument.[100]

In making the case against the unionization of farm workers, the same arguments are repeated: the perishable nature of agricultural products; the consequent need for uninterrupted harvesting and preparation for market; and the employers' lack of control over such conditions as weather, production, and prices. Opponents of coverage admonish that the nation must be protected from radical union leaders who would attempt to gain control of the country's food supply through domination of the farm work force; they argue that the National Labor Relations Board already had created chaos in the food packing industry among those employers covered by the NLRA.

The standby excuse of administrative difficulties is repeated by farm bloc witnesses who have described an illusory equality of bargaining power between farm employers and employees. Witnesses rarely appear on behalf of the farm workers.[101] Considering these pressures from the farm bloc, it is not surprising that farm workers have not fared well in legislative deliberations. Congress has refused to impede union efforts to organize the food processing industry by exempting its workers from the NLRA; in doing so, it has perpetuated the one departure from the general exclusion of farm workers. The process of organization in that industry has amply demonstrated that agriculture's fears of the labor movement were largely irrational, according to one study.[102] Farm workers in the fields still remain excluded from the provisions of the NLRA. An exception continues for those who pack, rather than pick, our crops.

The subject was debated again in 1965–66 before the Senate Subcommittee on Migratory Labor, which considered several bills affecting migrant laborers, including one that would have extended the NLRA for farm workers. The arguments in 1966 were the same as those used in 1939. This viewpoint was articulated by an American Farm Bureau Federation witness:

The unique feature of the employment relationship in agriculture is the vulnerability of the farmer to any work stoppage on his farm. . . . Come what may he must get his crops harvested. He must therefore accede to almost any demand upon him at harvest time which is necessary to prevent a work stoppage no matter how unreasonable or arbitrary the demand may be. Collective bargaining would not equalize the bargaining power of farmers and workers; it would make farmers subservient to labor union leaders.[103]

The same old arguments were paraded before the committee: the difficulty of absorbing added labor costs and the impossibility of passing them on to consumers, the fear that labor unions would have a sinister monopoly over agricultural labor and would control and manipulate the nation's food supply, and the specter of administrative difficulties. In addition, a few phantom problems were conjured: the unconstitutionality of the extension, a potential increase in unemployment that would hurt the very people it was designed to help, and the fears that farmers would be squeezed and agricultural business would be forced to move outside the United States. Instead of portraying the farm as an idyllic setting of harmonious labor relations, however, these witnesses emphasized the haphazard character of farm work, particularly its seasonal nature.[104]

The testimony from those opposing the exclusion was not much more helpful. Representatives of farm-allied unions, farm worker unions, and self-help and community action agencies did not constructively or specifically criticize the positions advanced by agriculture. These witnesses talked of abstract values like justice and equality under the law; they denied any rational basis for the exemption, but they did not address the farmers' real fears of strikes during harvest and the potential for union control of their operations.[105] They did not mention the 30 years of successful collective bargaining in the food processing industry nor the successful unionization of the dairy industry. Only one witness mentioned the field workers in Hawaii who had been represented for over 20 years by the International Longshoremen's and Warehousemen's Union (ILWU) and the fact that they have gained benefits comparable to those enjoyed by nonagricultural workers.[106]

Indeed, the Hawaiian experience provides a rebuttal to most of the farm bloc arguments. In 1945 the Hawaii legislature passed the Hawaii Employment Relations Act, which extended the rights and responsibilities of the NLRA to agricultural workers there. Within a year, the ILWU, which already had organized the dock workers, was accepted as the sugar workers' bargaining agent on all large Hawaiian plantations. After years of negotiating collective bargaining agreements and having only one sugar strike (in 1946), "conciliators and others close to the parties agree that bargaining today [in Hawaii] is as mature as anywhere in the United States and that the balance of power between management and the unions is approximately even."[107] This actual experience should have outweighed traditional fears; it is real evidence that there can be a stable, strike-free development of farmer–farm worker labor relations.

In 1967 the Senate Subcommittee on Migratory Labor held additional hearings on whether to extend the NLRA to agricultural workers. Many of the same witnesses testified and repeated their earlier testimony. But perhaps the most damaging statement of all came from Cesar Chavez, representing the United Farm Workers Organizing Committee. He testified against extending the existing NLRA to farm workers. Chavez wanted it both ways. He proposed a bill similar to the original Wagner Act that would provide recognition for farm worker unions, require good faith bargaining from employers, and freedom from employer interference and domination. But since his union was relatively new, Chavez felt it should be allowed to mature under the same conditons that governed industrial unions between 1935 and 1947, before the Taft-Hartley amendments added restrictions on union use of secondary boycotts and picketing. He painted a picture of employers bargaining in good faith through the harvest season, then refusing to agree to terms once most seasonal workers had left. Without the availability of consumer boycotts, the unions would have little leverage against the power of their employers.[108]

Again, farm workers received nothing. Their continued exclusion from the NLRA was best summarized by Professor Morris:

As the years have passed, the disadvantaged status of agricultural labor, particularly the seasonal farm worker, has not changed. The same forces that prevented legislation from being enacted twenty or thirty years ago are active today. . . . [Yet] the history of organized labor in the food processing industry . . . more than demonstrates the insufficiency, the irrelevancy, and the poverty of agriculture's position against legislation which would protect their workers in any attempt at self-organization.

The long exclusion of farm workers from the nation's labor legislation is not entirely a result of agriculture's political power. While it is undeniably a major factor, it must be admitted that the public at large, farm workers themselves, and particularly the forces of organized labor have, until recently, never resisted, nor even protested the flow of legislative events. Congressmen are not insensitive to the needs of the people. They are capable of resisting the pressures of special interests to achieve necessary legislation; but they need more support than they have received to date if they are to enact legislation to protect farm workers by equalizing their bargaining position.[109]

How the farm worker labor movement, not protected by federal law, floundered for half a century and how a union survived and eventually took root is the fascinating story that follows.

8

A MIRACLE IN THE MAKING

I⊤ WAS a logical evolution. Having been exploited by their fellowmen, overwhelmed by powerful forces in the marketplace, and ignored or disappointed by their representatives in politics and their benefactors in government, farm workers eventually would have to organize themselves to act collectively in their own interests and to become a social and political force in their own right. And they would have to accomplish this task without the help of federal laws and the administrative apparatus so critical to every other group of workers who unionized.

The story of this evolution is a melodrama that is still unfolding. It is not hyperbole to say that the evolution of the farm workers' union is a miracle in the making; history demonstrates that it is too soon to say more. One scholar called the farm labor movement "a never-ending saga," one that is likely to continue "until mechanization has eliminated the last farm laborer and all the orchards and vineyards have been ripped out to make way for jerry-built subdivisions."[1]

Fifty years of social history had set the scene. Early in this century, farm workers were unorganized, vulnerable, and unequal participants in the farm labor marketplace. All national labor relations laws as well as most major social welfare legislation since the New Deal excluded farm workers from coverage. The same worn-out arguments against farm worker unions are used whenever the subject is raised: the threat to consumers that food costs will rise sky-high; the farmers' fear that labor unions will manipulate the nation's food supply; and that classic bugaboo of social planners, administrative inconvenience.

The power and energy of the farm bloc never has been equaled by farm workers, who as a group generally have been unsophisticated, poor, and unrepresented. No one has presented their compelling case to the public very well nor pointed to the successful unionization of comparable industries.

Without a national labor law to govern their employment relations with farmers, growers, and ranchers, farm workers—who were an unlikely group of people to organize for collective bargaining purposes in any event—came to unionism late and only after bitter, intermittent attempts to do so had been regularly and violently challenged for a half-century.[2]

Until the mid-twentieth century, there were few union successes in organizing field workers. One labor historian reported, "The labor contract continued to be regarded as a personal bargain between equals, even when the employer was an absentee bank or land corporation bound by the rules of a trade association."[3] Little was done by agricultural employers to come to grips with the fundamental problems faced by agricultural workers, problems that periodically sparked bloody encounters and were likely to continue to do so.

Protective labor and welfare legislation ignored agricultural workers. There were few meaningful improvements regarding wages, living conditions, or job security; indeed, the very structure of farming in America continued to be predicated upon large supplies of cheap, mobile, passive seasonal laborers.

Until the problems of farm workers could be addressed realistically in a context where they themselves had a real role, the situation would remain explosive and the likelihood would continue that what should have been a matter of normal labor relations would become instead the waging of a class war. One historian of the farm labor movements prophesied:

> As long as wage levels and working conditions remain substantially inferior to those in urban occupations, labor unrest, unionism, and strikes will continue in rural areas. In the last analysis, farm laborers can gain economic security and improve their working conditions only if they can organize in large numbers as an economic and political pressure group.[4]

The story of the numerous attempts during the first half of the twentieth century to begin a farm worker union in the United States is one of violence, frustration, and failure. Time and again, different unions attempted to organize farm workers, only to be crushed by powerful landowners and their associations, invariably supported by local power structures, including the press, police, and politicians.[5]

As one reads about the different attempts to unionize farm workers, a recurring scenario evolves. Invariably, growers either allowed or promoted conditions so oppressive that hard-working laborers who ordinarily were passive and disorganized became susceptible to outside organizers who saw their work and circumstances as a ripe situation for political action. In turn, the growers—who as part of their local agricultural society had a powerful establishment behind them—instead of dealing with legitimate labor grievances, seized on worker demands as evidence of their bad faith, overreacted, intimidated organizers, and violently crushed all incipient union movements. Conditions continued or worsened; and, in repeating cycles, other organizing efforts would be initiated.

Until the efforts of Cesar Chavez resulted in the organization of the United Farm Workers in the 1960s, that same phenomenon recurred numerous times. The precipitating issues were always the same: discrimination, lack of social welfare benefits, uncertain availability of work, atrocious work conditions, and most of all, poor wages.

There is an irony about this cycle. Farmers have great and positive economic and political power, which could be used to ensure a satisfied, stable, proficient class of farm workers. Yet they use these potentially positive powers in a negative fashion; they are used in a selfish, short-term interest and eventually they are inimical to the long-term interests of themselves and their industry.

Farm workers have few economic powers, and they are negative ones. Work is seasonal; the products are perishable and their ability to waste crops is implicit. Rarely has this power been used, however, though the farm workers' claims to economic justice have no other practical force behind them.

Farmers deplore farm worker unions; yet they do nothing to avoid the only climate in which unions can thrive. They insist on the same provocative conditions that breed unionism, pushing a group unlikely to have taken such a course to turn to it in self-defense. Thus farmers have been forced to face the one power they cannot ignore or overwhelm by reason of their own tactics, and farm workers have been pressed to organize their unique work force to gain what rights they always should have had as a result of a normal marketplace operating in a proper system of private enterprise.

EARLY ORGANIZATION EFFORTS

The first concerted attempt to unionize farm workers was made by the Industrial Workers of the World (IWW or Wobblies, as they were known). Their utopian idea was to create a classless society by organizing the unskilled working classes to take over American industry. To Wobblies, what was involved was not a union movement but an utter class struggle. The Communist and Socialist parties took part in the IWW union movement. In their view, the American Federation of Labor (AFL) was a racist and elitist union that played into the hands of the middle and upper classes by adopting an unfair system and working within it. Their attitude was that "the state" was run by the wealthy management class, which exploited workers. Organized religion played along by helping the workers forget what was happening to them in the fields today in the hope that there would be a better tomorrow. Indeed, it was not until decades later that the major organized union movement (along with the Roman Catholic church) seriously supported local efforts to unionize farm workers.

For the first half of the century, organized labor concentrated its efforts and resources on the urban-centered trade and craft unions, in what one historian called "violent campaigns of raw self-help." The IWW at first dealt with unskilled workers in mass production in northeastern and midwestern cities. Then it turned to the farm workers, who had been neglected by the major unions.

One tactic always used by agricultural employers to frustrate the labor movement has been the employment of foreign workers. Poorer and more desperate than their American counterparts, the laborers of various underdeveloped foreign countries have been imported periodically to work for what by our standards were depressed hourly wage rates, under inhuman conditions. Asians from China, Japan, and the Philippines have been imported in large numbers to work on California farms and ranches. Braceros and other Mexicans have worked in large numbers in the Southwest. East and West Indians and Middle Easterners have also been imported to work in American fields in the place of more assertive American workers. American migrants have even been moved around by exploitative farm employers to break strikes and depress wage rates. In exploiting the poverty and lack of opportunity in other countries and other places, then, American farmers have been able to keep American farm workers at the very bottom of the economic ladder, working under intolerable conditions.

Some imported workers remained in the United States as a permanent part of the agricultural work force. While originally used to frustrate the incipient labor movement in the fields, they would eventually become the grandparents of the farm workers' labor movement.

The first recorded strike by farm workers in the United States was conducted by Chinese laborers in the Kern County, California, hop fields in 1884. In the early 1900s Mexican and Japanese workers struck, but the AFL refused to support them. Historians have attributed the failure of these first strikes to the alienation of the workers from the mainstream labor movement because of their strange languages and cultures.

Pressures would continue to grow. Agricultural employers pursued their profits, creating incendiary conditions that pushed workers beyond the breaking point. In addition to profits from their crops, many farmers made money by exploiting their laborers as well.

By 1915 the IWW had organized 40 groups under the Agricultural Workers Organization. Their leaders, however, were interested in proselytizing as much as in organizing; as a result, many were prosecuted for revolutionary and antiwar tactics as part of a broad social reaction to their movement.

By the early 1920s World War I had ended and so had the first agricultural labor union. Field workers were worse off than before; grower associations increased as farm worker labor organizations diminished in size and number.

As could be expected, conditions in American fields worsened. By the 1930s, there were more strikes; 140 have been chronicled. Following the Mexican Revolution in 1910, hundreds of thousands of Mexican farm workers had flooded into California, settling into barrios, seeking work in the fields, and organizing mutual aid societies to cope with their social problems. Though the farm employers were happy to have them as workers, whenever they struck to protest abuses, they were deported.

Cannery workers and field workers, especially in California, were brought together into an integrated agricultural union. But, for political reasons tangential to their union's agenda, the organizers were victimized by law enforcement authorities who were the handmaidens of the dominant community interests—the stores, banks, press, and legislators. In agricultural areas all these institutions were sympathetic to the growers; so the politics of the organizers defeated the cause of the farm workers.

Federal subsidies went to growers. Vigilante raiding parties victimized union organizers and farm workers. Workers who protested conditions were blackballed. Occasional minor victories were eclipsed by the overwhelming, reactionary responses of the growers. Farm workers would take two steps forward only to be pushed back three. Union organizers were equated with foreign interests; they were considered anti-American agitators. The prevailing propaganda was that a farm worker union would kill American agriculture.

This myth resulted in bad laws and pernicious law enforcement. Agriculture controlled the legislatures, which passed anti-union and antistrike laws. To unionize was considered a crime; a strike was deemed a conspiracy. The farm workers' case was portrayed as an attempt to control agriculture and revolutionize American economic relationships. Leaders of the unions that sprang up were persecuted and imprisoned; eventually their organizations faded away.

The Communist party founded the Trade Union Unity League in 1929 in another attempt to organize farm workers; again, there was a hidden agenda that was more meaningful to the organizers than to the organized. The Communist party had decided to discard its strategy of boring from within established unions and instead to start its own to fight capitalism on behalf of the exploited classes.

Sharecroppers and tenant farmers in Arkansas and nearby states were organized by the Socialist party's union to challenge the planters who were exploiting them. This vast culture of black workers was the by-product of the emancipation of slaves after the Civil War. They found, however, that this emancipation was not complete; they lived under total control of the owners on plantations, which were run like company towns.

Federal programs aimed at alleviating economic problems in the South supported the farmers and ended up hurting farm workers. Plantation owners were paid to plant less so they could raise prices and cut their roster of workers. Farms were vast; many were in the hands of absentee owners. Machines were brought in, and large numbers of workers were displaced.

The Southern Tenant Farmers Union was set up with funds from the Socialist party; eventually it had 25,000 members from Oklahoma, Texas, Missouri, Mississippi, and Arkansas. But union workers were harassed. Convicts were used in some states to replace them. Brief ties with traditional Committee of Industrial Organization (CIO) and AFL unions did not last; this rural union was too idiosyncratic and regional to mesh with the bigger, urban meatcutters' or packinghouse workers' unions.

The phenomenon by which urban intellectuals used the exploitation of farm workers as a foil in their class warfare and as a vehicle of propaganda in their attempts to create a better society characterized most early attempts to unionize farm workers. Decades later, Cesar Chavez would recognize this fatal flaw and build into his later and successful union the requirement that it be led and run by farm workers.

Other attempts to unionize farm workers failed in the 1950s and 1960s. The AFL organized cannery workers, and the Teamsters Union went after "everything on wheels." But there was continuing reluctance on the part of organized labor to deal effectively with the special, aggravated, and explosive problems of workers in the fields. As one AFL official in California said, "Only fanatics are willing to live in shacks or tents and get their heads broken in the interest of migratory labor."

In the 1930s, two catastrophic phenomena added to the explosive mix of conditions already existing in the California agricultural labor market. A national economic depression forced vast numbers of workers into unemployment; and extraordinary weather conditions in the Southwest created a dust bowl of Oklahoma, Texas, Arkansas, and Missouri.

This combination resulted in sudden and massive unemployment and the emergence of a labor force of over 300,000 uprooted workers who moved to California with their families, seeking to work its rich land. They came in droves, creating vast camps of oppressed and impoverished workers. They were ripe to be organized; and one after another the unions attempted to do so—the cannery workers, packers, CIO, AFL—but no effective and lasting unionization took place, and conditions worsened.[6] By 1940 a Senate Committee chaired by Senator Robert La Follette of Wisconsin was exposing to the nation the horrific living and working conditions of farm workers, which we since have come to know and indeed to view as their natural state.

In the long, sad history of the farm worker labor union movement, there is one successful episode. That was in Hawaii where sugar and pineapple plantation workers were organized by an extraordinary CIO labor leader, Jack Hall. Because Hawaii was surrounded by water, it was a natural place for the CIO to organize longshoremen and dockworkers. Because the longshoremen could stop the exportation of plantation crops, Hall was able to successfully organize the agricultural workers as well. To add field laborers to that powerful existing union was a natural step.

Five big companies had owned and influenced everything on the island. They imported workers from all over Asia and Europe and kept them oppressed, isolated, and disorganized. Hall's success in organizing the International Longshoremen and

Warehousemen's Union resulted in his gaining influence in the legislature. An Employment Relations Act was passed, giving the farm workers the right to unionize and providing them with welfare benefits. Soon the union had 30,000 members, making up a significant percentage of the population.

Hall ended the perquisite system by which the farm workers were paid in perks (homes, services, and the like), which tied them to employers and a system of enslavement. After some successful strikes, adequate contracts for sugar workers were obtained. The employers tried to raise the old specter of communism again, and the House Un-American Activities Committee gave union officials a hard time. When Hall and others were indicted for conspiracy to overthrow the government, he was told by the Federal Bureau of Investigation that if he would leave the island, charges would be dropped. Hall stayed and fought his conviction, which ultimately was overturned by the U.S. Supreme Court.

The union survived and by the 1950s was stronger than ever. Hall had created a political power force equal to that of the growers on the island. As a result, the farm workers had adequate health, education, welfare, and social services. The problems of mechanization were handled through pension and severance pay plans, medical care, and retirement programs. By the 1960s, though the work force had been reduced significantly in size, stoop labor had been eliminated and pay scales were at their highest level. As one book described it, Hall had "transformed an entire society from a virtual feudal territory controlled by huge financial interests into a modern pluralistic state with the most racially and ethnically mixed political leadership in the world."[7]

Farm workers had the evidence that if they organized and bargained collectively, they would be better able to insist on terms of work that would lead to a better life; at the same time, the proof was clear that their doing so would not wreak havoc with the rest of society.

While the major mainland efforts of unionizing agricultural workers took place in California (the largest agricultural state in numbers employed) and in the South in the wake of the plantation system, historically there were hundreds of nonunion spontaneous strikes led by indigenous farm workers in all agricultural states, along with numerous isolated efforts to unionize agricultural workers during the first half of the twentieth century. Between 1930 and 1940 alone, 178,000 farm workers participated in 275 strikes in 28 states, according to labor historians.

Sheep shearers organized the first established union of migrant agricultural workers. The Rocky Mountain Sheep Shearers Union organized the itinerant workers who moved through the network of large sheep ranches in Colorado and westward toward the Pacific. Here, employer-employee relationships were impersonal, seasonal work was done for distant markets, and the talents of the workers were highly skilled and thus available in smaller numbers. In addition, the workers dealt with a perishable product. For these unique reasons, a union could be organized and run in an effective manner.

The Mountain States Beet Workers were organized around the sugar beet industry that evolved in isolated western and midwestern areas, mostly in Colorado. Planting, topping, and harvesting sugar beets was submarginal work. As a result, migratory labor was used. The big sugar refining companies that controlled this business imported many Mexican workers.[8] Mexicans, who were discriminated against (as a poor and foreign caste) in Colorado, were hard to organize, though attempts were made. Union activity there was sporadic and ineffective.

In the Southwest (Texas, Oklahoma, and Arkansas) infrequent local attempts have been made to unionize cowboys on the cattle ranches, but they have not been successful. As ranches grew and working relationships became more impersonal and as markets grew more distant, the relationship between the hired hands who did seasonal work and the farmers changed radically. For this type of ranch worker, there was "a growing disparity in attitudes and wealth between the employer and himself," in the words of one historian. These conditions disposed some ranch hands to efforts to organize. Union activity never was notable in this area, however.

In Florida, citrus workers involved in the growing, picking, and shipping of that state's ocean of oranges were exploited for decades by big and powerful grower associations and by the political power of large absentee corporate owners. Yet the first union contract was not won in Florida until the 1960s when the United Farm Workers and the Coca-Cola company agreed to contracts covering large numbers of workers in the orange groves of Minute Maid, a Coca-Cola subsidiary.

In New Jersey, seasonal workers, brought in to harvest intensive crops of fruits and vegetables grown on small farms in the agricultural areas bordering the big cities, were controlled by labor contractors called padrones. Efforts to organize these workers have been greeted with adamant opposition by hostile farmers. Large numbers of Puerto Ricans have been brought in by grower associations and moved by the hundreds of thousands from farm to farm around the state. Their government acts like a union, providing growers with large numbers of farm workers whose contracts they negotiate en masse.

Union activity for farm workers in New Jersey—indeed in all the East Coast agricultural areas—has been minimal. In New England, the culture of large tobacco and cranberry crops calling for the importation of migrant and seasonal labor has resulted in some attempts at unionization, especially in areas near the big cities. Here again, foreign workers (West Indians and Portuguese bravas from Cape Verde), women and students, Boy Scouts, and unemployed workers have been brought in by farm owners who are unwilling to raise their pay scales and improve conditions for the career farm workers. No unions have been successful here.

In the Great Lakes region, migrants are brought in for short seasons as dairy workers and for harvest of small cash crops such as onions and sugar beets. Often working in strongly antiunion, one-industry towns, farm workers here frequently encounter form contracts imposed by absentee companies on the local growers' associations, who in turn impose them on the individual workers. Again, union activity has been sparse in this area.

The struggle of farm workers has continued in the United States. It has been a struggle for existence; for economic justice; and in most cases for the barest minimum wages and tolerable working conditions to do the hardest, most undesirable, yet necessary work. The gestation period for the birth of an effective union and the conditions of that maturation process have been extraordinary. Life in America has changed radically during the first half of the twentieth century, but farm workers' problems and needs have remained static.

THE UNITED FARM WORKERS

The past is prologue; the real story of the farm worker union movement is taking place in the present, predominantly in California. There are several roots of the United Farm Workers union (UFW). In a broad, historic sense this union can be viewed as the successful result of over 50 years of struggle by generations of industrious but exploited farm workers all over the United States. To some extent as well, its success can be personalized as the product of the heroic leadership of Cesar Chavez. In some sense, both assessments are correct.

The UFW union movement was spawned during a two-decade period beginning in the early 1950s. At this time the right leadership and a congenial blend of timing and events came together in an appropriate political climate. The farm workers found their leader and created their organization—one of many social movements that emerged out of the conscience of America during this tumultuous time. Chavez has called his union movement La Causa—the cause—and indeed it has to be as much a cause as a union.

The story of this union has taken place mostly in California, although it is a show that, like the mobile workers in its cast, is ready to go on the road. The first organizational step came with the formation of the Agricultural Workers Association in 1958 by a priest in California who was moved by the sense of community among the thousands of demoralized, disorganized, and isolated farm workers. In 1959 the AFL-CIO organized an Agricultural Workers Organizing Committee, pledging (as others had before) to push an all-out drive to organize farm workers.

The political climate was right. There was a liberal state administration in California. And, in addition, there was the necessary personal spark to ignite this movement, as there had not been in prior situations. This was the presence of Chavez and a handful of his associates, all of whom were becoming active social organizers on the scene at that time.

Since farm workers were scattered and on the move, they were hard to organize. In addition, because so many were immigrants (in California, most were Chicanos and Filipinos), they viewed organized labor (like government programs) as something that did not work for them.

Cesar Chavez had come to California from Arizona with his family when misfortune forced them to leave their small family farm in search of work. He matured in barrios and migrant camps throughout California. Like so many of his fellow Chicanos, he and his family worked in the fields when jobs were available. He finished high school and a hitch in the Navy with no specific life work in mind.[9]

Chavez eventually found work as a community organizer in California under the tutelage of Fred Ross, a veteran organizer and disciple of Saul Alinsky. Ross recruited Chavez in 1952 when he was working in apricot orchards near San Jose. He would mature into an avid man with an uncompromising vision of what was needed for farm workers to organize successfully and with the single-mindedness of an obsessed purist.

He was a classical example of the right man in the right

**By the melon fields,
Coachella,
California, 1970.** (Chris
Sanchez)

place at the right time. He knew personally about the perversions of the labor contractor system and the exploitation of piece rate payments. He had experienced the depravities of farm labor and the personal humiliations suffered by Chicano farm workers. He was a driven and self-educated man, who had experienced a farm worker's life.

Chavez was particularly touched by the writings of Gandhi and Thoreau and the experiences of Martin Luther King, Jr., whose views about nonviolence (and in the case of Gandhi, about the power of the boycott) would inspire his leadership of the union in later years. In addition, Chavez's strong religiousness gave him both succor and support when the Roman Catholic church became one of the union's strongest and most influential allies. Chavez told one writer that he found inspiration in the example of St. Paul, whom he viewed as "a terrific organizer who would go and talk to the people right in their homes—sit there with them and be one of them."[10] There are frequent references to St. Francis and the Virgin Mary of Guadalupe in union literature. The union's Mexican heritage is personified in the posters and other memorializations of Emiliano Zapata and Pancho Villa.

Chavez worked with Ross, Dolores Huerta, Gilbert Padilla, and a small cadre of Chicano organizers who later would become the leadership of the emerging UFW. He would handle poverty, frustration, and the opposition of his better organized opponents with patience and vision that approached saintliness.

Eventually, Chavez found the Community Service Organization (CSO) which had sponsored his early organizing work, to be too middle class and detached from the reality of farm workers' lives to suit him. Having learned his organizing lessons and the strengths of his opponents, Chavez resigned from the CSO in 1962 to begin the National Farm Workers Association (NFWA), which would become what is now the United Farm Workers of America, AFL-CIO.

In 1965 the embryonic union joined forces with Filipino farm workers in strikes against Delano, Calif., grape growers. At this time, Chavez's NFWA had 1,200 member families. The NFWA joined the AFL-CIO Agricultural Workers Organizing Committee in September 1964. It fought the Delano area grape growers, using the techniques of civil rights and peace groups. This battle would continue for five years, causing a nationwide boycott and strike that gained the union national friends and attention. Eventually, in 1966 the NFWA and the Agricultural Workers Organizing Committee merged into the UFW.

The battle between the union and the California growers continued. Chavez managed to turn defeat into victory, and growers proved they were as ingenious as they were adamant. The national boycott developed when a major Delano grape grower, attempting to avoid union pressures, sold grapes in New York state under his colleagues' labels. The only way for the union to cope with this tactic was to attempt a national boycott of all California table grapes. Even so, the growers managed to get President Richard Nixon to buy unsold grapes for the Defense Department and send them to Vietnam.

Lettuce growers tried to avoid dealing with the UFW in 1970 by signing sweetheart contracts with West Coast teamsters. Grape growers did the same. By 1973, conditions in the California fields were explosive. Thousands of UFW strikers and supporters were jailed; some were killed. But the worse the situation became, the more it turned into a public battle into which others than the growers and the farm workers were drawn. Again, its greatest adversities ultimately would bring to the young union its major allies and successes.

During these years as a young man on the move, Chavez matured in a unique way. He read a great deal and developed a philosophy that governed his life-style and work. To this day, he is a man growing and evolving in a way that characterizes people of special accomplishment. His views about money and political action, along with his obsessive devotion to the cause of farm workers, were the root of the tactics of his flowering union; his ties to the church, the civil rights movement, and liberal politics would engage him and the union along with their needed allies in subsequent battles against overwhelming odds.

Participation and sacrifice were the keys to developing a successful union, Chavez had concluded. He would not make the error earlier union organizers made and use outside "experts" to run this organization. He would insist on farm workers themselves running their own union. He would—and still does—resist sources of outside money being used to fund the union's daily work. "It is only when you get into the whole idea of love, and sacrifice, and service," he told an audience of Health, Education, and Welfare Department employees, "that we begin to get it together. Money doesn't get us there."

The farm workers themselves—poor as they were—had to pay to belong to the new union. However little the payments may have been, these few dollars were meaningful contributions in the views of the donors themselves; as such, their acts were likely to keep them committed to the union cause. Chavez's views of sacrifice are repeated so constantly one cannot mistake their relevance to his strategy:

We cannot organize farm workers with money. It will take sacrifice and a lifetime of work. If we are unwilling to sacrifice a little bit more on top of the suffering we already experience then we will never change the conditions which enslave us and which stifle the hopes of our children.

All union staff (Chavez included) are paid only a modest weekly stipend (it was raised from $5 to $10) plus room and board for their work. Even if he could change this, he would not. Chavez insists it is the union's freedom from economic dependence that is its saving grace. He has converted the farm workers' poverty from a tragedy to a resource. "We have nothing else to do with our lives except to build our union. . . . We will never give up," Chavez has said.

Conscientiously and steadily for years, Chavez drove down all the remote and dusty roads to the shacks and gathering places, to fields and meeting halls, to talk endlessly with his constitutents. He drew them into his cause; as they became part of a movement, the cause became theirs. He preached self-abnegation, personal sacrifice, brotherhood and sisterhood, and nonviolence. He fasted; he worked endlessly; he organized. And he built his union.

A union it is, though some observers think it is not. From his audacious but humble beginning, Chavez concentrated on providing farm workers, who acted collectively, with crucial benefits that were meaningful to them—burial insurance and low interest loans, for example. In the early years of the union he was as committed to the pragmatic battles as he was to techniques of nonviolence.

Chavez has two German Shepherds he keeps at his headquarters, La Paz, in Keene, Calif. They are named Huelga (Strike) and Boycott and are the symbols of his success. Those concepts are the traditional weapons of the union; weapons Chavez has used brilliantly and effectively. As the union grew, so did the mystique of Chavez, a man whose growing power as a social crusader was belied by his frail and simple presence.

He fought fiercely; others had done so before, but he combined the will to fight with a unique ability to draw upon the spiritual motivations of his allies and associates, which carried them through frightening and defeating periods. To hear Chavez speak is to understand how he can lead so effectively. He has the sureness, commitment, and total dedication that works like an irresistible magnet on anyone but his most ardent enemies. And he has the complete credibility of a person who "has been there" and is incorruptible.

His turn-the-other-cheek, Taoistic approach precluded his opponents from claiming anything but the most temporal victories. Chavez would only respond to some parochial but heated battle lost by saying, "We never lose; there are temporary setbacks, but we can't lose. We have no money or power, but we have all the time. There are more of us than them. Ultimately we will win. Money and power cannot buy us. Our justice will come." "The greater the oppression," Chavez told a church audience, "the more leverage nonviolence holds." Therefore, his leadership of the union movement would be predicated on the notion that satisfaction comes only from giving one's life to the nonviolent struggle for justice. That philosophy made his defeat impossible despite the overwhelming strength of his opponents.

> We know that most likely we are not going to do anything else the rest of our lives except build our union. For us there is nowhere else to go. Although we would like to see victory come soon, we are willing to wait. In this sense time is our ally. We learned many years ago that the rich may have money, but the poor have time.

His notions about money were as deeply felt and as critical to his approach to organizing as his attitudes about nonviolence. Recalling how other union efforts had failed, Chavez reminded his followers that there are other ways to get things done than with money. "There isn't enough money to organize poor people," he has said. "When we started organizing our union, we knew we had to depend on something other than money." Someone earning a good salary, Chavez points out, cannot organize because he depends on money.

> Money is not going to organize the disadvantaged, the powerless, or the poor. We need other weapons. That's why the War on Poverty is such a miserable failure. You put out a big pot of money and all you do is fight over it. Then you run out of money and you run out of troops. It's just like those revolutions. If you haven't got the money you haven't got the troops.[11]

Chavez invested instead in sacrifice, which proved invaluable and contagious.

His views were very long range ("in organizing, you see results years later") and tied to personal involvement. He went to the poorest of the poor in the barrios and "they opened their homes and gave us their hearts," he said, although "we had nothing to give them except the dream that it might happen."

The farm workers followed his example and tied themselves to the union. Middle-class America watched, was appealed to, and wanted to help. They gave their bodies, their labor, and their money; though Chavez would only accept all this help in his own way. By 1975 a Harris poll showed that 17 million American adults were honoring the grape boycott, 14 million people were not buying lettuce, and 11 million were boycotting Gallo wines. The consumers of America, the very ones the critics of farm worker organization had argued would be hurt by the unions, became their allies.

Union headquarters is like a retreat. At an old sanatorium covering several hundred acres near Keene in the rugged Tehachapi mountains outside Bakersfield, Calif., a few hundred workers live and work in a collection of trailers, small cottages, and simple buildings. Most meals are communal, and chores are shared by everyone. There is an atmosphere of fellowship, peacefulness, and joy; at the same time there is a quiet but fierce dedication to the work and goals of the union. People have died at this union's work; the mission is a deadly serious commitment, which all these people share. There is an excitement, a certainty, and a total involvement that is shared by all.

The church played a key role during the UFW's time of testing. The strong Roman Catholic church in California, to which Chavez had a long and personal commitment, and the California Migrant Ministry (CMM), the ecumenical Council of Protestant Churches that historically had concerned itself with social services for farm workers, formed a powerful ally with the emerging union at a critical time.

The Reverend Wayne "Chris" Hartmire, longtime director of the CMM, was a key person during these times; he is still a union ally. In Hartmire's judgment, the church was but one, though important, of several external social forces, such as the civil rights movement, that helped give rise to the formation of the union. Its presence precluded red-baiting claims of hostile growers; provided sources of necessary volunteers, food, and money at critical times; added inspiration and succor to the strikers; and eventually helped attract the national attention that provided the new union with the protection of allies and public scrutiny. The church made the union's problems the problems of all of us: "We reject the heresy that churches and synagogues are to be concerned only with so-called 'spiritual matters,' " a church committee reported; the farm workers' grievances were "a fundamental injustice which we dare not evade."[12]

Early in his tenure with CMM (now the National Farm Worker Ministry), Hartmire had concluded that the church could not preach a dogma it did not practice in the real world. Through his direction of the CMM in the 1960s, the church became an active ally and supporter of Chavez and his union officials. While local churches, many of whom were captives of area growers, complained about the prounion activities of the CMM, it received major support from church headquarters in the big cities.

The Roman Catholic church became involved in the union struggle as a result of the interest of individual church members, especially in the Delano area. Its small and ad hoc support grew. In 1969 a group of Hispanic priests went to the National Conference of Bishops with a boycott appeal. A special commission was set up, and it mediated the first farm worker strikes in Coachella and Delano.

The original church role of reconciliation gradually became one of participation. The bishops arbitrated the jurisdictional agreement between the Teamsters Union and the UFW after a major lettuce boycott in Salinas, Calif., in August 1970. When the Teamsters broke the agreement and raided the grape fields beginning in April 1973, the church officially threw its support behind the UFW strike; and the Roman Catholic church, Protestant churches, and Jewish denominations joined in supporting Chavez and his fledgling union.

In an important and insightful paper chronicling these days, Hartmire analyzed his church's role.[13] He had discovered early in his career with the CMM that because the farm workers were not active in the local churches, their voices were not being heard. Thus churches wittingly or unwittingly were adding their weight to the prevailing community attitudes toward oppressed people.

Agribusiness was thriving in California. Five percent of all California farmers paid 60 percent of the farm labor wages, and only 6 percent of the farms accounted for 75 percent of the acreage in 1959. Because the growers and the people they influenced were men and women and not angels, Hartmire concluded, their decisions could only be related to their own economic self-interest. He saw numerous examples to assure him that, essentially, government (as all of life in general) in agricultural counties was run by the agricultural employers.

The CMM decided to assist and befriend the leaders of the CSO, which at this time was the major voice of Chicanos in the

Southwest. By 1962 they were supporting the leadership that was "building a militant and democratic farm workers' union that would be composed of farm workers, paid for by farm workers and run by farm workers." With students and civil rights activists, the church became part of an emerging labor movement.

To do this, it was necessary to survive a great wrenching in the church. Hartmire had decided that moral suasion was not enough; that for the church to serve its constituents in a rapidly changing world, it could not act from "the pulpit alone or from the position of safety or purity." To do so, he concluded, would be to preserve the institution by ignoring the people that the institution existed to serve. Yet, for the church to act, it could not avoid conflict "with the custodians of the established power order."

The predicament Hartmire described was a classic example of institutionalization, a process in which all institutions must make fundamental decisions on whether to preserve themselves or to work for the constituents they were created to serve when a situation arises in which doing both is impossible. Church activists in California were accused by their critics of involving themselves in an economic war aimed at the redistribution of power to secure social justice for a poor and weak group. The church's social activists argued that to do less would be dishonest; it would be no more than "salving the conscience while hanging onto an unjust social system that benefits 'our kind of people' at the expense of the poor."[14]

In its earlier efforts to help farm workers—for example, in the battles over the bracero program—the church had narrowed its base of support. Having accepted CMM leadership in farm labor matters for 45 years, the church in all conscience could not capitulate to the growers later when the going got tough. As Hartmire reported, since the growers could not prove that the CMM was guilty of "mismanagement, immorality or incompetence," they had no good argument against its work in aiding farm workers. "Having been dragged into the farm labor struggle by their unruly child (the CMM), [it] could not back away and say no to a basic human quest for justice and opportunity."

After entering the all-out warfare over the union, the boycott, and the strikes, there were fears that the CMM might be pressured out of existence by influential members of the church who either were growers or were sympathetic to them. Growers and their representatives in the church at first were embarrassed and later outright annoyed by the presence of the CMM in this struggle. Local congregations pressured denominational offices to stay out of the fray, but the CMM persevered and succeeded in keeping the church active in the battle. Hartmire has written about the contribution of the church people in this struggle:

The most important thing that can be said about this "churchly" support is that it helped; it helped keep a very brave people alive and strong in an important struggle for social justice. These Christians did not come with sermons or admonitions or membership cards. They did not need to identify themselves because farm workers knew who they were and farm workers tend to know better than we do what it is that God's people should be doing. The ministry of Jesus is highly visible and easily identified when it is in fact done—and not only talked about.[15]

Despite this important commitment and participation by the activist wing of the church, much time was spent at the institutional level fending off attacks against the CMM, attempting to assuage grower constituents, and maintaining some institutional balance. Indeed, as Hartmire reports, this dynamic force did limit the church's participation in the struggle to some extent:

Interpretation and explanation, as crucial as they are in a time of strife, *do detract* from the energy and resources that can be applied to the needs of the world. The enormous quantity of interpretation required in this instance speaks very clearly about who has power in the church. We are a long way from losing our heads over the needs of suffering men. We *are* in danger of losing our integrity as the Body of Christ because of captivity to the prevailing power orders of this society.[16]

In his recapitulation of these exciting days, Hartmire eloquently articulated the excruciating balance that was in play during those times. In assisting the underdog in a major confrontation, the church was painfully aware that the very power interests who had to be moved were in the pews with those who sought change. The church really was being asked to put up or shut up—to help one group of constituents attain the kind of justice the church preached for all, at a time when doing so would conflict with those with power.

The farm workers were militant and aggressive, but they were motivated by nonviolence and had strong ties to the church. They persisted in operating within the system, though it was one that had denied them justice for so long and to which they had none of the access their opponents had. They had to depend on justice and on the institutions of society that concern themselves with justice. In doing so, they forced an agonizing decision on the church. In Hartmire's words, the farm workers forced the church to think "not only in terms of what is institutionally possible, but first and foremost in terms of what is truly helpful."

´[S]ervanthood is a very hard thing for churches to do. When the chips are down, we who are responsible for decisions about church resources decide first in terms of what is institutionally appropriate and only second in terms of what is truly needed by those who are seeking life in the world.[17]

Despite the pressures of its powerful farmer constituents, in its moment of truth the church did not turn its back on the striking farm workers. How could the church of Jesus Christ explain its failure to help in the causes it espoused when its help was critically needed? One local clergyman pointed out to his colleagues who were pondering the risks of their position that all they could lose was their jobs, and that, in the context of the fundamental struggle that was going on, was not such a big risk.

Hartmire saw the question to be: Has God called the CMM to serve the churches or to serve farm workers? The CMM could rationalize taking sides on the ground that the growers were the ones who really forced the conflict by "resisting a reasonable and non-violent attempt to bring about necessary social change." Thus the CMM forced the institutionalized church into what it viewed to be a higher form of servanthood to its needy constituent members. Despite what it viewed to be resistance, which is built into the institution, Hartmire said, "We were driven by the circumstances of our work to put the highest priority on the needs of the people and only a secondary priority on the needs of the institution."

This story is told at length not only because it is the story of the evolution of a major ally of the farm worker union movement but also because it is a unique example of institutional legitimacy. Other institutions—government, some of the press, major league unionism, the professions—failed to do what the church did for farm workers because they could not or would not perceive the choice as Hartmire and his colleagues did and because they took the customary, institutional easy way out when crises arose.

By 1971 a National Farm Worker Ministry had begun; it was composed of 40 individual church organizations that wanted to support the union. Churches were assigning lay and clerical "worker priests" to official jobs in the union.

La Causa was also invigorated by the attentive coverage of the national media, which was following the successful appeals of the Chavez fasts and marches, and by the support of well-known celebrities such as Robert F. Kennedy. It was included in the pre-

Picketing, California, 1968.
(Bob Thurber)

ferred lists of the "radical chic," and eventually it won the sponsorship of the AFL-CIO and the interest of the general public whose concerns about the problems of the poor and disadvantaged flourished during the Johnson administration. The bumper stickers on the station wagon of the little old lady, on the sports car of the young (consciousness 2) professional, and the back of the (consciousness 3) hippie's used camper proclaimed the boycotts of lettuce, grapes, and Gallo wine. These pressures, initiated in the fields of California, were to be felt in faraway markets. When sales are cut by 10 to 15 percent, the growers' profits are gone and the boycott is effective.

Around the time of his election as governor of California, word had come to Jerry Brown from East Coast supermarket interests that the time was ripe for reform. As California secretary of state, Brown had walked with Chavez in Calexico. His interest in farm workers' problems was widely known. The UFW boycott was working; there was general impatience in the food industry with all the lawsuits, marches, and trouble in the supermarket parking lots.

Ideology was not important. It was time to get the interested parties together and work things out. The two chief unions concerned with organizing farm workers—the UFW and the Teamsters, which had made a big push to unionize farm workers in California for several years—were obviously interested. So were the growers who felt that, since some regulation was inevitable, they had better be part of the process. They formed an ad hoc bargaining team.

In the spring of 1975 the institutional parties were brought to the governor's office but kept in separate rooms; with Brown hammering at compromise and shuttling between rooms like Henry Kissinger in the Middle East and state Agricultural Commissioner (now state Chief Justice) Rose Bird drafting a bill modeled on the NLRA, an agricultural labor relations bill was hammered out in three weeks time.

The UFW was worried about (and they were granted) time limits for union elections and certifications because their constituents were on the move and work was seasonal. The growers were worried about and got some limitations on secondary boycotts. After a draft bill was agreed upon, the negotiating parties had one firm condition, according to LeRoy Chatfield, Brown's chief agent in the negotiations: no changes were to be made in the consensus bill to be sent to the legislature.

All sides were exhausted and agreed to the rules for the remaining fight. After eight committee hearings in both houses of the state legislature, the bill was passed unchanged. As one legislator wailed about Brown, "That man kept us here till we passed the law." So it was that an industry that had been unregulated for 80 years shared power for the first time with the work force in a peaceful way.

The new legislation intoned the official policy of the state and articulated the hopes of farm workers everywhere:

In enacting this legislation the people of the State of California seek to ensure peace in the agricultural fields by guaranteeing justice for all agricultural workers and stability in labor relations.

This enactment is intended to bring certainty and a sense of fair play to a presently unstable and potentially volatile condition. . . .[18]

Its name—the Alatorre-Zenovich-Dunlop-Bergman Agricultural Labor Relations Act of 1975—sounded more like the Stanford backfield than the controversial legislation that might prove to be the model agricultural labor relations law in this country. The statute declared the state's policy to be to encourage and protect the rights of agricultural employees to full freedom of association and self-organization in negotiating the terms and conditions of their employment. Farm workers were empowered to bargain collectively, free from interference.[19] It is unclear whether the law is the historic event that protagonists in this contentious social drama claim; the final act is yet to come. However, my recent view of the scene convinces me that the California Agricultural Labor Relations Act will be the successful major test case demonstrating that the historic exclusion of farm workers from the union movement has been unnecessary and unwise.

Brown had made no promises about prospective Agricultural Labor Relations Board (ALRB) members. He chose Roger Mahoney, a bishop from the Fresno diocese, as chairman; he added his negotiator, Chatfield, an ex-UFW staffer, along with a Chicano having no UFW ties, a law professor who had represented the Teamsters, and a former lobbyist for the California Agricultural Council. Though the claim later was made that the board had a UFW bias, Chairman Mahoney) pointed out in a 1976 white paper, "Setting the Record Straight," that in the first busy year of operations when the board issued 72 decisions, there were dissenting opinions in only 5.

The board's problem was not harmony, it was money. Its first annual budget was a modest $1.3 million; that sum was used up quickly. Within its first five months, the ALRB held 414 elections under the new act; the National Labor Relations Board (NLRB) had conducted only 300 elections nationwide during its first two years of activity. In its first 5 months of operations, the ALRB received 873 unfair labor practice charges, issued complaints in 250 cases, and held 62 hearings.

A million and a quarter dollars more was borrowed by the ALRB from a state emergency fund; it soon was depleted also. The legislature was asked for a supplemental budget. This step required a two-thirds vote, compared to the single majority needed to get the act itself passed.

The growers pressed the legislature, seeing an indirect way to win the war after having lost the earlier battle against unionization. In the first five months under the new law, unions had won 93 percent of the elections. The bankrupt board held out for a while; some staffers collected unemployment insurance and food stamps and continued to work. When I talked with Chavez at La Paz at this time, he said, whimsically, that for the first time in his life he found himself rooting for the bureaucrats who were trying to get re-funded.

That battle for funds was lost. The 50 percent vote needed in the liberal California legislature to pass the law could not be stretched to the 67 percent needed for a supplemental budget. The ALRB was out of business before the end of its first year.

Down but never out, Chavez and the union conceived Proposition 14, an attempt by public initiative to make the ALRB permanent and not subject to legislative whims and political fashions (if passed, it would have taken another public vote to undo the ALRB). The campaign to get sufficient signatures went well; the union got 720,000 names—200,000 more than they needed. Proposition 14 went onto the ballot. Calls for its passage and its defeat went onto countless car bumpers and into mounting media messages.

The growers ran a tough, expensive media campaign, orchestrated by the powerful advertising agency, Spencer and Roberts. Seizing on the sanctity of private property as an issue, the opponents of Proposition 14 zeroed in on the relatively subsidiary question of access by union organizers to farm employees living in camps on employers' property. They effectively hammered at the notion that Proposition 14 was going to legalize trespass and violate all people's rights to be left alone on their private property.

The Supreme Court of California had approved the union's demand to have limited access to workers, before and after working hours and at lunch breaks, to recruit and campaign. That decision was appealed to the U.S. Supreme Court. The union's fear of the prevailing Supreme Court and its fear that the ALRB's bankruptcy was an omen of its weakening position in the state legislature had prompted the search for a quick shot in the arm.

Proposition 14 was that strategy. "We were dead in the water," one UFW official told me after it was over, "and we had to risk going back to the people with our cause."

Despite the big push by the UFW to counteract the growers' media blitz attacking Proposition 14, which was aided by a television endorsement by Governor Brown, the proposition was soundly defeated by almost a 2 to 1 margin (62–38 percent).

Nonetheless, the union's activity had borne fruit. Before the Proposition 14 vote, the legislature re-funded the moribund ALRB. The governor immediately restaffed the agency, which quickly resumed its work under the chairmanship of a former NLRB member named, coincidentally, Jerry Brown. The U.S. Supreme Court refused to reconsider, and thus left standing, the California Supreme Court's decision upholding union access to workers in the fields; the ALRB then issued a regulation adopting that case law as its access rule. Soon the UFW and the Teamsters signed an agreement ending their bitter feud over organizing farm workers, giving the UFW exclusive rights to organize workers in the fields and the Teamsters the right to organize allied workers whose jobs are more compatible with those of their members. The Teamsters have closed their field offices and have not petitioned for any new elections.

The move by the UFW was accelerated to organize the farm workers of California. By the summer of 1977, elections were taking place and the UFW was winning most of them. Rapidly, tens of thousands participated in union elections. Fears of abuses, chaotic employment relations, and consumer losses were proved to be unfounded.

As a substantial constituent of the AFL-CIO and as an organization that had proved its mettle and its staying power in the hurly-burly of state politics, the UFW became a powerful political force in the state. It aimed to deal with all the social problems of farm workers. Then the plan was to move the action eastward—to Arizona, Texas, Florida, New York, New Jersey, Michigan, and other centers of farming activity.

Three other states have passed farm labor collective bargaining laws: Idaho, Arizona, and Kansas. Reportedly, Massachusetts, South Dakota, Wisconsin, and Minnesota are considering legislation. Other states—Texas and Oregon for example—have controversial laws pending. Critics think the laws in Texas and Oregon were employer conceived and favor employers. The UFW is fighting them.

In Idaho a 1943 Farm Picketing Act was declared unconstitutional by the Idaho Supreme Court because it penalized lawful acts of peaceful picketing. A 1970 Agricultural Labor Act was passed, but one reviewer concluded that the act is employer oriented and primarily intended to prevent collective bargaining by imposing insurmountable requirements for elections.

In 1972 the Arizona legislature passed a law that so outraged UFW officials they have sued to have it declared unconstitutional. The law, though it purports to be a farm labor law, has been called a ruse to frustrate effective organization by imposing defeating conditions regarding such action:

[I]t appears that a union's ability to organize and campaign effectively [is] jeopardized by the Arizona law. . . . The only explanation . . . seems to be a desire on the part of the Arizona Legislature to impede the workers' ability to organize and to facilitate the growers' efforts to counteract the unions' organizational efforts and resist unionization.[20]

In April 1978 a three-judge federal court in Phoenix declared the Arizona law unconstitutional in its entirety and enjoined the state from enforcing it. The case was appealed to the U.S. Supreme Court, which reversed the lower courts[21] and sent the case back to the U.S. District Court in Arizona for further consideration of several of the issues (election procedures, consumer publicity, and criminal sanctions). The court also decided that two of the issues raised were not justiciable (the challenges to the access rule and the arbitration provisions). These delays inevitably will slow the union movement in Arizona, and this approach may well become appealing to states that are not sympathetic to the farm worker union movement.

For these reasons, the UFW is opposed to new state legislation in the creation of which it has not participated. It is also against a federal law that would include farm workers under the National Labor Relations Act (NLRA). Instead, the union prefers the slower, surer, state-by-state passage of favorable farm labor relations laws. The UFW view is that unless legislation comes when farm workers are organized and prepared to take advantage of it, as in California, it will serve only the growers' interests.

CORRECTING INEQUITIES

The federal government recently has recognized the historic inequity that excluded farm workers from the original NLRA, despite the irrationality of doing so to an industry whose interstate character is so clear. Despite the uniquely changing quality of both farm products and farm labor, there are no sound marketing or social reasons for making this one distinction in the dispensation of federal protective regulation.

Several approaches for correcting this inequity are under consideration. One would be to add farm labor to the general coverage of the NLRA. This would allow farm workers to organize and collectively bargain under the supervision of the NLRB. Proponents argue that this approach fosters collective bargaining by bringing the full force of the federal government behind union elections and organizing activities. Those opposed to this approach do not want the slow, ineffective, sometimes hostile federal bureaucracy involved in early organizing efforts. They point out that some of the most effective union organizing in recent times has been conducted outside the NLRA. Chavez holds this view, arguing that the UFW would lose the boycott and other beneficial tactics if it was brought under the act, and that the NLRA would disenfranchise many farm workers who are transitory employees.

Another approach would be to design a special act for farm workers; the idea here would be to provide a labor relations law without the restrictions (such as the one against boycotts) that later labor laws applied to unions. The Chavez theory is that most unions were allowed to organize originally under the Wagner Act without the later restrictions; therefore, the farm workers should have the benefit of such an act also, at least for a while.

The third approach would be to design a national agricultural labor relations act like California's, which provides general state regulation of labor relations in the agricultural industry through tailoring the administration of the act to the unique nature of the world of agriculture. (Strong enforcement provisions and speedy elections, for example, to cope with the fast harvest seasons and the migrancy of farm workers). Staff with expertise concerning agriculture would be necessary under any of these three approaches.

In Washington there were signs that the Carter administration would be sensitive to the problems of farm workers. The UFW registered 320,000 new voters, mostly minority members, in a 1976 election drive for the Democratic National Committee. President Carter was aided in his campaign by Chavez. A silent, politically important group was becoming vocal and active. By background and reputation, the new secretary of labor could be expected to show a special interest in rural affairs. The Democratic party platform endorsed the right of agricultural workers to organize and bargain collectively and urged the adoption of appropriate federal legislation to ensure this goal. Numerous industrial relations bills were proposed before Congress, some establishing a special agricultural labor relations act, others extending NLRA coverage to farm workers. Hearings were planned to consider how to authorize collective bargaining and unionization of farm workers.

Only when farm workers have the bargaining power that was established decades ago for the rest of the American work force will this silent minority be enabled to participate with agricultural employers in solving the social and economic problems of their labor market.

AFTER THE "MIRACLE"

It was not long, however, before the romance and the excitement of the early union battles wore off, and the hard job of building a union began. Soon, some of the union's supporters were asking whether La Causa was an effective cause but an ineffective union and whether the skills with which Chavez had led his essentially Chicano movement could be translated into a nationwide union organization involving blacks and whites as well as Mexican-Americans.

The front page of the *Washington Post* reported in January 1978 that "the UFW has moved into the less glamorous, highly technical world of nuts-and-bolts unionism, and its record so far is less than inspiring." It quoted a grower who stated that UFW leaders were "social activists and agrarian reformers, not union leaders." A May 1976 article in the *New Republic* had concluded that "having won union recognition, he [Cesar Chavez] does not know quite what to do with it."

A visit to the UFW La Paz headquarters early in 1978 convinced me that the charge that the union was faltering was exaggerated. The union was celebrating its sixteenth anniversary when I was there, the same day as Chavez's fifty-first birthday; it was evident that both were well and prospering in their work.

Union members bristled when questioned directly about these criticisms. Key officials pointed out that the white urban middle class (students, the church, and the media, for example, along with their contributors) has supplied key help to the movement; that Chicanos successfully organized black farm workers in Florida; and that the union's executive board includes a Filipino, a black, a white, and two women as well as Chicanos. They are all longtime union spark plugs, not just figureheads to give an illusion of union democracy.

Cesar Chavez.

Chavez himself, in long conversations continuing for several days, stressed that the union is focusing now on administration, organization, management systems, and programs. "Our job now is to build the union. The fight is moving from the picket line and the boycott to the hearing room and the courts," he told the union convention in August 1977.

Wages for agricultural workers in the vineyards and lettuce fields have tripled since the union has begun collective bargaining. The perverse contractor system has been replaced by seniority and the hiring hall. Grievance and arbitration procedures have been created.

Programs are being created to enrich farm workers' lives. Every union contract provides that a certain sum (usually several cents) per hour per worker goes to provide educational and social services programs. Trusts are also created with these funds, which are contributed to by employers as well. Benefits follow workers wherever they go, even as far away as Mexico, Yemen, and the Philippines. Already in place is a comprehensive family medical program, an interstate network of health clinics, a pension fund, an education and economic development fund that bankrolls a network of campesino centers providing services for farm workers, a national farm workers' service center that is developing new facilities, microwave communications systems linking union field offices, language training programs, and even a farm workers' vacation fund.

Chavez is aware that the need now is to develop basic social services for his constituents; indeed, this is what the union is busy doing in California, along with attempting to sign up 200,000 new members in the next few years. There are plans to move the union's action eastward when this is done—to go into other major agricultural areas outside California. The lettuce boycott of the late 1970s has slowed down this eastward movement, sapping the union treasury and monopolizing staff efforts. But successful results are beginning to be seen in new and better contracts. And the union has time.

Chavez understands that his personal role has changed. He will always be the charismatic leader of the farm workers; this is an extraordinary man of vision, with unique leadership qualities. But meeting with Chavez now, one realizes that he is not simply a symbol or a guru. On a long drive in the middle of a rainy night to address 900 striking farm workers in Oxnard, Calif., who would vote the next day to join the UFW, Chavez spent almost three hours thrashing out with a staff member what was to be a new transportation program for the union. He had studied the inanities of motor vehicle pools and the far-from-romantic needs for transportation program planning with the same thoroughness and intensity with which he had earlier studied Ghandi's writings about nonviolence.

I questioned Chavez about cultism in his union. What will happen when he is not the union's leader, and what is the union doing to develop new leaders? He reminded me that from the beginning he has forced responsibility upon farm workers to run their union. To others he has said, "Now we have to get the workers, especially the younger ones, to learn the mechanics of operating the union. We want to train them to be professionals, to negotiate and administer the contracts we have already won."

There are other important and visible officers in this army of workers, and they have authority and responsibility. Chavez always will be the saint of the farm workers; but if he is, he also is working hard to build a church and a constituency that will survive him. Chavez adds that it is his belief that the issues concerning the union are too deep rooted not to survive the man who leads it.

A visitor to union headquarters can observe groups of students attending a daily course on labor law history, agriculture and business economics, collective bargaining and negotiating theory and techniques, and other subjects necessary for the training of competent union officials. As one writer who has followed the UFW closely for years has observed, it is now a union "firmly rooted in traditional trade union, collective bargaining soil." The union headquarters is a beehive of activity. The atmosphere is kindly and personal and congenial; but the agenda is all business. Training, printing, accounting, and planning is going on; this is not a rarefied society of dreamers. Chavez has admonished that the union's decisions must be made by prepared executives, not by pressures; by dealing with relevant opportunities, not urgent crises.

The union has been building ties with its allies in the labor movement, actively supporting the Coors beer strikers, for example, in their boycott. The union is engaged in a major battle with the powerful University of California Board of Regents, which has used vast amounts of public funds to develop techniques for mechanized farming at the behest of powerful grower groups in the state. Before the regents, in the press, at the legislature in Sacramento, and through its network of storefront boycott offices, the union is engaged in a sophisticated fight over the need for social planning to deal with the human fallout of mechanization.

Throughout 1979 the union battled major lettuce growers in California in another prolonged, bitter struggle for recognition and better wages. With strikes and a boycott, the union eventually was able to secure better contracts with most of the lettuce growers.

Getting new members and new contracts and building a network of benefits for farm workers is the preoccupation of the union now. It has turned down several offers by major film studios to be the subject of popular movies that would have gained the union large amounts of publicity and money; it refused because the project would have caused too great a digression from the routine but necessary work of union building. The work of the union is focused on bread-and-butter issues vital to farm workers' lives, such as getting the hourly wage rate for melon picking raised from $2.65 to $2.97 and providing cold water and toilet facilities to workers in the fields.

Some outsiders still attribute the UFW's success to its ephemeral appeal to elements of "radical chic"; at the same time, some insiders are complaining about the centrist and establishmentarian drift of union politics. Ironically, some former staff members do not want what they describe as a George Meany bread-and-butter union because they prefer to become a socialist force. Cesar Chavez is trying to institutionalize the management and administrative techniques needed to organize and build a real union. Despite what its critics and even some of its friends may be saying, the United Farm Workers union is not a Mexican masquerade; it is a young union working hard to be a good union.

9

THE END OF THE STREAM

WHAT DOES THE FUTURE hold for migrant farm workers? Are they at the end of the stream? Will the trend toward larger farms and mechanization of farming end the need for migrant laborers? Must government deal with these quarter million impoverished, worker citizens (and their dependent families) as a continuing welfare class? These workers historically have been excluded from most public assistance, discriminated against by their government, abused by their employers, and forbidden to organize. Will they now be forgotten and disappear?

I think not. However American farming practices evolve, there inevitably will be a need for some unskilled, temporary farm laborers to negotiate the vast and delicate seasonal harvest process. The pools of farm workers may diminish; they should stabilize, but they will not disappear entirely. Nor will they diminish to the point where any problems they pose could be deemed so minimal as not to warrant public attention.

Seasonal work can be stabilized. Migrant work can be coordinated. Farm workers can be trained to work out of the stream, sometimes in more skilled farm work. But some farmers inevitably are going to need temporary workers to handle the relatively small or unmechanized harvests that will always be a part of the nation's food supply.

The questions now are, What attentions to which problems are necessary, and how and by whom can solutions be assured?

There is a direct remedy for the historic exclusion from key federal programs that farm workers have suffered. That is for appropriate House and Senate committees to hold hearings, gather testimony, and eventually legislate a Farm Worker Bill of Rights. Coverage of all social welfare legislation should be extended to apply equally to farm workers.

There is no good reason why such fundamental programs as workmen's compensation, minimum wage and age laws, and unemployment insurance should not cover farm workers to the same degree as they cover all others. Rationales for exclusion are inapt and specious. This bill of rights also should assure that farm workers never again will be excluded as a class from the coverage of comparable social welfare laws.

How to assure that laws, once passed, are administered in a nondiscriminatory fashion is a more difficult challenge, as the case study in Chapter 5 demonstrates. One answer is to save government's role for the few specific problems that require a national approach or federal funding. Wherever possible, the actual administration of programs should be contracted to the private sector, preferably to relevant client groups. This client-oriented approach reduces the tendency toward institutionalization that historically has burdened farm worker programs at the big government agencies such as Health, Education, and Welfare and the Department of Labor.

Some of what government has accomplished ultimately can be handled better by the national farm workers' union; the central function of job placement, running dayhauls, and controlling farm labor contractors are examples. Monitoring of government programs should be done by farm worker advocates, as the Special Review Committee recommended in its final report to the court regarding the Department of Labor.

There are some situations where government is uniquely able to provide the assistance farm workers would find useful. As their union evolves and becomes more sophisticated, it could assume even these responsibilities. There have been models for programs the federal government could conduct until the day the union could take over their administration. Two chief examples concern the travel and housing problems of migrants.

THE ANNUAL WORKER PLAN

If government could possibly serve migrant farm workers, it has had a unique opportunity. By establishing a network to manage the migrant streams in the interests of farmers and workers alike, government could have performed a necessary and helpful role. It had and it wasted one good chance.

Traveling, as migrant farm workers do, with little information or means is fraught with inevitable problems. A grower may have the need for a worker and a worker for a job, but the two may never know of each other's need and availability. A worker may be hired to do work that is not there when he arrives at great cost; the problem could arise from causes the farmer could not control (weather could kill or delay a crop) or from situations he created (overhiring to be sure of plentiful, cheap laborers). There are many comparable examples. Before migrants were organized and able to traverse the tricky currents and sharp rocks of their streams of labor (some growers have associated to deal with common problems and bargain with greater power), the government could have administered an interstate system to inform and facilitate these journeys. Indeed, the model was there.

In New Jersey after World War II, the State Farm Labor Service began prearranging local employment for Florida farm workers who migrated northward during the growing season. In 1948 the New Jersey experience was broadened into an Eastern Seaboard Plan, which was an attempt to coordinate and schedule the employment of farm workers along the entire East Coast, from the citrus harvest in Florida during the winter months, to the spring and summer crops in the Carolinas, to the later apple harvests in New York and New England.

Prior to the development of the Eastern Seaboard Plan in 1948, there was no real organized attempt by the federal government to coordinate the employment of migrant farm workers moving interstate from job to job. The majority of the migrants left their homes in Florida and wandered from one place to another seeking employment. They often congregated in one place, while a neighboring area was suffering from a lack of labor. This chaos caused farm workers to lose valuable employment time looking for jobs, ultimately decreasing their income, while at the same time it caused a shortage of available agricultural labor to meet grower demands.

The successful Eastern Seaboard Plan was expanded nationwide in 1954 in what became known as the Annual Worker Plan (AWP). The AWP was administered by the Labor Department's Employment Service and actually was run through each state's network of local offices. The number of farm workers involved the first year of the plan was approximately 97,000. The number grew steadily until 1967, when the number participating peaked at approximately 193,000.

After that time, the number of farm workers covered under the AWP declined sharply. During the five-year period between 1972 and 1976, approximately 199,000 participated, slightly more than in the single year of 1967. The lowest number of farm workers in the AWP was approximately 28,000 in 1973.

The AWP was designed to schedule a succession of agricultural jobs for migrant farm workers or crews prior to the start of the yearly growing season. The plan made good sense; it served three purposes. First, it offered longer and more continuous employment and, consequently, a higher annual income. Second, it guaranteed growers a dependable labor supply at the right time. Third, it provided the Employment Service with information about the whereabouts and activities of the farm workers it tried to match with grower demands for agricultural labor. It gave this government agency a useful reason for being; it provided a real service for a needy and hardworking clientele.

The Employment Service's interstate clearance system provided farm employers with the ability to recruit workers over a vast area. An employer could simply place an order with the local Employment Service office, specifying the type of job, dates of employment, number of workers needed, the rate of pay, and any other pertinent terms and conditions of employment. The recruitment order then would be sent out to other states that could be expected to have people interested in farm work in the area where the employer was located.

Minimum federal standards had to be met by employers seeking to recruit in this manner. These regulations were designed to insure that the recruitment of distant workers would not undercut the competitive position of local workers. Minimum housing standards were required of employers wishing to use the Employment Service to recruit migrants.

Job orders were placed into the interstate clearance system in three ways. Florida and a few other states used what is called the "pooled interview" approach. Employment Service staff from demand states took job orders from employers in their states and then met with crew leaders or family groups in supply states to work out a seasonal schedule and itinerary for the workers. They briefed the crew leaders on crop prospects, wage rates, and working and living conditions. In a second method, used in midwestern and northwestern states, recruitment and completion of work schedules was performed by Employment Service representatives of demand states, using worker information provided by supply states. In a third version of interstate migrant recruitment, interstate clearance orders were sent out by demand states, while recruitment and scheduling was done by representatives of the supply states.

As the growing season progressed, adjustments in the farm worker's schedule might be necessary to compensate for unforeseeable difficulties such as an early crop or bad weather. Local Employment Service staff might have to make new arrangements or reschedule a crew to other crops in other areas. Some states had temporary information stations on major migrant travel routes; workers might be relocated as crop activities changed. The migrant farm worker could obtain needed information from these offices about weather, crop conditions, wage rates, and maps showing harvest timetables and the most convenient travel routes.

The use of the AWP declined in the 1970s as a result of two factors: one was bureaucratic perversity; the other was employer duplicity. State Employment Service personnel in the demand states had to spend significant time and financial resources to coordinate all the scheduling under the plan; but they did not receive credit for all this work under the Labor Department's funding formula. Thus there was a financial disincentive for local Employment Service offices to participate in the AWP. In addition, the ability of the staffs in supply states to schedule continuous employment for farm workers depended upon growers in demand states making employment commitments in advance of the growing season. But many East Coast growers have been reluctant to submit their job orders sufficiently in advance of the growing season because they prefer foreign workers. To some extent, also, the decline of the AWP was related to the practices of free-wheeling crew leaders who did not make use of the Employment Service.

The AWP is no longer functioning. One survey in 1975 found that less than 1 percent of individual farm workers and 10 percent of crew leaders surveyed believed they were covered by the AWP. Most of the arrangements for farm worker employment takes place outside the Employment Service system as a result of direct arrangements between crew leaders and the growers, it was found. According to Labor Department insiders, there are no plans to resuscitate the AWP. As far as farm workers were concerned, perhaps the chief systemic service government could provide, which. was not a salve for wounds or an emergency giveaway, fizzled and disappeared.

Our court-appointed Special Review Committee (a majority of us) wanted to consider renewal of AWP by the Department of Labor. Eventually, it could have been conducted by the farm workers' union. Planning can decrease many of the vicissitudes of the migrant life and can stabilize the seasonal labor force. It makes sense.

MIGRANT FARM LABOR CENTERS

Migrant housing is a blight on the American landscape and one of the tragic circumstances of migrants' lives. Because these people generally are very poor, their permanent housing often reflects their meager life-styles. Their "homes" on the road, however, are shocking. Migrant housing is among the most horrible living conditions I have ever seen, anywhere.

One of the reasons for this situation is that while they are in transit, migrants have to find temporary housing, often very short-term, in areas where they are unwanted and good temporary quarters are not available. The employers often do not provide housing; and, when they do, it usually is minimal at best and often substandard, unsafe, and unhealthy.

Communities often are unwelcoming to migrants. A bulletin from a farm worker organization reported that the San Antonio City Council rejected a zoning proposal to permit the construction of 75 migrant housing units that could have been built with federal funds. Opponents feared that the city's education costs might escalate as a result and that social "trash" would be attracted to the community. Migrant advocates were not able to persuade the city council that the program, which would have resulted in the migrants' owning their housing and becoming useful citizens, was worthwhile.[1]

Growers have attributed the appalling housing to the lifestyles of the migrants themselves. Commonly, farmers say that they provide their temporary workers with simple but adequate housing only to find it destroyed, unkempt, and deteriorated. "These people live like animals and destroy the places we provide for them" was a common complaint by employers. The problem becomes cyclical.

In this regard, one personal experience is notable; it suggested a potential, systemic solution to one of the housing problems of migrants.

Late in 1950, with funds from the Office of Equal Opportunity, a Migrant Farm Labor Center was opened at Hope, Ark. This is a small (population 8,100) rural town chosen because it had been a habitual stopping-off place for migrants traveling from their homes in southern Texas to short-term jobs in the Great Lakes region and in the Northeast. Traditionally, farm workers piled into their cars, left their homes in the Rio Grande Valley in Texas, and drove to their temporary jobs in the north during the harvest season. At the end of a long day's drive, they would find themselves in the region around Hope, Ark. Exhausted, they would stop at the sides of roads, in parks, along streams, anywhere they could find; they would collapse, eat, clean up as best they could, sleep awhile, and continue their journey. This situation was hardly desirable for the farm workers, and it was a cause of concern in the local communities where they stopped as well.

To cope with this situation, the city of Hope provided a small parcel of land (for $50 they gave a 99-year lease), and the federal government made a grant of a few hundred thousand dollars through the state Employment Service to build 21 simple housing units and a campsite. For ten months each year, migrants on the way to jobs could stop at this rest center, rent a four-bed trailer for a dollar a night, and stay in clean though austere, overnight quarters. There were community showers where families could clean up, a place to do laundry, and a picnic area where they could cook their meals and eat before retiring to a pleasant place for a good night's sleep. The modest fees paid for most of the upkeep of the rest center (to approximately $40,000 a year from rentals was added a federal stipend to meet the $73,000 annual budget). The migrants departed the next day refreshed, feeling that they had been treated like human beings, and they posed no threat to the community.

It was interesting to see how immaculate these people kept their temporary homes and how fully and gratefully they used the cleaning, cooking, and rest facilities. That experience belied the common story I had been told by farmers about migrants living like animals. At the Hope Rest Center, migrant farm workers were treated like civilized human beings and they reacted in kind.

The key was the attitude of the proprietors. Neither distant nor condescending, a small, bilingual sympathetic staff was serving people they admired. "We respect these people," one staffer said to me as he showed me around. "They come here on their way to doing backbreaking work. You go to the supermarket shelf to pick your national brand cans of vegetables; well, these are the people composing the labor force that picks this food you eat. We admire them. They are workers; they are not looking for a dole. I hate the idea of their not having a decent place to stay on the road." This kind of approach and attitude must be contagious; the Hope Rest Center was a beehive of activity, but everyone was pleasant, the atmosphere was kindly, and the maintenance adequate.

Across the road from the rest center, a Baptist mission had opened its own center, which welcomed the migrants—especially the children—and provided them with a place to play games and buy used clothes. It also provided a referral service to local public and private social welfare and health services organizations that the migrants might need. Most of the funds to run the mission came from the proceeds of the soda fountain at the Rest Center, so the workers in effect were paying for their own care. The highway the migrants traveled provided a metaphorical separation of church and state in the provision of aid to weary transient workers.

The whole scene was one of good sense, goodwill, and public service in its best sense. The public costs were relatively small, while the public benefits were significant. In 1959, the first year of operation, 1,119 people used the facility at Hope. The numbers have grown steadily since then—as high as 56,513 in 1970 and reaching a total overall use of 387,499 by 1972. With some planning and the wise use of a relatively modest amount of public funds, a small network of comparable facilities could be built at established stopping places in the migrant stream.

In the late 1970s, an architect in California developed and built a prototype for an inexpensive, movable form of what he called "disposable architecture." These forms of temporary shelter were designed to replace the cars that the "ditchbankers" used as their homes as well as their transportation. The houses could be used singly or in groups to provide "flash peak" camps for the bigger farms during the harvest season.

With Office of Equal Opportunity funds, he designed small but adequate structures that inculcated the special needs of the potential users. They were simple concrete modules. The costs were low enough (under $1,000 per unit) to be amortized in 5 years, so that the danger of needing to institutionalize the structures after their purpose was served could be avoided.[2] Such overnight, basic facilities could be supplemented by ongoing social service agencies whose programs are designed to assist farm workers. Charges could remain very low, while still covering the costs of running such centers.

Indeed, from such a base—as was the case at Hope—some farm workers might choose to take advantage of local opportunities and leave the migrant stream to seek permanent nonagricultural employment. During their stay information was provided by the center staff to migrants concerning available jobs, government assistance, and other relevant news and services.

A commonsense, economic use of federal assistance in ways that would thoroughly benefit a needy clientele at the same time that it might prove a wise investment for the general public makes good sense and good public policy. Specific, useful projects such as

Paper and plastic foam shelters designed by Sanford Hirshen and Sim Van der Ryn of Berkeley, California. 1968. (Bob Thurber)

the AWP and migrant centers provide an economic, functional, and human role for government. In both cases, migrant participation would be critical. Eventually, the programs could be contracted to farm worker groups such as the union, which could run them in the private sector, which is where and how such programs should be run.

LAW ENFORCEMENT

Farm workers need law enforcement from the government. If the many laws already on the books were truly enforced, their world would be more welcoming. Money marked for appropriate public purposes should be channeled to those in need who are the real objects of the government's bounty. Less public money should be spent to run bureaucracies. And the many existing laws pertaining to the various aspects of migrants' lives must be enforced.

Consider just a few examples. Occupational Safety and Health Administration regulations exist in abundance, but lack of enforcement apparatus has rendered the agency inactive in securing safe workplaces for farm labor. The same problem keeps the Department of Labor from enforcing such basic laws as those governing minimum wages. The failure to implement immigration laws to protect American workers from foreign competition is another example.

An all-out effort to enforce the existing adequate laws—managed by a committed, adequately funded and staffed farm worker ombudsman or inspector general—could result in immediate improvement in the quality of farm workers' lives.

Farm workers are a class of citizens whose needs are known and for whom adequate remedies exist, but they have been denied the full and real protection of law enforcement by responsible agencies of government. This policing function is uniquely governmental, as the administration of most programs demonstrably is not. Despite good intentions and some good examples, as a general rule, government has excluded migrant farm workers from the dispensation of its beneficence and has discriminated against them in the administration of relevant programs.

Better and more legal services programs for migrants would help. One report to the United States Civil Rights Commission noted that "migrants, perhaps more than any other group, have historically been confronted with the greatest need for, but the least access to, legal services." Perhaps I reveal a lawyer's abiding faith in the efficacy of the advocacy role; but from experience I know that aggressive representation can make a big difference in assuring disenfranchised people their rights. As the same report noted, laws are meaningless unless they are used for their beneficiaries.[3]

COLLECTIVE ACTION

Farm employers have organized and planned to control the economics of the farm labor market, while opposing, often violently, comparable attempts by the workers. Foreign labor markets have been exploited to keep wage rates low—with government acquiescence and encouragement.

Government can provide emergency assistance and encourage self-help efforts. But farm workers cannot rely on government to ensure the economic justice which they seek. For this, they must organize in their own self-interest and build an adequate power base that will provide them with both voice and muscle. The union alone holds out the prospect of providing this base.

Mack Lyons, Cesar Chavez, and Juan Flores sing "Nosotros Venceremas" after Lamont, Calif., pickers vote to strike. (Bob Thurber)

Thinking back to that brief, unplanned visit to the union hiring hall in Avon City, Fla., mentioned in the introduction of this book, I can now comprehend what it was that avid, young union organizer was trying to tell us. The problems farm workers have had are not unique; other poor people have experienced them, though rarely in such extremes. The seasonal and impermanent nature of farm work, its unskilled character, the invisibility and impotence of the workers themselves, and their vulnerability to manipulation all exacerbate natural problems and create extreme distress.

Collective action is the key. In fact, the bigger the farms, the more useful unions can be in guaranteeing a predictable, steady labor supply. The essence of collective bargaining is a stable work force. The power of unions is rooted in job control.

The hiring hall is a critical feature of the union's unique ability to solve farm workers' problems. It should be viewed by employers as an ally, not necessarily an adversary. Union control of jobs would eliminate the need for crew leaders and thus the abuses emanating from that questionable system. Employers and employees could stabilize their working relationships and better satisfy their needs through the kind of organization a union would provide.

Collective action will permit social services programs for workers at the same time that it secures some semblance of economic justice for individual workers. A union permits broad-scale negotiations with large employers, as the longshoremen were able to do in Hawaii. It eliminates labor contractors and precludes the use of foreign workers as scabs. A union also provides workers with a needed voice in public policy debates affecting its constituents. A union will have staying power; it will last when fashions and politics change. Finally, the presence of an effective union should confine the battle between employers and employees to the inevitable, smaller economic skirmishes and avoid the bitter confrontations that were fought earlier in this country between farm worker organizers and farm employers.

Chavez prefers a state-by-state approach to unionization. Some problems are peculiar to specific locales, and indigenous, participatory union building is central to the United Farm Workers (UFW) success. Thus, as a start, the union now prefers to work for the adoption of good state agricultural labor laws and boards, as it did in California, in other key agricultural states such as Texas, Florida, Arizona, New Jersey, and Michigan. A federal labor law might make sense later; but for now, the UFW prefers its own slow but sure pace. Its success suggests that the strategy should be respected.

The effectiveness of the UFW in California will spread; the time is right for the unionization of farm workers. The union movement is where the answers lie for farm workers—to the limited extent that any answer exists.

Limited government assistance; an end to historic discrimination; strong law enforcement; and a competent, well-administered union are the keys to the improvement of the migrant farm workers' destiny. The time has come for real reform.

A question lingers. Will this rich and idealistic country continue to countenance the despair of one poor but hard-working caste? Will we respond at long last to the just pleas of these workers who gather the food that feeds us? The harvest is "the end of the age," a biblical parable declares, "and the harvest workers are the angels." It is time that these angels were honored on the earth they work and that the age of their deprivations be ended at last.

N O T E S

PREFACE

1. Raymond Barrio, "The Plum Plum Pickers," excerpted in G. Carlsen and Anthony Tovatt, eds., *Insights: Themes in Literature* (New York: McGraw-Hill, 1973), p. 511.

CHAPTER 1

1. For treatments of the subject of migrant workers in Europe, see John Berger and Jean Mohr, *A Seventh Man: Migrant Workers in Europe* (New York: Viking, 1975); S. Castles and G. Kosack, *Immigrant Workers and Class Structure in Western Europe* (New York: Oxford Univ. Press, 1973). The 1957 Treaty of Rome established a European Economic Community that, among other things, governed the movement and rights of workers within member states.
2. Cletus E. Daniel, "Radicals on the Farm in California," 49 *Agricultural History* 629–46 (Oct. 1975).
3. National Association of Farmworker Organizations Annual Meeting, March 24–27, McAllen, Texas; speech reported in *The National Farmworker* (April–June 1980), p. 2.
4. Conrad Fritsch, "Characteristics of Agricultural Employment and Agricultural Labor Market Operations, 1976," unpubl., in USDA files.
5. J. C. Roetheli and G. P. Zepp, "An Analysis of Costs for Selected Orange Harvesting Systems in Florida," University of Florida, Econ. Rep. 65, 1974.
6. Burton F. Cargill and George E. Rossmiller, "Horticultural and Engineering Outlook of Fruit and Vegetable Harvesting Mechanization, in *Fruit and Vegetable Harvest Mechanization and Manpower Implications,* Rural Manpower Center, Michigan State University, 1969, pp. 75, 76.
7. "Structural Characteristics of Flue-Cured Tobacco Farms and Prospects for Mechanization," ERS, USDA, Rep. 277, 1975.
8. Cesar Chavez, "How UC's Machines Shortchange California Farmworkers," *Los Angeles Times,* Apr. 2, 1978, pt. 5, p. 3.
9. National Commission on Technology, Automation, and Economic Progress report, "Technology and the American Economy," vol. 1, Feb. 1966, p. 110.
10. Tony Dunbar and Linda Kravitz, *Hard Traveling: Migrant Farm Workers in America* (Cambridge, Mass.: Ballinger, 1976), p. ix.
11. "Where Have All the Farm Workers Gone? The Statistical Annihilation of Hired Farm Workers: An Analysis of the Federal

Effort to Define and Count Migrant and Seasonal Farm Workers,"
Rural America, Sept. 1977.

12. Gene A. Rowe and Leslie W. Smith, "The Hired Farm Working
Force of 1974: A Statistical Report, ERS, USDA, 1975. This survey
includes only farm workers who reside in the United States during
the mid-December survey week and who did or expected to do any
farm work during the calendar year.

13. John H. Southern, "National Agricultural Labor Policy Considerations," 48 *American Journal of Farm Economics* 1123 (Dec.
1966).

CHAPTER 2

1. Senate Committee on Labor and Public Welfare, Subcommittee on
Employment, *Hearings on H.R. 26 6346;* Subcommittee on Poverty
and Migratory Labor, *Hearings on S. 2070, S. 3202,* 93d Cong., 1st
sess., 1974, p. 155.

2. "Farm Labor Contractors' Regional Act of 1963," 7 U.S.C. §
2042(b).

3. Tony Dunbar and Linda Kravitz, *Hard Traveling: Migrant Farm
Workers in America* (Cambridge, Mass.: Ballinger, 1976), p. 36.

4. 1974 Senate Hearings, pp. 61–622.

5. Ronald B. Taylor, *Sweatshops in the Sun* (Boston: Beacon Press,
1973), pp. 45, 49.

6. Willard Heaps, *Wandering Workers* (New York: Crown, 1968), pp.
103–5.

7. Ibid., p. 97.

8. Ibid.

9. 1974 Senate Hearings, pp. 48–49.

10. Dale Wright, "I Saw Human Shame as a Migrant Worker," *New
York World Telegram,* Oct 14–24, 1961.

11. Loretta Schwartz, "The Plight of America's Five Million Migrants," *Ms. Magazine,* June 1978, p. 66.

12. 1974 Senate Hearings, p. 2.

13. Ibid., p. 53.

14. Ibid., p. 34.

15. "Farm Labor Contractors' Registration." 7 U.S.C. §§ 2041–2055,
1964; Ch. 52. This chapter makes reference to the following sections of this act: § 2044(a)2–3, Issuance of certificate of
registration—persons qualified; § 2042 (b), Definitions; § 2042 (d),
Definitions; § 2044 (a) (4), Issuance of certificate of registration—
persons qualified; § 2050 (a), Civil relief, federal court jurisdiction;
and § 2050 (c), Record keeping.

16. 1974 Senate Hearings, p. 230.

17. In 1969, 2,043 crew leaders met with the secretary of labor; 2,842 in
1970; 2,900 in 1971; 2,142 in 1972; 1,855 in 1973.

18. 1974 Senate Hearings, pp. 37, 107.

19. Jean Giraudoux, *The Madwoman of Chaillot,* adapted by M.
Valency (New York: Random House, 1949).

CHAPTER 3

1. Robert Coles, *Children of Crisis: Migrants, Mountaineers, and Sharecroppers* (Boston: Little, Brown, 1972), p. 434.
2. Senate Committee on Labor and Public Welfare, Subcommittee on Health and Subcommittee on Migratory Labor, *Joint Hearings on S. 3762,* 92d Cong., 2d sess., 1972.
3. House Committee on Interstate and Foreign Commerce, Subcommittee on Health and Environment, *Extension of Health Program Authorities, Feb. 22-24, 1977,* Hearings on H.R. 3538, 3539, 3598, 95th Cong., 1st sess., 1977.
4. Centaur Management Consultants, Inc., Recommended Standard for Housing of Agricultural Workers, 1976.
5. 1972 Senate Hearings.
6. Senate Committee on Labor and Public Welfare, Subcommittee on Migratory Labor, *Hearings on Migrant and Seasonal Farm Workers' Powerlessness,* 91st Cong., 1st and 2d sess., 1970.
7. R. Schmidt, "The Migratory Farm Worker in the U.S.," Congressional Rep. Serv., H.D. 5856 (1975).
8. 1972 Senate Hearings.
9. Peter E. Danns and Samuel Johnson, "Politics in the Development of a Migrant Health Center," 229 *New England Journal of Medicine* 894 (1975).
10. Ann Northrop, "Government Farmworker Policies—Slim Pickings," *Ms. Magazine,* June 1978, p. 68.
11. P.L. 87-692, 87th Cong., 2nd sess. Sept. 25, 1962, amending S. 310, Public Health Act.
12. P.L. 94-63, Title IV, 94th Cong., 1st sess., July 29, 1975.
13. Department of Health, Education, and Welfare, "The Migratory Health Program," pamphlet, 1976; also see HEW, "Promoting Community Health," HSA 77-5000, 1976.
14. L. P. Reno, "Pieces and Scraps: Farm Labor Housing in the U.S.," report of the Rural Housing Alliance, 1970.
15. Danns, "Politics."
16. Coles, *Children of Crisis,* p. 427.
17. Robert Coles and Jane Coles, *Women of Crisis* (New York: Delacorte, 1978); excerpt, *N.Y. Times Magazine,* Mar. 26, 1978, p. 18.
18. Reno, "Pieces and Scraps," p. 11, quoting Peter Krame, *St. Petersburg Times.*
19. Ibid., n. 7, pt. 8-A, p. 5063.
19. Ibid., pt. 1, p. 3.
21. Rural Housing Alliance, proposal for a grant from the Department of Labor for the study of housing for migratory agricultural workers, 1977-78, pp. 45-50.
22. "Occupational Safety and Health," P.L. 91-596, 29 U.S.C. §§ 651-678, 1970.
23. "Wednesday's Children," report on programs funded under the migrant amendment to Title 1 of the Elementary and Secondary Education Act, National Committee on Education of Migrant Children, New York, 1971.

24. "Promises to Keep: the Continuing Crisis in the Education of Migrant Children," National Child Labor Committee, 1977.
25. M. Guido, report to the National Child Labor Committee, unpubl., on file at Goldfarb, Singer, and Austern, Washington, D.C., n.d.
26. "Wednesday's Children," p. 92.
27. Coles, *Children of Crisis.*

C H A P T E R 4

1. Several years later in June 1975, the National Association of Farm Worker Organizations asked a congressional subcommittee to shift the administration of the farm worker programs from the Labor Department to the Community Services Administration because the latter would be more sympathetic to farm workers. Testimony of Tom Jones, before House Subcommittee on Labor and HEW Committee on Appropriations, *Hearings, May 20, 1975,* 94th Cong., 1st sess., 1975.
2. Stanley Ruttenberg and Jocelyn Gutchess, *The Federal-State Employment Services: A Critique* (Baltimore: Johns Hopkins, 1970), p. 1.
3. Statement of Gregory J. Ahart to House Committee on Government Operations, Subcommittee on Manpower and Housing, May 24, 1976.

C H A P T E R 5

1. The Migrant Legal Action Program was founded to perform backup research services for the migrant legal projects around the country. The California Rural Legal Assistance group was the most active and notorious of the two. A symbol of anarchy during the Reagan, Nixon, Agnew years, the CRLA was the lightning rod for opponents to the idea of Office of Equal Opportunity legal services—a view that would be revised later when Governor Jerry Brown appointed many CRLA alumni to key positions in state government during his administration.
2. 250 Farm Workers, et al., v. Shultz, et al., C-70 481 (U.S. Dist. Ct., No. Dist. Calif., Apr. 22, 1970), Judge Zirpoli; Gomez v. Florida State Employment Service, 417 F. 2d 569 (5th Cir., 1969).
3. Plaintiffs moved to add the CETA program to the coverage of the consent order. The defendants objected. I studied the subject, sought advice from my consultants, and ultimately decided not to support the motion. The judge sat on the motion and in effect, by his inaction, ultimately denied the motion without ever ruling on it.
    CETA had replaced the Manpower Development Training Act and the Economic Opportunity Act. The new agency administered a special migrant program that dispensed significant amounts of money to private migrant organizations and public organizations on a competitive basis. In addition, the secretary of labor had the right under CETA to make discretionary funds available for farm

NOTES

workers. Migrant and seasonal farm workers composed about 2 percent of CETA's population of grantees, and they received about about 5 percent of CETA's funds.

Adding so great a program as CETA to our case would have overwhelmed us if our assignment already did not do so. The Special Review Committee could and indirectly did affect CETA programs for the benefit of farm workers; under the circumstances it was the best we could have done.

4. Stanley Ruttenberg and Jocelyn Gutchess, *The Federal-State Employment Service: A Critique* (Baltimore: Johns Hopkins, 1970), p. 1.

5. Cunningham v. English, 175 F. Supp. 764 (D.D.C., 1958), 269 F. 2d 517 (D.C. Cir.), 361 U.S. 897, 361 U.S. 905 (1959).

6. The Labor Department objected to hearings and fought even using that word. We were to use euphemisms like "participant" instead of witness and "special meeting" rather than hearing, so no judicial qualities would attend our work. But everyone knew what we were doing and used the right words when they were not being quoted.

7. Susan Hall and John Ripton, "Human Chattels," *The Record,* Aug. 21, 1978.

8. See the statement of Director Gregory Ahart, House Committee on Government Operations, Subcommittee on Manpower and Housing, *Hearings on the Operation of the Federal-State ES System,* 94th Cong., 2d sess., May 24, 1976.

9. U.S. Employment Service, report on on-site reviews of rural manpower service operations in 15 states, July, Aug., and Sept. 1973.

10. Abram Chayes, "The Role of the Judge in Public Law Litigation," 89 *Harvard Law Review* 1282 (1976).

11. Ibid., p. 1284.

CHAPTER 6

1. 2 U.S.C. Congressional and Administrative News 3329; S. 748; 8 U.S.C. § 1182(a)(14); P.L. 89-236, 89th Cong., 1st sess., 1965.

2. Truman Moore, "Slaves for Rent: The Shame of American Farming," 215 *Atlantic Monthly* 111 (May 1965).

3. N. R. Gilmore and G. W. Gilmore, "The Bracero in California," 32 *Pacific Historical Review* 218, 271 (Aug. 1963).

4. S. W. Coombs, "U. S. Harvest Provides Seasonal Work for Mexican Farmers," 15 *Americas* 4, 7 (Dec. 1963).

5. Gilmore and Gilmore, "The Bracero in California," p. 272.

6. H. G. Hirsch, "Termination of the Bracero Program," USDA, ERS, Foreign Agr. Econ. Rep. 34, June 1967, p. 1.

7. Gilmore and Gilmore, "The Bracero in California," p. 218.

8. Coombs, "U.S. Harvest Provides Seasonal Work."

9. Moore, "Slaves for Rent," p. 113.

10. "Where Braceros Once Worked," *Business Week,* Jan. 16, 1965, p. 42.

11. Coombs, "U.S. Harvest Provides Seasonal Work."

12. A. McClellan and M. Boggs, "Illegal Aliens: A Story of Human Misery," 81 *The Federationist* 17 (Aug. 1974).
13. Hirsch, "Termination of the Bracero Program," p. 2.
14. McClellan and Boggs, "Illegal Aliens," p. 2.
15. Coombs, "U.S. Harvest Provides Seasonal Work."
16. M. E. Leary, "As the Braceros Leave," *Reporter,* Jan. 28, 1965, p. 45.
17. Ibid.
18. "Where Braceros Once Worked."
19. "When the U.S. Barred Foreign Workers from Farms," *U.S. News and World Report,* May 31, 1965, p. 75.
20. Coombs, "U.S. Harvest Provides Seasonal Work."
21. Hirsch, "Termination of the Bracero Program," p. 2.
22. Ibid., p. 5.
23. Ibid., pp. 2, 3, 4.
24. David S. North, "The Border Crossers," Report of the Transcentury Corporation, Washington, D.C., 1970, is an excellent and thorough study of this subject.
25. Vernon M. Briggs, Jr., *Chicanos and Rural Poverty* (Baltimore: Johns Hopkins, 1973), p. 34.
26. Jones, "Alien Commuters in the U.S. Labor Markets," Spring *International Migration Review* 83 (1970).
27. Michael J. Piore, "The New Immigration and the Presumptions of Social Policy," paper delivered to IRRA meeting, Dec. 29, 1974.
28. Preliminary report, Domestic Council Committee on Illegal Aliens, Dec. 1976.
29. Office of the attorney general, "Illegal Immunization: President's Program," Feb. 1978, p. 2.
30. B. Smith and R. Newman, "A Study of the Institute for Urban Studies."
31. Testimony of Jerry Rowland, state monitor advocate, SRS Hearings, pp. 9, 10.
32. House Judiciary Committee Hearings, 92d Cong., 1st sess., ser. 13, pt. 1, 1971, p. 30.
33. Wayne A. Cornelius, presentation to the Carnegie Endowment for International Peace, Washington, D.C., Aug. 10, 1977.
34. Center for International Studies report, "Mexican Migration to the U.S.," MIT, C/76-12, 1976; "Illegal Migration to the U.S.," MIT, C/77-11, 1977.
35. Wayne A. Cornelius, "When the Door Is Closed to Illegal Aliens, Who Pays?" *New York Times,* June 1, 1977, p. 21.
36. I.N.S. Regulations, 8 C.F.R.; S. 214.2(h)(3)(i), S. 214.2(h)(2)(ii); I.N.A. S. 214(c); 8 U.S.C. § 1184, § 1182(a)(14)(B) (1965).
37. 26 Stat. § 1084 (1891).
38. Pesikoff v. Secretary of Labor, 501 F.2d 757 (D.C. Cir., 1974).
39. U.S. District Court for the District of Columbia, Special Review Committee memorandum, Apr. 21, 1976, p. 4, quoting John Wesley White, director of the Florida Division of Employment Security, letter, Oct. 13, 1975.
40. Ibid., quoting Edward J. Trombetta, Florida secretary of commerce, letter to the Labor Department.

41. 8 U.S.C. § 1182(a)(14)(B) (1965).
42. Frederick County Fruit Growers' Association, Inc., v. Marshall, et al., 436 F. Supp. 218(W. D.Va., 1977).
43. 20 C.F.R. § 653.108(c) (5); 41 F.R. 48250, Nov. 6, 1976, as amended at 42 F.R. 62134, Dec. 7, 1977; 43 F. R. 10312, Mar. 10, 1978 (1979).
44. The Court cited Patterson Orchard v. Marshall, 77-147 (D.Vt., June 30, 1977), as supporting its position, a case decided about the same time.
45. Frederick County Fruit Growers' Association, Inc., v. Marshall, et al.
46. J. R. Kerney, "Puerto Ricans Stranded," *Washington Post,* Sept. 17, 1978, p. C-1; C. Dickey, "Puerto Rican Apple Pickers Tangled in Bureaucracy," ibid., Sept. 27, 1978, p. C-6.
47. J. Horrigan, "Puerto Rican Workers Lose Ulster Orchard Jobs," *Poughkeepsie Journal,* Sept. 12, 1978.
48. U.S.C. § 101(a)(15)(H-2) of the Immigration and Nationality Act of 1952; 8 U.S.C. § 1101 (a)(15)(H)(ii) (1976).

CHAPTER 7

1. Declarations of Ernesto Soria, Guillermo Hernandez, and Jose Alvarado, Senate Committee on Education and Labor, Subcommittee on Agricultural Labor, *Hearings on Workmen's Compensation for Farm Workers,* 92d Cong., 1st sess., 1971.
2. Gutierrez and Gallegos v. Glaser Crandell Co., 202 N.W. 2d 786 (1972).
3. National Commission on State Workmen's Compensation Laws, report, July 1972, p. 44.
4. Ibid., p. 15.
5. Interdepartmental Workers' Compensation Task Force, Division of State Workers' Compensation Standards, "Coverage of Agricultural Workers," July 1976.
6. "Casual" is often defined as not in the usual course of business. Whether migrant labor is casual varies from state to state.
7. The 12 leading agricultural states based on the value of farm products sold, listed in descending order, are: California, Iowa, Texas, Illinois, Minnesota, Nebraska, Kansas, Indiana, Wisconsin, North Carolina, Missouri, Ohio. See "Workmen's Compensation Laws and Equal Protection: Does *Gallegos* Portend the Demise of the Agricultural Exclusion?" 1973 *Duke Law Journal,* at p. 705, n. 3.
8. National Commission report, p. 44.
9. Ibid.
10. *Accident Facts,* (Chicago: National Safety Council, 1971), p. 23.
11. National Commission on State Workmen's Compensation Laws, "Compendium on Workmen's Compensation," Washington, D.C., 1973, p. 016.
12. Carl J. Schramm, "Workmen's Compensation and Farm Workers in the United States," Supplemental Studies for the National Com-

mission on State Workmen's Compensation Laws, vol. 1, pp. 148–49.

13. Conrad F. Fritsch, "Occupational and Nonoccupational Fatalities on U.S. Farms," USDA, ERS, Agr. Econ. Rep. 356, p. 10.
14. Schramm, "Workmen's Compensation," p. 155.
15. M. Duckor, "Legal Problems of Agricultural Labor," 2 *University of California, Davis, Law Review* 141 (1970).
16. Senate Committee on Labor and Public Welfare, Subcommittee on Labor, *Fair Labor Standards Amendments of 1974,* S. 93-690, 93d Cong., 2d sess., 1974, p. 4.
17. *Legislative History of the Fair Labor Standards Amendments of 1966,* P.L. 89-601, H.R. 13712, prepared for the Senate Committee on Labor and Public Welfare, Subcommittee on Labor, 89th Cong., 1st sess., 1965; H.R. 1366, p. 102.
18. S. Jacobsen, "Labor Legislation and the Agricultural Laborer," 11 *Industrial and Labor Relations Forum* 143 (Summer 1975).
19. Irving Kovarsky, "Congress and Migrant Labor," 9 *St. Louis University Law Journal* 328 (Spring 1965).
20. Harry Schwartz, "On the Wage Structure of Agriculture," 57 *Political Science Quarterly* 411, 412–13 (1942).
21. Bowie v. Gonzalez, 117 F. 2d 11, 18 (1st Cir. Ct., 1941).
22. *FLSAs of 1974,* p. 5.
23. Ibid., pp. 5–6.
24. Senate Committee on Labor and Public Welfare, Subcommittee on Labor, *Hearings, Amendments to the Fair Labor Standards Act,* 89th Cong., 1st sess., 1965, pt. 1, p. 33.
25. Ibid.
26. Ibid., p. 95, pt. 2, p. 993.
27. Ibid., p. 1,003.
28. Ibid., p. 1,005.
29. Ibid., Testimony of Blue Carstenson, p. 1026.
30. Senate Committee on Labor and Public Welfare, Subcommittee on Labor, *Fair Labor Standards Amendments of 1972,* S. 92-842, 92d Cong., 2d sess., 1972, p. 2.
31. "The Farm Worker: His Need for Legislation," 22 *Maine Law Review* 213, 223 (1970).
32. *FLSAs of 1974,* p. 28.
33. Ibid., pp. 28–29.
34. *FLSAs of 1974,* p. 30.
35. Jacobsen, "Labor Legislation and the Agricultural Laborer," p. 143.
36. Statement of Senator William Hathaway to Senate Committee on Labor and Public Welfare, Subcommittee on Labor, *Hearings, Agricultural Child Labor Provisions of FLSA, 1975,* 94th Cong., 1st sess., 1975, p. 2.
37. *FLSAs of 1974,* p. 30.
38. *FLSAs of 1972,* p. 21.
39. *FLSAs of 1974,* p. 30.
40. Ibid., p. 31.
41. Supplemental views of Jacob Javits and Harrison Williams,

Legislative History of the Fair Labor Standards Amendments of 1966, P.L. 89-601, S. 1487, to accompany H.R. 13712, 89th Cong., 2d sess., 1966, p. 163.

42. Ibid., p. 165.
43. *FLSAs of 1974,* p. 30.
44. Ibid.
45. Statement of Hon. Vera Katz, Senate Committee on Labor and Public Welfare, Subcommittee on Labor, *Hearings, Agricultural Child Labor Provisions of FLSA, 1975,* 93d Cong., 2d sess., 1974, pp. 15-25.
46. Statement of Rafael Palleo Ciddio, ibid., pp. 27-31.
47. W. Haber and M. Murray, *Unemployment Insurance in the American Economy* (Homewood, Ill.: Irwin, 1966), pp. 26-27.
48. "Federal Unemployment Tax Act," 26 U.S.C.A. § 3302(c).
49. Haber and Murray, *Unemployment Insurance,* pp. 27-29.
50. For a general history of unemployment compensation in the United States prior to the Social Security Act of 1936, see ibid., 61-75.
51. H. Doc. No. 397, 73d Cong., 2d sess., 1934; quoted in Haber and Murray, *Unemployment Insurance,* pp. 76-77.
52. Haber and Murray, *Unemployment Insurance,* p. 77; A. Schlesinger, Jr., *The Coming of the New Deal* (Boston: Houghton Mifflin, 1958), p. 304.
53. Schlesinger, *The New Deal,* p. 305.
54. Report to the President of the Committee on Economic Security (Washington, D.C.: USGPO, 1935).
55. Haber and Murray, *Unemployment Insurance,* p. 158; statement of Roger Rossi, Employment and Training Administration, Department of Labor.
56. "Farm" was defined to include greenhouses and fur-bearing animal raising farms, while "agriculture" was defined to include harvesting of maple sugar and turpentine, mushroom growing, poultry hatching, cotton ginning, and certain irrigation functions. See Haber and Murray, *Unemployment Insurance,* p. 157.
57. U.S. Congressional Code and Administrative News, 1970, pp. 3616-3617.
58. 26 U.S.C.A. § 3306(k), § 3121(g).
59. Ibid. Production and harvesting of maple syrup, maple sugar, or mushrooms or hatching of poultry, unless performed on a farm, were excluded from the definition.
60. U.S. Congressional Code and Administrative News, 1974, pp. 6758, 6761; ibid., 1975, pp. 379-80.
61. H.R. 94-755, "Unemployment Compensation Amendment of 1975," p. 38.
62. H.R. 10210 provided coverage for agricultural workers whose employers hired four or more on 20 days in different calendar weeks or who paid $5,000 in quarterly wages for agricultural services. The provision applicable to nonfarm employers requires them to pay taxes if they employ one or more workers in 20 different weeks or pay quarterly wages of $1,500. 26 U.S.C.A. § 3306(a).
63. H.R. 94-755, p. 38; W. Bauder, J. Elterich, R. Farrish, and J.

Holt, "Impact of Extension of Unemployment Insurance to Agriculture," Pennsylvania State University, College of Agriculture, Bull. 804, Jan. 1976, pp. 143, 145, 156, 149.

64. Senate Committee on Finance, *Hearings on H.R. 10210,* 94th Cong., 2d sess., 1976, pp. 122–23.

65. Ibid., pp. 100–101.

66. *Congressional Record,* July 20, 1976, H. 7325, 7407; Senate Hearings, 1976, p. 215.

67. See Conference Report 94-1745, "Unemployment Compensation Amendments of 1976" (Washington, D.C.: USGPO, 1976).

68. Statement of staff member of Senate Committee on Finance to my researcher.

69. Haber and Murray, *Unemployment Insurance,* p. 158; Rossi, statement.

70. Rossi, statement; statement of Leonard Lasser, Center for Community Change, Washington, D.C.

71. Lasser, statement.

72. Rossi, statement.

73. S. Seaver, J. Elterich, W. Bauder, R. Emerson, J. Holt, R. Warland, B. Wood, and C. Fritsch, "Economic and Social Considerations in Extending Unemployment Insurance to Agricultural Workers," Pennsylvania State University, College of Agriculture, Bull. 806, Feb. 1976, p. 59.

74. Bauder et al., "Impact of Extension," p. 143.

75. Hawaii, Minnesota, California, the District of Columbia, and the Commonwealth of Puerto Rico currently have provisions in their unemployment compensation laws that provide coverage for agricultural labor. California's law became effective on January 1, 1976. While the District of Columbia does not exclude agricultural workers, there is no agricultural labor in the jurisdiction that would benefit by the provision.

76. Seaver et al., "Economic and Social Considerations," p. 56.

77. A. Morris, "Agricultural Labor and National Labor Legislation," 54, pt. 2 *California Law Review* 1945 (Dec. 1966).

78. Woodbury, "Limits of Coverage of Labor in Industries Closely Allied to Agriculture under Codes of Fair Competition under NIRA," Division of Review, NRA, Wood Materials, 45A, p. 4.

79. Morris, "Agricultural Labor," p. 1946.

80. Woodbury, "Limits of Coverage," p. 3.

81. Morris, "Agricultural Labor, p. 1947.

82. House Committee on Ways and Means, *Hearings on H.R. 5644,* 73d Cong., 1st sess., 1933, p. 4.

83. Morris, "Agricultural Labor," p. 1948.

84. Woodbury, "Limits of Coverage," pp. 2–3.

85. Morris, "Agricultural Labor," p. 1950.

86. This irrational definition has continued through today in the Fair Labor Standards Act, 52 Stat. 1060 (1938), as amended, U.S.C. §§ 201-19 (1964), in §3(f), which is also the definition of agricultural employee under the NLRA. See "Amendments to the Fair Labor Standards Act," p. 95, for this definition.

87. Morris, "Agricultural Labor," pp. 1950–51.

88. Ibid., p. 1951.

89. The one exception was Congressman Vito Marcantonio; Morris, "Agricultural Labor," n. 54, p. 1951.
90. S. 2926, 73d Cong., 2d sess., 1934.
91. § 2(3) of NLRA, 49 Stat. 450 (1935), 29 U.S.C. § 152(3)(1964).
92. Testimony of Dr. William Leiserson to the NLRB, "Legislative History of the National Labor Relations Act," 1949, p. 269.
93. S. 573, 74th Cong., 1st sess., 1935, p. 7.
94. See testimony of Norman Thomas, *"Amending Migratory Labor Laws,"* Senate Committee on Labor and Public Welfare, Subcommittee on Migratory Labor, *Hearings on S. 1864, S. 1865, S. 1866, S. 1867,* 89th Cong., 1st sess., 1966, p. 463.
95. H.R. 969, 74th Cong., 1st sess., 1935, pp. 27–28.
96. Jacobsen, "Labor Legislation and the Agricultural Laborer," p. 138.
97. Leiserson, testimony, p. 3202.
98. Morris, "Agricultural Labor," p. 1954.
99. E. E. Witte, *Development of the Social Security Act* (Madison: Univ. of Wis. Press, 1962), p. 153.
100. Morris, "Agricultural Labor," p. 1956.
101. Ibid., pp. 1977–78.
102. Ross, "Agricultural Labor and Social Legislation," 1941, p. 241, unpublished thesis in University of California, Berkeley, library. Cited in Morris, "Agricultural Labor."
103. Testimony of Matt Trigs, Senate Committee on Labor and Public Welfare, Subcommittee on Migratory Labor, *Hearings, Migratory Labor Legislation on S. 8, S. 195, S. 197, S. 198,* 90th Cong., 1st sess., 1967, pp. 95–96.
104. Morris, "Agricultural Labor," pp. 1978–82.
105. Ibid. p. 1983.
106. Testimony of Harry Bridges, president of ILWU, *Hearings, Migratory Labor Legislation,* p. 324.
107. Curtis Aller, "Labor Relations in the Hawaiian Sugar Industry," Institute of Industrial Relations, University of California, Berkeley, 1957, pp. 60, 107.
108. Senate, *Hearings, Migratory Labor Legislation,* pp. 361–80.
109. Morris, "Agricultural Labor," p. 1989.

CHAPTER 8

1. Ernesto Galarza, *Spiders in the House and Workers in the Field* (Notre Dame: University of Notre Dame Press, 1970), p. xi.
2. For an interesting analysis of this subject, see ibid.
3. Stuart Jamieson, "Labor Unionism in American Agriculture," Department of Labor, Bureau of Labor Standards, Bull. 836, 1954, p. 46.
4. Ibid., p. 411.
5. Two excellent publications describe this phenomenon: ibid., and Richard Meister and Anne Loftis, *A Long Time Coming: The Struggle to Unionize America's Farm Workers* (New York: Macmillan, 1977).
6. These days are described in the now classic book by Carey

McWilliams, *Factories in the Field: The Story of the Migratory Labor in California* (Camden, Conn.: Shoe String, repr., 1969).

7. Meister and Loftis, *A Long Time Coming.*

8. The anthropological and sociological story of this phenomenon is told by James Michener in his bestseller about Colorado, *Centennial* (New York: Random House, 1974), pp. 673–727.

9. There is a growing literature about Chavez. He considers the best source to be Jacques E. Levy, *Cesar Chavez: Autobiography of La Causa* (New York: Norton, 1975). Other sources are: Ronald B. Taylor, *Chavez and the Farm Workers* (Boston: Beacon, 1975) and Peter Matthiessen, *Sal Si Puedes—Escape if You Can: Cesar Chavez and the New American Revolution* (New York: Random House, 1970).

10. Meister and Loftis, *A Long Time Coming,* pp. 112–13.

11. "Cesar Chavez on Money and Organizing," transcribed from a talk given by Chavez to a group of church people, Oct. 4, 1971, at La Paz, Calif.

12. Statement of interfaith team that visited Delano, Calif., at invitation of CMM, quoted in *Ave Maria* (national Catholic weekly), Jan. 29, 1966, p. 18.

13. Wayne C. Hartmire, Jr., Director, California Migrant Ministry, "The Church and the Emerging Farmworkers Movement: A Case Study," July 22, 1967.

14. Ibid., p. 10.

15. Ibid., p. 23.

16. Ibid., p. 28.

17. Ibid., p. 35.

18. Section I, SB 1 Calif., 1975–76 sess.

19. 3.5 A.L.R.A. S.1140.2.

20. Wayne P. Fuller, "Farm-Labor Relations," 8 *Idaho Law Review* 66 (1971).

21. Babbit, et al. v. United Farm Workers Union, et al., 78-225; 47 *Law Week* 4659 (June 1979); 442 U.S. 287 (1979).

CHAPTER 9

1. A weekly farm worker advocacy bulletin published by the National Association of Farmworkers Organizations in Washington, D.C., MOVIDAS, August 22, 1980.

2. This work is described in S. Van der Ryn and S. Hirshen, "Synopsis of Our Experience in Housing Design and Community Planning for Rural Areas," Feb. 1966, on file at the offices of Goldfarb, Singer, and Austern.

3. North Carolina Advisory Commission report to the United States Civil Rights Commission, "Where Mules Outrate Men, Migrant and Seasonal Farmworkers in North Carolina," May 1979, p. 18.

I N D E X

Abrego, Bruno, 136
Aders, Robert, 95–96
AFL-CIO, 126, 156, 166, 186, 188, 198, 201
Agribusiness, 4, 8, 15, 53, 156, 193
Agricultural Adjustment Act (AAA), 169–71
Agricultural Labor Subcommittee, U.S. House of Representatives, 64
Agricultural Labor Relations Board (ALRB), 199–201
Agricultural Workers Association, 186
Agricultural Workers Organizing Committee (AWOC), 180, 186, 188
Alinsky, Saul, 186
Amalgamated Meatcutters and Butchers Workmen of North America, 156
American Farm Bureau Federation, 118, 156, 166, 173–74
American Federation of Labor (AFL), 179–82
American GI Forum, 67
American Medical Association, 151
Annual Worker Plan, 83–84, 210–13, 217

Bell, Griffin, 130–31, 145
Bergland, Robert, 14
Bickel, Alex, 112
Boycotts. *See* Unions/Unionization, strikes/boycotts
Braceros. *See* Foreign competition
Brennan, Peter J., 69
Brown, Jerry, 101, 198–99, 201

Cahn, Edgar, 70, 90, 95
California Agricultural Labor Relations Act, 199
California Migrant Ministry (CMM). *See* National Farmworker Ministry
California Rural Legal Services, 31, 60, 101
Carter, Jimmy, 107, 125–26, 130–33, 145, 203
Castillo, Leonel, 130
Center for Community Justice, 97
Certified foreign workers. *See* Foreign competition
CETA. *See* Department of Labor, U.S.
Chatfield, Leroy, 198–99
Chavez, Cesar, 13–14, 34, 36, 85, 175, 178, 182, 185–86, 188–92, 196, 198, 200, 203–4, 206–8, 220
Chayes, Abram, 112–13

Civil Rights Act, 68, 155
Civil Rights Commission, U.S., 218
Civil Service Commission, U.S., 106
Claus, Carin, 109
Coca Cola Company, 184
Coles, Robert, 26, 33, 38, 50–51, 89
Collective bargaining, 218–20. *See also* Unions/Unionization
Committee on Economic Security, 163
Committee of Industrial Organizations (CIO), 181–82
Communist party, 179, 181, 183
Community Services Administration, U.S., 44, 54, 55n.1, 188
Congressional Record, 170
Connery, William, 172
Cornelius, Wayne, 132–33
Council of Protestant Churches, 192
Council of State Government, 151
Crew leaders, 9–10, 19–32, 137–38, 142–43, 167–68, 212, 219
  characteristics and role, 19–28
  cruelty and abuse, 24–28
  evolution, 19
  exploitation, 4, 12, 25–28, 30–31
  free-lancing, 20, 213
  government definition, 22
  government regulation, 20, 22, 28–32, 29n.15, 30n.17, 65–66, 92, 108–9, 168
  recruitment practices, 10, 20, 23–24, 26
  safety violations, 24–25
  transporting practices, 20, 23–25, 29–30

Daniel, Cletus: *Radicals on the Farm in California,* 5
Dayhaul, 66, 84–85, 210
Department of Agriculture, U.S., 12–13, 15–17, 28, 43, 117, 121, 157–59, 169
  Economic Research Service, 17, 17n.12, 120–21
Department of Defense, U.S., 189
Department of Health, Education, and Welfare, U.S., 35, 37, 46, 49, 54–55, 210
Department of Justice, U.S., 72–74, 76, 79, 96–97, 126. *See also* Federal Bureau of Investigation; Immigration and Naturalization Service
Department of Labor, U.S., 29, 54, 62–64, 66–71, 86, 88–91, 94–113,

Department of Labor, U.S. (*cont.*)
118, 128, 134, 136–39, 141–45, 151, 154–57, 159–60, 165, 167, 210, 213, 218
Bureau of Labor Statistics, 59, 139
CETA, 55, 69n.3, 111
consent order, 72–73, 76, 78, 80, 82–83, 86, 89, 91, 96, 98, 101, 103–9, 111
discriminatory practices, 82, 96, 108
Employment Security Automated Reporting System (ESARS), 86, 88–89
Employment Service, 10, 16, 19, 28, 55–113, 117–18, 136–37, 142, 145, 211–13, 215
Employment Standards Administration, 30–31, 99, 109, 157–58
Employment Training Administration, 55, 106, 109
Farm Labor Services Division, 29–30, 63
Occupational, Safety, and Health Administration (OSHA), 35–36, 44–45, 66, 93, 99, 105–6, 108–10, 151–52, 217
secretary's 13 Points, 66–69, 90, 105–8
Dunlop, John, 95, 138

Eastern Seaboard Plan. *See* Annual Worker Plan
Economic security, farm workers. *See* Unions/Unionization
Education, farm workers, 45–51, 214
attitudes, 46–50
effect of unionization, 206
Elementary and Secondary Education Act, 46
government programs, 46–50, 53–55
major problems, 46–51
National Child Labor Committee, 46–50
National Committee on the Education of Migrant Children, 46
surveys, 16, 46–49
Education and Labor Committee, U.S. Senate, 171–72
Elementary and Secondary Education Act, 46
Employment, farm workers, 3–4, 8, 10–11, 219. *See also* Department of Labor, U.S.
conditions, 4, 11–12, 26, 211
convicts, 181
discrimination, 4, 61,64–65, 68, 70
Exploitation, 4, 65, 70, 134, 137–38, 159, 161, 179–82, 185. *See also* Foreign competition; Crew leaders, exploitation

family involvement, 3, 10, 15, 17, 19, 46, 157–58, 166, 212
government regulations, 68–73, 113, 210–13, 215
pensions, 206
social welfare, 4–6, 8, 14–15, 54, 122–24, 127, 180, 206, 209, 216, 220. *See also* Social benefits, exclusion
statistics/data, 12–18, 17n.11, 23
training, 206, 209. *See also* Department of Labor, U.S., CETA
transportation, 8–10, 66, 207, 210
unemployment, 16, 18
unionization. *See* Unions/Unionization
wages, 3, 8–9, 12, 17, 27, 29–30, 84, 105, 108, 167–68, 171, 206. *See also* Miminum wage laws
Employment Security Automated Reporting System (ESARS). *See* Department of Labor, U.S.
Energy Research and Development Administration, 111
Environmental Protection Agency, U.S., 35–36

Fair Labor Standards Act, 153–58, 160–62
Farm bloc, 162, 172–74, 176
Farm Labor Contractor Registration Act of 1963 (FLCRA). *See* Crew leaders, government regulation
Farm Labor Service, 65
Farm Picketing Act, 201–2
Farm Worker Bill of Rights, 209–10
Federal Bureau of Investigation (FBI), 183
Finance Committee, U.S. Senate, 164, 166
Food Marketing Commission, U.S., 15
Ford, Gerald, 124
Foreign competition, 114–46, 179, 180–81, 184–85, 213, 218, 220
bracero program, 28, 115–21, 127, 145, 179, 194
certification of foreign workers, 108, 121, 133–46
commuters/green carders, 121–22
coyotes, 22, 124
Domestic Council on Illegal Aliens, 124–27, 130
illegal aliens, 16–17, 29, 114–15, 121–33, 144, 147
immigration laws, 65, 115, 117, 121–23, 126, 130–35, 218
problems, 114–15, 119–20, 122, 124, 126–28, 130–39, 144, 146
Freedom of Information Act, 96
Fuentes, Humberto, 34

General Accounting Office, U.S., 58, 89
Giraudoux, Jean: *The Madwoman of Chaillot,* 31–32.
Government Operations Committee, U.S. House of Representatives, 89
Grange, The, 118
Gutchess, Jocelyn, 73–74, 86

H-2 Program, 145–46
Hall, Jack, 182–83
Hartmire, Wayne "Chris," 192–96
Hatfield, Mark, 161
Hawaii Employment Relations Act, 174, 183
Health, farm workers, 33–40
  ailments, 34–35, 43
  attitudes toward care, 34–39
  average life span, 34–35
  children, 34–35, 43, 159, 160–61, 162
  clinics, 37–38, 206
  dilemma, 33–35
  effects of environment, 3, 34–35, 65. *See also* Housing, farm workers
  fatalities, 34–39, 151, 159–60
  funds, 37–38, 152
  government programs, 36–39, 53
  hearings, 36–37
  injuries, 34–36, 159–60
  Migrant Health Act, 36, 38
  National Advisory Council, 37
  National Center for Health Statistics, 36
  pesticides, 4, 12, 34–36, 45, 65–66, 105, 151
  Public Health Act, 36
  public health departments, 37, 216
  Special Health Review Sharing Act, 37
  statistics, 34–38
  treatment, 37
Herrera, Salvador, 9
Hodgson, James D., 66–67
Housing, farm workers, 40–45, 105–6, 110–11, 210, 214–15
  conditions, 12, 40, 42–45
  Department of Housing, U.S., 44
  disposable architecture, 216
  employers' attitudes, 43–44
  government programs, 43–45, 53, 212
  government regulation, 42–45
  Housing Act (1949), 44
  public reaction, 40, 42, 214–16
  statistics, 40, 42–45
Huerta, Dolores, 188

Illegal aliens. *See* Foreign competition
Immigration and Naturalization Act, 66
Immigration and Naturalization Serv-

ice, 68, 117, 121–23, 129–30, 135, 145. *See also* Department of Justice, U.S.
International Association of Industrial Accident Boards, 151
International Longshoremen's and Warehousemen's Union (ILWU), 174, 182–83
International Workers of the World (IWW), 169, 178–79
Interstate and Foreign Commerce Committee, U.S. House of Representatives, 34

Jamaican Regional Labor Board, 142–44
Javits, Jacob, 160
Johnson, Lyndon B., 52, 54, 147, 155, 198
Judiciary Committee, U.S. House of Representatives, 130

Kendrick, J. B., Jr., 14
Kennedy, Robert F., 196
King, Martin Luther, Jr., 188
Kolberg, William, 55

La Causa, 186, 196, 198, 204
La Follette, Robert, 182
Landrum-Griffin Amendments, 169
Law enforcement and compliance, 62–64, 217–20. *See also* Special Review Committee, enforcement and compliance
Legal services, 218. *See also* Migrant Legal Action Program
Lillesand, David, 139–41

Mahoney, Roger, 199
Marcantonio, Vito, 172
Marshall, Ray, 127, 130–32, 144–45
Mechanization, 4–5, 8, 11–18, 118, 120, 151, 176, 181, 183, 207, 209
Migrant Health Act. *See* Health, farm workers
Migrant health clinics. *See* Health, farm workers
Migrant Legal Action Program, 60, 60n.1, 62–64, 67, 72, 74–78, 145
Migrant streams, 3–19, 40, 46, 49, 74, 82, 122, 137, 210–11, 216. *See also* Employment, farm workers
  displaced workers, 5, 12–13, 15, 17
  end, 209–20
  European migrants, 5, 5n.1, 11
  migrant farm labor centers, 214–17
Minimum age laws, 65–66, 109, 148, 158–62, 170, 210
Minimum wage laws, 65–66, 109, 148,

Minimum wage laws (*cont.*)
   152–58, 170, 210, 218. *See also*
   Social benefits, exclusion
Monitor advocate system. *See* Special
   Review Committee, enforcement
   and compliance
Morris, Austin P., 171–75
Mountain States Beet Workers, 184
Murphy, George, 120

NAACP, 67
NAACP, et. al. v. *Secretary of Labor
   Hodgson, et. al.*, 67–113. *See also*
   Special Review Committee
National Academy of Sciences, 86
National Association of Farmworker
   Organizations, 9, 34, 75, 144–45
National Center for Health Statistics.
   See Health, farm workers
National Committee on the Education
   of Migrant Children. *See* Educa-
   tion, farm workers
National Conference of Bishops, 193
National Farmers Union, 156, 210
National Farm Workers Association
   (NFWA), 188
National Farmworker Ministry, 146,
   192–96
National Industrial Recovery Act
   (NIRA), 169–71
National Labor Relations Act (NLRA),
   168–75, 171n.86, 198, 202–4
National Labor Relations Board
   (NLRB), 199, 201, 203
National Safety Council, 36, 151, 159
Nelson, Gaylord, 55
New Deal Farm Security Act, 44
New England Journal of Medicine, 35
New Republic, 204
New York Times, 11, 16
Nixon, Richard M., 54–55, 67

Occupational Safety and Health Ad-
   ministration (OSHA). *See* Depart-
   ment of Labor, U.S.
Office of Equal Opportunity, U.S.
   (OEO), 44, 46, 52–55, 96, 106, 214,
   216
Office of Management and Budget,
   U.S. (OMB), 124–25
Off-shore labor, 133–37, 144
Old Age, Survivors, and Disability In-
   surance   Program   (OASDI),
   163–64

Packwood, Robert, 161
Padilla, Gilbert, 188
Perkins, Frances, 163
Political powers, farm workers. *See* Un-
   ions/Unionization

Power, Jonathan, 133
Powerlessness, farm workers, 40, 79,
   147–48, 191, 219
Provenzo, Anthony, 129–30
Public Health Act. *See* Health, farm
   workers
Puerto Rico, government of, 139–43

Recio, Louis Silva, 140
Richey, Charles, 67–72, 80, 90, 95–96,
   104, 106, 108–9, 112
Rocky Mountain Sheep Shearers Union,
   184
Roman Catholic Church, 179, 188,
   192–93
Romero, Fred, 75, 78, 80, 82, 101, 106,
   141
Roosevelt, Franklin D., 42–43, 163
   Economic Recovery Program, 163,
      169–72
   New Deal era, 56, 147–48, 153–54,
      169
Roosevelt, James, 53
Ross, Fred, 186, 188
Rural America, Inc., 17
Rural Housing Alliance, 111
Rural Manpower Service, 64–65, 67
Ruttenberg, Stanley, 72

Sherman, Larry, 62–63, 74, 78, 105
Shriver, Sargent, 53
Social   benefits,   exclusion, 147–77,
   209–10
Social Security Act, 56, 65, 172
Social Security Administration, 118,
   131, 144, 148, 162–63, 167–68
Southern Tenant Farmers Union, 181
Special   Review   Committee, 73–113,
   210, 213
   activities and goals, 73, 78–85, 88–
      89, 91–92, 94–95, 99, 101–2, 104,
      107, 110–12
   author's participation, 74–80, 91–92,
      94, 98, 101, 103–5, 107
   case settlement, 109–10
   data gathering, 80–86, 88–89, 99,
      103, 108, 110
   enforcement and compliance, 73, 76,
      80–83, 86, 88–95, 96, 101–5,
      108–9
   findings and recommendations, 73,
      80–81, 86, 88–89, 94–95, 97,
      100–102, 104–13, 139, 210
   hearings, 77n.6, 79–83, 88, 91–93,
      102–3, 105, 108, 111, 128–30,
      136, 142
   staff and organization, 73–79, 91
Special Review Staff report, 64–67
State Farm Labor Service, 211

Steinbeck, John: *Grapes of Wrath,* 64
Sundquist, James, 53

Taft-Hartley Amendments, 169, 175
Teamsters Union, 76, 182, 193, 198–99, 201
Thomas, Norman, 171–72
Trade Union Unity League, 181

Un-American Activities Committee, U.S. House of Representatives, 183
Unemployment assistance, 164, 168
Unemployment compensation, 164–68
Unemployment Compensation Amendments of 1976, 163
Unemployment insurance, 56, 144, 148, 162–68, 163n.56, 164n.59, 165n.62, 168n.75, 210. *See also* Roosevelt, Franklin D.
Committee on Economic Security, 163
Unemployment tax, 56, 162, 165, 167
Unions/Unionization, 4, 176–208, 218–20
activities, 14, 85, 89, 201, 213, 217, 220
arguments against, 173–79, 194–95, 200, 202–3
church's role, 192–96
collective action, 218–20
economic powers, farm workers, 4, 170–71, 177–79, 181, 185, 218, 220
evolution, 5–6, 176–82, 184–86, 188, 190, 192–94, 196, 198–99, 203–4, 210
issues concerning, 15, 31, 36, 118, 120, 145, 178, 218–19
laws, 177, 181, 202–4, 220
political powers, farm workers, 4, 16, 33, 53, 153, 160–61, 168, 170–71, 175, 178, 180, 183–84, 186, 198–204, 220
problems faced by organizers, 13, 114, 122, 148, 169–71, 174–75, 177–91, 194–96, 198–205, 207–8, 218–19
strikes/boycotts, 114, 180, 183, 188–89, 193–94, 198, 205, 207
success, 177, 182–85, 189–91, 205, 207–8, 220
United Farm Workers of America, 13–14, 28, 31, 34, 36, 178–79, 184–86, 188–89, 192–93, 198–99, 201–4, 206–8, 220
United Farm Workers Organizing Committee, 175
University of California Board of Regents, 14, 207
Usery, Willie, 138

Villa, Pancho, 188

Wagner, Robert, 170–72
Wagner Act, 169, 171, 175, 203
Wagner-Peyser Act, 56, 59, 62–64, 68, 73, 100–101, 104
War Food Administration, U.S. *See* Foreign competition, bracero program
Washington Post, 204
Ways and Means Committee, U.S. House of Representatives, 164–65, 170, 172
White, Richard C., 145
Williams, Dave, 139
Williams, Harrison, 53, 160
Wirtz, Willard, 119–20, 144, 155–56
Workmen's compensation, 147–52, 150n.7, 210

Zapata, Emiliano, 188

THE AUTHOR

RONALD L. GOLDFARB is a partner in the law firm of Goldfarb, Singer & Austern in Washington, D.C. A nationally known lecturer, consultant, and critic, he has written extensively for newspapers, magazines, and professional journals and is the author of five books on subjects concerning the administration of justice. His experience in 1975 and 1976 as chairman of the Special Review Committee established by the U.S. District Court for the District of Columbia to review compliance with the order of the court in *NAACP, Western Region et al.* v. *Brennan et al.* concerning the provision of services to migrant and seasonal farm workers by the U.S. Department of Labor inspired him to write this book.